ADVOCACY AND OPPOSITION
an introduction to argumentation

ADVOCACY AND OPPOSITION

an introduction to argumentation

Karyn C. Rybacki

Northern Michigan University

Donald J. Rybacki

Northern Michigan University

Prentice-Hall, Inc. Englewood Cliffs, New Jersey 07632

Library of Congress Cataloging-in-Publication Data

Rybacki, Karyn Charles, (date)
  Advocacy & opposition.

  Bibliography: p.
  Includes index.
  1. Persuasion (Rhetoric) 2. Debates and debating.
I. Rybacki, Donald Jay, (date). II. Title.
III. Title: Advocacy and opposition.
P301.5.P47R93 1986   808   85-12358
ISBN 0-13-018193-5

Editorial/production supervision
  and interior design: Marianne Peters
Cover design: Wanda Lubelska Design
Manufacturing buyer: Barbara Kelly Kittle

Printed in the United States of America
10 9 8 7 6 5
ISBN 0-13-018193-5 01

Prentice-Hall International (UK) Limited, *London*
Prentice-Hall of Australia Pty. Limited, *Sydney*
Prentice-Hall Canada Inc., *Toronto*
Prentice-Hall Hispanoamericana, S.A., *Mexico*
Prentice-Hall of India Private Limited, *New Delhi*
Prentice-Hall of Japan, Inc., *Tokyo*
Prentice-Hall of Southeast Asia Pte. Ltd., *Singapore*
Editora Prentice-Hall do Brasil, Ltda., *Rio de Janeiro*
Whitehall Books Limited, *Wellington, New Zealand*

CONTENTS

Preface   xi

1   What Is Argumentation?   1

The Nature of Argumentation   *1*
The Usefulness of Argumentation   *5*
Limitations on the Use of Argumentation   *7*
Applications of Argumentation   *8*
The Historical Development of Argumentation   *10*
Ethical Standards for Argumentation   *12*

   The Research Responsibility   *12*
   The Common Good Responsibility   *13*
   The Reasoning Responsibility   *14*
   The Social Code Responsibility   *14*

Learning Activities   *15*
Suggested Supplementary Readings   *16*

2   What Do I Need to Know before
I Can Begin to Argue?   17

Presumption   *17*
Burden of Proof   *21*
Prima Facie Case   *22*
Learning Activities   *28*
Suggested Supplementary Readings   *29*

3   What Am I Going to Argue About?   30

The Nature of Propositions   *30*

Selecting Terms for Definition   *31*
Specifying Direction of Change   *32*
Identifying Key Issues   *35*

The Process of Definition   *38*

Rules of Definition   *38*
Terms Needing Definition   *40*
How to Define Terms   *41*

The Classification of Propositions   *43*

Propositions of Fact   *43*
Propositions of Value   *44*
Propositions of Policy   *45*

Phrasing the Proposition   *47*
Learning Activities   *49*
Suggested Supplementary Readings   *50*

4   How Do I Construct My Argument?   52

The Primary Triad   *53*

Claims   *53*
Grounds   *56*
Warrant   *58*

The Secondary Triad   *60*

Backing   *61*
Qualifiers   *62*
Rebuttals   *63*

Learning Activities   *65*
Suggested Supplementary Readings   *65*

5   How Do I Prove My Argument?   67

Types of Evidence   *68*

Evidence of Fact   *68*
Evidence from Opinion   *72*

Tests of Evidence   *74*

Tests of Facts   *74*
Tests of Opinion Evidence   *80*
General Tests of Evidence   *81*

The Discovery of Evidence   *83*

Books   *84*
Periodicals   *84*
Newspapers   *85*
Government Documents   *86*
Almanacs, Fact Books, and Other Resources   *86*

Recording Evidence   *87*
Learning Activities   *89*
Suggested Supplementary Readings   *90*

6   How Does the Reasoning Process Work?   91

Argument from Cause   *92*
Argument from Sign   *97*
Argument from Generalization   *99*
Argument from Parallel Case   *101*
Argument from Analogy   *103*
Argument from Authority   *105*
Argument from Definition   *108*
Argument from Dilemma   *109*
Learning Activities   *110*
Suggested Supplementary Readings   *114*

7   What Should I Avoid?   115

Fallacies in Reasoning   *116*

Hasty Generalization   *116*
Transfer   *117*
Irrelevant Arguments   *118*
Circular Reasoning   *119*
Avoiding the Issue   *119*
Forcing a Dichotomy   *120*

Fallacies of Appeal   *121*

Appeal to Ignorance   *121*
Appeal to the People   *122*
Appeal to Emotions   *122*
Appeal to Authority   *124*
Appeal to Tradition   *125*
Appeal to Humor   *125*

Fallacies in Language   *126*

Ambiguity and Equivocation   *127*
Emotionally Loaded Language   *127*
Technical Jargon   *128*

Learning Activities   *129*
Suggested Supplementary Readings   *130*

8   How Do I Argue Fact Propositions?   **131**

Analyzing the Fact Proposition   *133*

Locating the Immediate Cause   *133*
Investigating Historical Background   *133*
Defining Key Terms   *134*
Determining the Issues   *134*

Advocating Propositions of Fact   *136*

Determining the Primary Inference   *136*
Building the Prima Facie Case   *137*
Preempting Opposing Arguments   *139*
Preparing the Argumentative Brief   *140*

Opposing Propositions of Fact   *142*

Evaluating the Primary Inference   *143*
Using Presumption to Dispute the Primary Inference   *143*
Refuting by Denial and Extenuation   *144*

Learning Activities   *148*
Suggested Supplementary Readings   *149*

9   How Do I Argue Value Propositions?   **150**

The Nature of Values   *150*

Locus of Value Conflict   *151*
Processes of Value Change   *152*
Factors That Promote Change   *153*

Characteristics of Value Propositions   *155*
Analyzing the Value Proposition   *156*

Locating the Immediate Cause   *156*
Investigating Historical Background   *156*
Defining Key Terms   *158*
Determining the Issues   *158*

Advocating Value Propositions   *159*

Define the Value Object   *159*
Identify the Hierarchy   *160*
Specify the Criteria   *161*
Measure the Object   *163*

Opposing Value Propositions   *167*

Establish Strategy   *167*
Examine Definitions and Hierarchy   *168*
Challenge Criteria   *168*
Refute Measurement   *169*

Learning Activities   *173*
Suggested Supplementary Readings   *174*

10   How Do I Argue Policy Propositions?   175

Analyzing the Policy Proposition   *177*

Locating the Immediate Controversy   *177*
Investigating Historical Background   *177*
Defining Key Terms   *178*
Determining the Issues   *179*

Advocating Policy Propositions   *180*

Advocacy of the First Stock Issue   *180*
Advocacy of the Second Stock Issue   *182*
Advocacy of the Third Stock Issue   *183*
Patterns of Organization   *185*

Opposing Policy Propositions   *191*

Establish Strategy   *191*
Examine Definitions   *192*
Refute the Reason for Change   *192*
Refute the Consequences of Change   *193*
Offering Counterproposals   *195*
Patterns of Organization   *196*

Learning Activities   *200*
Suggested Supplementary Readings   *201*

Appendix   **202**

Debate Formats   *202*
Speaker Responsibilities   *204*
Burden of Clash   *207*
Cross-Examination   *208*
Flow Sheeting   *210*
Debate Judges   *210*

References   **212**

Index   **215**

PREFACE

While there are a number of books in the field of argument, we have made every effort to de-mystify the process of argumentation by treating it as a form of communicative behavior that occurs in contexts other than intercollegiate debate. To this end, we have included chapters demonstrating how issues of fact and value may be argued as legitimate ends in and of themselves, rather than just as a part of policy debate. Insofar as has been possible, we have avoided the jargon of debate, thus the focus on advocates and their opponents rather than affirmative and negative teams.

Chapter 1 defines the nature of argumentation, its place in society, and concludes with a discussion of ethics. Chapter 2 covers the three concepts central to the process of argumentation: presumption, burden of proof, and the prima facie case. Chapter 3 introduces the student to propositions and explains how they may be defined. Chapter 4 reviews the Toulmin model of argument and indicates how it may be used in the construction of arguments. Chapter 5 focuses on types and tests of evidence, as well as the means for locating and cataloging evidence for retrieval. Chapter 6 addresses reasoning from cause, sign, generalization, parallel case, analogy, authority, definition, and dilemma. Chapter 7 deals with argument gone awry as a result of fallacies of reasoning, appeal, and language. Chapters 8, 9, and 10 draw the material from the seven preceding chapters together and address the analysis of fact, value, and policy propositions. The techniques and strategies for arguing on behalf of, and against, each type of proposition are presented along with extended examples illustrating these techniques and strategies.

This book is written with the beginning student in mind. For instructors who want to do more than policy debating in their argumentation classes, each chapter offers some suggestions in the form of learning activities. We believe this book is appropriate for teaching both oral and written argument, and have included materials geared specifically to written argument in both the learning activities and the lists of suggested supplementary readings.

Though this book is a joint effort, its form and content have been shaped by more hands than ours alone. We would like to take this opportunity to publicly acknowledge the profound influence of some of these unseen hands. Douglas Ehninger and Jack Howe introduced us to argumentation and taught us much. Stephen Toulmin's writing opened our eyes, affected our thinking, and stimulated the insights which we now share with others. Our students, who have endured two earlier self-published editions, have been full of suggestions, many of which have found their way into this effort. Our reviewers, John Lyne of the University of Iowa and Dr. Warren Decker of George Mason University, were helpful with their input. We must thank Christine Ulness, our Prentice-Hall representative, and Speech Editor Steve Dalphin for "discovering" us. Without them, this would be the third self-published edition. Finally, a special thank you to our Production Editor, Marianne Peters, for her understanding and support in guiding us through the production process unscathed and on time.

1

WHAT IS ARGUMENTATION?

The way you conceptualize "arguing" or "having an argument" may influence your attitude toward this textbook and the course in which it is being used. Having been involved in the process of argumentation for many years, your authors never cease to be amazed at the misconceptions that exist about the value of argumentation. Recently a student asked us to fill out recommendation forms for employment with a certain organization. One category on the form concerned perceptions of whether or not this person was "argumentative" in nature. As this textbook unfolds, we hope that, unlike the personnel officers of that organization, you will see that being "argumentative" is not necessarily a negative trait.

THE NATURE OF ARGUMENTATION

To discover argumentation, all you have to do is look around you. You will be challenged and assaulted by many attempts to influence your beliefs and to direct your behavior to someone else's desired end. Some efforts will be aimed at your emotions, prejudices, and superstitions, but some will use information and reasoning in an attempt to influence you. Almost every person we encounter, friends, family, teachers, employers, the mass media, advertisers, editorialists, and politicians, offers arguments imbedded in persuasive appeals to encourage us to think as they do or behave as they wish. From the apparently trivial matter of choosing a breakfast cereal to the more vital decision of what career to pursue, we are constantly exposed to the argumentation of others.

Every day of our lives, each of us authors dozens of written and oral messages intended to influence the beliefs or direct the behavior of others. If you have ever asked a friend to lend you five dollars, a teacher to let you turn in a paper a week after it was due, your boss for the afternoon off, or if you have ever written a letter to the editor, you have probably engaged in argumentation. Some of your appeals may have been aimed at the emotions, prejudices, or superstitions of the persons you were trying to influence, but some probably targeted the more rational sides of their beings. It may not be unreasonable to say that were it not for argumentation, we would have very little to hear or say, read or write. As a matter of fact, what you have just read is an example of argumentation.

Argumentation is a form of instrumental communication relying on reasoning and proof to influence belief or behavior through the use of spoken or written messages.

Examination of this definition allows us to begin to understand argumentation's purpose, targets, and methods, and its relationship to persuasion. Hart and Burks (1972) suggest that all communication falls into one of two categories: expressive or instrumental. The primary purpose of expressive behavior is to allow the communicator to ventilate, to let his feelings be known, to allow his "real self" to express itself freely. The expressive communicator focuses on "self," articulating personal feelings and desires, and may not be terribly concerned about the effect these messages have on the "other." The primary purpose of instrumental communication is change—to influence what the "other" thinks or does. The instrumental communicator attempts to adopt a dual perspective (Phillips, Butt, & Metzger, 1974), considering how the expression of the ideas of the "self" will be received by the "other." Argumentation is a form of instrumental communication precisely because it is concerned with how the "other" will respond. It is intended to produce change in the "other," either in belief or behavior or both.

Obviously, the target of argumentation is the "other," but there are several potential "others" to whom argumentation may be directed. The first, most obvious, "other" is your opponent, the person whose belief or behavior you wish to change. However, the "other" may also be a nominally disinterested, or at least neutral, third party who possesses the power to constrain the behavior, and possibly even the beliefs, of your opponent. We engage in argumentation directed at this third party to encourage her to render a decision which will produce the change we desire in our opponent.

Finally, the "other" can be a part of our "self." In the process of intrapersonal decision making, we frequently engage in an internal dialogue, listing the pros and cons of two mutually exclusive courses of action or contradictory schools of thought. Thus, the target of argumentation is one of several possible "others" who has the power to ensure the desired change in belief or behavior.

While the medium of argumentation is speaking or writing, the method of argumentation rests on the dual nature of communication as either expressive or instrumental; the latter is superior. Instead of seeking to alter the "other's" thoughts or actions in response to an expressive disclosure of the feelings of the "self," practitioners of argumentation adopt the dual perspective referred to earlier. In so doing, the arguer's "self" sets forth reflective, critically formulated statements of his beliefs, which appeal to sources of belief in the "other." Such instrumental communication confronts the sensibilities of listener or reader directly, laying out an analysis of the relevant data upon which the request for an alteration of belief or behavior is based. In argumentation, one tries to take the "other" into account and to construct messages reflecting an understanding of his point of view. Expressive disclosures of "self" have the result that both parties in the dispute fail to see any point of view aside from their own.

Anyone who has witnessed or participated in the following sort of dialogue will instantly recognize why we claim that instrumental communication, or argumentation, is the superior method of altering belief or behavior. Consider these two expressive youngsters:

BARTHOLOMEW: Can I play ball with you?
CHADWICK: No!
BARTHOLOMEW: Why?
CHADWICK: Cause.
BARTHOLOMEW: But why?
CHADWICK: Mom! Bartholomew is bugging me. Make him leave me alone!

In many ways, this fictitious dialogue possesses superficial characteristics which might suggest that it is argumentation. Verbal messages are employed in an attempt to promote changes in belief and behavior, and the first two forms of the "other" are addressed. But this encounter fails as an example of argumentation through its method of communication, which is predominantly expressive. Bartholomew and Chadwick know in their heart of hearts that they are right, and they do not consider what the "other" might be thinking or why he might be thinking it. Even Chadwick's solicitation of aid from a nominally neutral third party reflects a concern only for "self" and its free expression. The probable result:

MOM: Chadwick, be nice to your little brother. Now you take him along, and let him play. Do you hear me!

Both youngsters learn something from this experience. Chadwick is probably less likely to take such problems to Mom in the future, since her neutrality has become suspect in his eyes. Bartholomew, however, may develop a strategy which renders even this defense useless: Go straight to Mom whenever the prospect of a ball game arises. Chadwick's only defense rests on his discovery of instrumental communication and his ability to adopt a dual perspective. At that point he discovers argumentation and possibly the winning argument.

CHADWICK: OK Mom, it's just that the guys I play with are all my age and some of them are bigger than me. I was just worried that Bartholomew might get hurt, since we play tackle.

The need of the "self" to be free of Bartholomew is still addressed by this argument, but two conflicting needs within the "other" are aroused. First, Mom's concern for her younger son's safety is addressed directly. Second, her desire that her older son not be deprived of socializing experiences with his peer group is imbedded in the subject of the entire conversation. While she may decide that tackle football is too dangerous for both of them, Chadwick's use of dual perspective and instrumental communication gives him a chance to affect a change in belief and behavior.

The ability to develop, maintain, and employ a dual perspective in your communicative behavior is something you developed long before reaching college. The study of argumentation takes this facility and further refines and develops it. Specifically, we will be examining means of urging changes in the beliefs and behaviors of "others" based on appeal to the rational, as opposed to the emotional, side of their natures. At this point it will be helpful to distinguish argumentation from the larger category of communication designed to influence belief and behavior—persuasion.

Recall our earlier discussion of your role as both consumer and creator of messages intended to influence belief and behavior, in which we indicated that these appeals might be directed at emotions, prejudices, superstition, or reason. A message may be intended to produce a response which is either predominantly affective or predominantly cognitive. Another form of instrumental communication, persuasion, concerns itself with the study of messages and responses to messages, which are both affective and cognitive in their appeal. Eisenberg and Ilardo (1980) suggest that the function of persuasion is to change minds by any means short of physical force and that the principal criterion for evaluating persuasion is its effectiveness in inducing change. Argumentation concerns itself with the study of messages, and responses to messages, aimed at the cognitive domain. Eisenberg and Ilardo suggest that the function of argumentation is to establish conclusions through the use of reasoned discourse, and that the principal criterion for evaluating argumentation is its logical cogency. Thus, while the goals of argumentation and persuasion may be similar, the paths followed to reach these goals may not be. Argumentation and persuasion may upon occasion utilize the techniques of message making, but persuasion is a much broader category of attempt at influence, and the worth of argumentative and persuasive messages is judged by different means.

When you engage in communication, whether you are using argumentation or some other form of message construction, you are engaging in behavior that is governed by rules. One set of rules that we use in American society to make sense out of messages is the rules of English grammar. In addition to the rules we learn in acquiring our native tongue, individual communication contexts may have their own particular rules of what is appropriate or meaningful in communication practice. Communicators may employ instrumental or expressive behavior, creating and using rule sets as broadly applicable as those used in public speaking or as narrowly defined as the rules that govern communication in a particular family. We learn these communication rules through formal instruction or through informal modeling of the behavior of those around us. Some rule sets are applicable to more than one context. Because argumentation may occur in a variety of communication contexts, the communication rules for effective argumentation you will learn from this textbook may be appropriate in several contexts beyond the argumentation classroom.

THE USEFULNESS OF ARGUMENTATION

In distinguishing between argumentation and persuasion it is not our purpose to suggest that argumentation is the superior form of communication behavior. Because changes in belief and behavior often have serious consequences, we believe there are good reasons to study and employ methods of argumentation in many everyday situations that call for decision making. For both pragmatic and philosophic reasons, argumentation studies are well worth your time and effort.

First, argumentation is a reliable method for arriving at the "truth." Beliefs and behaviors arrived at through argumentation result from careful examination of facts and expert opinion, not from responses colored by emotion and prejudice, or by habitual predetermined responses caused by triggering stimuli (Ehninger, 1974). Beliefs and behaviors resulting from emotion, prejudice, or triggering stimuli stand the test of time only by serendipity. When you reach a decision through argumentation, you are more likely to feel good about it because it will stand up both to your scrutiny and to the criticism of others. To test this premise, pretend you are buying a new car. Which decision-making process will produce the most satisfaction in the long run, buying a car because the color appeals to you or buying the car with the best track record for safety, mileage, performance, and factory support?

Second, the use of argumentation increases personal flexibility (Ehninger, 1974). When you base belief or behavior on the dictates of an authority figure, tradition, custom, or prejudice, you may be unable to adapt to environmental changes that challenge that belief or behavior. We see humor in an individual's inability to cope with change, laughing at an Archie Bunker or a George Jefferson. When we are that person, however, the situation is less amusing. Beliefs and behaviors arrived at through argumentation are less inclined to rigidity, for rather than relying on traditional patterns, the practitioner of argumentation searches out and develops new patterns of belief and behavior as new situations and new problems arise. Developing argumentation skills is a means of coping with a future in which new knowledge and new ideas may make our "truth" seem invalid.

The third pragmatic reason for the use of argumentation is found in the willingness of the listener or reader to change belief or behavior because he has played a part in the argumentation process. When you change as a consequence of an argument you have heard or read, you are acting of your own volition, not because the argument's author has imposed his will upon you (Ehninger, 1974). Because argumentation is a two-way process, a dialogue between you and those whose beliefs or behaviors you wish to influence, much of the resistance that would be present if you attempted to impose change upon them is defused.

There are also philosophical reasons for the use of argumentation that supplement the pragmatic reasons. First, communication is generally regarded as a liberal art. When we discuss the liberal arts, we are typically concerned with those disciplines that civilize and humanize us. Argumentation is a civilizing, humanizing process, since its practitioner must respect both his own rationality and that of his reader or listener. Argumentation treats people as rational beings rather than objects, incapable of thought.

A second philosophical justification for the use of argumentation is apparent when we examine the use of persuasion in our society. Listen to the network news or read one of the national news magazines. It will not take long to find references to "mere rhetoric," or "presidential rhetoric." What the media are really criticizing is not rhetoric or persuasion but how it is practiced. We are suspicious of persuaders who seek knee-jerk responses based on emotions, prejudices, or superstitions. By contrast, argumentation overcomes one of the objections to contemporary persuasion by treating its consumer as a rational person. The arguer seeks not to manipulate the receiver, but to offer her the opportunity to participate in the process by respecting her ability to think.

For the humanizing influences of argumentation to occur, its practitioners must accept substantial personal risk. Argumentation occurs in response to controversy. The potential advocate must make a choice: to retreat from controversy by taking secure refuge in his established beliefs, or to confront the controversy, exposing his beliefs to unknown challenges that might result in their disconfirmation and alteration (Eisenberg & Ilardo, 1980). The potential advocate, realizing the risks involved, may decide that the potential payoffs from successful argumentation and the probability of achieving success are insufficient to warrant the risk.

One of the ways in which the individual grows is through confronting new ideas and change. As is true of any encounter in which a portion of the "self" is disclosed, argumentation carries risks that, if confronted, can result in substantial personal growth. Philosopher Henry Johnstone, Jr. (1965) sees argumentation, and its attendant risks, as an essential part of the development of a healthy, fully functioning "self." For Johnstone, there is "self" only when there is risk, and the risk found in argumentation "is a defining feature of the human situation" (p. 17). Thus, accepting the risk of engaging in argumentation is not only a means of making our ideas acceptable to others and thereby achieving interpersonal goals, but it is also a vehicle for intrapersonal growth, testing our ideas so that we may reject those we discover to be unsound or irrelevant.

LIMITATIONS ON THE USE OF ARGUMENTATION

It is possible to find negative examples of persuasion, such as the demagoguery of a Hitler, and argumentation also has its limitations, since it is practiced by fallible human beings whose motives may not always be above reproach. To achieve its fullest humanizing potential, argumentation depends on the ethics of its practitioners. An unsound argument or one based on shallow or inadequate proof can, through skillful oral and written presentation, be made to appear valid. Thus, as with other means of altering belief or behavior, argumentation can be subject to abuse.

Ever since the first textbooks on argumentation and persuasion were written, scholars of communication have been concerned with the use of argumentation to promote the selfish ambitions of the individual rather than the good of the group or society. Plato, concerned with the practice of rhetoric in ancient Athens, urged his students to practice *dialectic,* the use of questions and answers to arrive at truth, instead of argumentation and persuasion. Plato felt that arguments were mere flattery in the guise of rational thought. Aristotle, influenced by Plato, also warned students that appeals based solely on emotions were unethical. Two thousand years later, the problem remains. Automobiles are sold on the basis of sex appeal, household cleansers are marketed on the basis of social disapproval, and politicians are packaged on the basis of form rather than substance.

Since we have listed the virtues of argumentation as a means of influence, you may wonder why the manufacturers of automobiles and household cleansers and the campaign managers of political candidates do not insist on carefully reasoned arguments to gain the public's acceptance. The second limitation of argumentation explains why. The process of argumentation is time consuming. In subsequent chapters, you will learn about the process of phrasing propositions, defining terms, conducting research, and constructing arguments. Changing belief or behavior through rational processes takes time. Although the ethics of resorting to emotion to transmit the message may be questionable, it can be achieved in a thirty-second spot or in a single picture. After all, would you want your favorite TV program interrupted for half an hour while someone proves why "ring around the collar" will make you a pariah?

In a very real sense, frustration over the second limitation of argumentation can cause its practitioners to engage in ethically questionable behavior. The time necessary to marshall sufficient evidence to support a position and ensure its logical consistency can make all the more alluring the siren song of stimuli that trigger an emotional response. In subsequent chapters dealing with the evidence and reasoning on which argumentation is based, we will provide a set of guidelines, or minimal standards, for sufficiency. As a creator of arguments, you should employ these standards rigorously in evaluating your own work. As a consumer of argumentation, you should be equally rigorous in using them, testing what you hear and read to ensure it is not emotive discourse masquerading as argumentation.

The potential abuses of argumentation notwithstanding, we need the ability to argue in order to communicate successfully. We have poked fun at commercials that seem to misuse persuasion and argumentation because most of you are familiar with these examples. Realize that these same techniques, which may seem creative or merely annoying in the commercials, create serious problems when used to "sell" a point of view on public policy issues such as nuclear weapons, the environment, or education.

APPLICATIONS OF ARGUMENTATION

The most common applications of argumentation are found in situations where the individual discovers goals to be achieved or tasks to be completed that he is incapable of accomplishing alone. To implement new programs or change existing ones, to gain support for developments in thinking and theory building, to create new laws or alter existing legislation, an individual with an idea is dependent on the support of others. In seeking this support, he must communicate not only his goal but the evidence and good reasons that make it worthy of the support of others. To do this, people commonly engage in argumentation. Real-world examples demonstrate this and reinforce our earlier claim that argumentation is an instrumental rather than an expressive form of communication.

The first example, which affects a large number of Americans each year, is found in the criminal justice system. While both prosecuting and defense attorneys have goals, albeit conflicting ones, concerning the conviction or acquittal of the defendant, they are incapable of achieving these goals without the assent of a nominally disinterested third party, the jury. The disinterest of the jury may be more than nominal, since *voir dire* is used to weed out potential jurors who have already formed an opinion or who might be predisposed to make a decision based on some triggering stimulus, such as the race or age of the defendant, rather than the facts of the case. Because the system rests on societal values concerning the right to fair trial, the presumption of innocence until guilt is proven, and the preferability of freeing a possibly guilty individual to convicting an innocent one, the defense is given certain advantages, not the least of which is *pretrial discovery*.

Pretrial discovery allows the defense to request to see the evidence on which the prosecution's case rests. After inspecting the basis, in evidence and in reasoning, for the case against his client, the defense lawyer may choose among alternative defenses, instrumentally determining which best serves his client's interests. Many of the concepts discussed in the next chapter—the prima facie argument, presumption, and burden of proof—are applied in criminal and civil proceedings every day. Although you may have no intention of becoming a lawyer, serving on a jury, being a criminal, or a victim, the second example represents the kind of argumentation to which we are regularly exposed and may even engage in ourselves.

Political campaigns, especially presidential campaigns, afford us an opportunity to observe political argumentation practices. In a larger sense, political campaigns are persuasive because they deal with the images of candidates in addition to the issues. However, one aspect of political campaigning emphasizes argumentation—candidate debates. Debates allow voters to hear the candidates' stand on the important issues of the day. The tradition of political debating began with the series of debates between Abraham Lincoln and Stephen Douglas in the 1858 race for the Illinois Senate seat. In those debates, a single issue, slavery, dominated argumentation. Recently debates between presidential candidates have become common.

In 1960 Richard M. Nixon and John F. Kennedy met in the first debates between presidential candidates that were also the first televised debates. In 1976, Gerald Ford and Jimmy Carter participated in a series of televised debates; the 1980 presidential campaign offered debates between Ronald Reagan and John Anderson, while Anderson's independent candidacy was still viable, and later a Carter-Reagan debate. The 1984 presidential campaign featured extensive televised debating among the Democratic contenders for the nomination, and later two debates between Ronald Reagan and Walter Mondale, and a debate between the vice presidential candidates. What has characterized presidential debates has been a broad consideration of both domestic and foreign policy issues. America's role overseas, the use of military force, and the support of repressive regimes friendly to the United States have been important foreign policy issues in these debates. Economic and industrial policy, defense spending, and social issues such as abortion and the rights of women and minorities have been debated in election years.

Argumentation is also frequently employed in society's attempt to deal with controversies such as that of evolution science versus scientific creationism. The controversy is between a scientific explanation that life on earth evolved and the fundamentalist view that life appeared as an act of divine creation. Examples of arguments from the evolutionist's point of view are found in *Scientists Confront Creationism*, edited by Laurie R. Godfrey (1983). The book offers the arguments of several scientists and affords the reader an excellent demonstration of using arguments to establish fact: the earth is ancient, geology and paleontology disprove the idea of a single global flood, the second law of thermodynamics does not disprove evolution, and there is a close evolutionary relationship between human beings and apes. Each issue is approached by addressing the scientific response to the creationists' claims.

Issues about which people disagree abound in our society. We have the opportunity to observe or participate in argumentation on almost every subject or interest. We do not deny the desirability of expressive communication in some controversies. In the context of achieving change, argumentation, which is instrumental, is an effective means of communication and an important part of persuasive communication.

THE HISTORICAL DEVELOPMENT OF ARGUMENTATION

In this text we emphasize a model, or structure, for creating arguments developed by the English logician Stephen Toulmin. It is offered primarily as a means of organizing ideas in a form that listeners or readers will find most appropriate. As evidenced by our references to Plato and Aristotle, the study of argumentation has an extensive foundation in the genesis of our discipline. To gain a better understanding of contemporary argumentation theory and its evolution, it is worthwhile to look briefly at some of the earliest theories of argumentation and the societal forces that precipitated them.

The formal study of argumentation began in ancient Greece. Citizenship in the democracy of Athens required communication skills. Each male freeborn citizen might be called upon to serve the state in the deliberative processes of the assembly or the judgmental processes of the courts. He might also find himself acting as prosecutor or defense attorney, since the Greek judicial system required each party to the action to represent himself. The Greeks also engaged in public speaking on ceremonial occasions.

The study of communication skills necessary to fulfill these requirements—*rhetoric*—was an important part of formal elementary education. The foundations of argumentation, as studied today, were laid in those ancient schools. Rhetoric was conceived as a humane discipline, grounded in choice, that was primarily designed to persuade or change the listener. The communicator's function was to influence choice by developing meaningful probabilities, or arguments, in support of a claim that was being contested. Emphasis was placed on the claims that occurred in the courts, since so much speaking involved arguing one's own case.

One of the greatest of the Greek rhetoricians, Aristotle, viewed the practice of argumentation as central to human nature, "for to a certain extent all men attempt to discuss statements and to maintain them, to defend themselves, and to attack others" (Roberts, trans., 1954, p. 19). Aristotle had defined rhetoric as the ability to find, in a given situation, all the means of persuading an audience to believe a proposition. This involved more than just building workable arguments. The responsibility of the communicator was to investigate everything his audience might be moved by—their emotions, their political beliefs, and those sources of information which they most respected. The responsible communicator would choose the most ethical, the most nearly true, of all of these available means of persuasion.

In their refinement of Greek rhetoric, Roman authors identified four kinds of questions crucial to legal disputes: (1) questions of fact—did the accused commit a crime; (2) questions of definition—if the accusation is theft, might not the act have been just borrowing; (3) questions of justification—if the act were theft, did the accused steal out of dire need; and (4) questions of procedure—was the charge properly made (Fisher & Sayles, 1966). The nature of these legal controversies, and the need for judges to determine which party to the dispute more nearly represented the "truth," was a driving force behind the development of rhetoric in Greece and Rome. While rhetoric was developed in the legal context, its study produced workable theories of argumentation and persuasion applicable to controversies in other contexts as well.

Theories of communication, then as now, included the content of the message, its context, and its potential consequences. In studying argumentation, we are concerned with that part of rhetorical theory relating to message content, its logic, form, and structure. From the body of classical writings on communication come the following propositions identifying what is involved in argumentation: (1) arguments are a series of logically related statements, (2) arguments use reasoning in writing and speaking, (3) arguments use reasoning to induce belief, (4) arguments rely on their author to discharge certain ethical responsibilities, and (5) arguments constitute a means of persuasion.

ETHICAL STANDARDS FOR ARGUMENTATION

Because consumers of argumenation often lack the time or resources to verify every statement made, the creator of arguments bears a heavy ethical burden, for that which is made to seem most probable or believable is that which is most likely to gain acceptance. Just like other forms of communication, argumentation has the potential for great good or evil. Communication is a social act that implies moral obligations to one's audience (Nilsen, 1974), whether that audience is the world or a single individual. Our communication is often judged as good or bad by the audience on the basis of how well we meet those moral obligations. This is the essence of speaker credibility.

Like other forms of communication, argumentation is a matter of choosing what to say. In preparing argumentative cases, you will research a topic, decide which claims and proofs to offer, and decide how to arrange your materials for the most impact. Whether your end product is deemed ethical or unethical will ultimately be determined by your audience. Because we live in a society that holds freedom of thought and speech as a seminal value, ethical communication practices are aimed at protecting the rights of free speech while at the same time respecting the rights of audiences.

Stanley G. Rives (1964) suggests that those who engage in argumentation in a democratic society have three ethical obligations: "(1) the responsibility to research the proposition thoroughly to know truth, (2) the responsibility to dedicate his effort to the common good, and (3) the responsibility to be rational" (p. 84). To these we add a fourth obligation: the responsibility to observe the rules of free speech in a democratic society.

The Research Responsibility

An ethical arguer will thoroughly research the proposition to discover as much as possible of what is probably true of the subject. Although no one expects you to find everything on a given subject, your responsibility is to prepare your argumentative cases as thoroughly as you can. Ethical argumentation requires you to be well informed. This means knowing the subject not only from your viewpoint but from opposing viewpoints as well. It means using to the best advantage the resources available to you.

The research responsibility also requires you to use the facts and the opinions of others honestly. Remember that when you think something through, something you have witnessed, read, or heard, you filter the information through your unique cognitive maps of experience. You decide how you will interpret reality. In deciding, you have the ability to distort or confuse the facts. Your ethical obligation is to avoid consciously distorting information, thus misleading your audience. What is wrong with distortion, especially if it is done in pursuit of a worthy goal? Simply this, you violate the trust of your audience and create the possibility of not being considered a credible source in the future. During the 1960s and 1970s, the arguments used by government officials to justify the Vietnam War and the Watergate coverup created a crisis of belief that caused many Americans to question the veracity of any government official on any subject.

Beyond being honest in reporting facts and opinions, you should never fabricate research. Making up information is deceptive and unethical. With information available on almost any subject, a diligent exploration of printed resources will yield what you need to prove your arguments.

Realize that probable truth may exist on both sides of a controversy. Issues in human affairs are seldom one sided. Indeed, we define something as controversial when at least two conflicting, legitimate points of view regarding it exist. Just because information does not jibe with your point of view does not mean that such information is a "lie."

The Common Good Responsibility

An ethical arguer has, as her objective, the welfare of the society. Many issues argued involve resolving which policy is best, which course of action should be taken. The responsible arguer always creates argumentative positions that stress the benefits of a course of action to society, attempting to determine the course of action that will bring about the greatest common good. In controversies over values, argumentation focuses on the value or value system that ought to prevail for the common good.

The responsibility to seek the common good is a tricky ethical proposition. What appears good to one individual may appear evil to another. The issue of abortion on demand illustrates the problem. For some, the right to an abortion is an essential right of choice, consistent with the societal value of freedom of choice. For others, abortion constitutes murder of the unborn, a violation of the rights of the fetus. Which set of rights is preeminent? The answer is ultimately up to the individual based on his values. This issue illustrates the importance of thorough research, for determining the common good is not always an easy task. While research may not provide answers in every instance of conflicting values, it will at least help you to better understand the values or policies in conflict.

Ethical behavior demonstrates one's character, and the tradition in communication is that a prerequisite of good character is placing the audience's welfare above your own interests. Therefore, ethical argumentation attempts to satisfy acknowledged public wants and needs. You rarely hear a presidential candidate state, "Vote for me because I want to be president." Rather, the candidate asks for votes on the basis that he best represents the will of the electorate.

One aspect of ethical argumentation that promotes the common good is that we live in a society of laws and are obliged to respect these laws. Changing a law is often the basis for debate and discussion and the responsible arguer advocates that we change laws rather than break them. Although it is possible to point to exceptional cases, such as the civil rights protests of the 1960s in which "morally repugnant" segregation laws were violated for the purpose of drawing attention to their unjustness, generally the responsible argumentative position is to advocate change. You may, for example, feel that laws against the possession and use of marijuana, laws requiring the wearing of safety equipment, or laws regulating the purchase and consumption of alcoholic beverages are unjust, but to advocate violating them is to advocate anarchy. A responsible arguer makes a case by demonstrating a law's injustice, rather than deprecating the concept of the rule of law in society.

The Reasoning Responsibility

An ethical arguer uses sound reasoning in the form of logically adequate arguments supported by facts and expert opinions. Good or sound reasons are the premier rule of argumentation and rhetoric according to modern theorists (Golden, Berquist, & Coleman, 1983). To engage in communication is to use and to respect its rules. When translated into practice, this requires the arguer to assume responsibility regarding the form that her message takes. The rules of argumentation will be discussed in subsequent chapters on research practices, constructing arguments, testing their quality, and organizing them into a case format. While you do not need to be a slave to rules, ethical argumentation requires that you know and use them as a means of addressing the rationality of your audience.

The Social Code Responsibility

An ethical advocate respects the rights of other arguers and the audience in order to preserve freedom of speech in a democratic society. Freedom of speech means everyone is entitled to a point of view, even if it is different than yours. Those with opposing viewpoints have an equal right to be heard and deserve the courtesy you expect for yourself. This is a form of "the golden rule" appropriate to communication. Remember, sometime you may be the one who has the opposing view, and your right to be heard will be jeopardized if only majority opinions are allowed free expression.

One social code of argumentation is that while criticism and refutation are important parts of the process, they should be directed toward the arguer's reasoning and proof, not his person. Character assassination is not good argumentation because it diverts attention from the issues and does nothing to further the rationality of your position. Point out the misinterpretations or mistakes in the other person's position but do not accuse him of little intelligence for having offered them.

Earlier we said that communication was rule-governed behavior. In addition to rules telling us about word order, idea organization, and rational thinking, there are rules of social custom that govern communication behavior. Discover these for the context in which you are arguing and avoid violating them. Because a word is in your vocabulary does not mean its use is appropriate in every communication context. Social customs include dressing appropriately and avoiding slang expressions and poor jokes. A social code that is becoming increasingly important in a number of different communication contexts is avoiding language that discriminates on the basis of age, sex, race, ethnic origin, or personal characteristics. Because social customs vary greatly, being ethical means being flexible and determining what conduct is appropriate before a given audience. Remember, you will be judged on the basis of how well you operate within the social customs of the group before which you are speaking.

Many different standards of ethical behavior may be in operation at any given time. Rules of law, religious codes of conduct, situational ethics, and professional codes of behavior can determine what is appropriate in any given situation. Standards of ethics should not be taken as absolutes, however, since they seldom fit every instance of behavior, especially when you are considering what would be the greater good. We have suggested some standards that will serve you well in practicing argumentation.

When we engage in argumentation to influence the belief or behavior of another, we usually find ourselves demonstrating what is possible or probable, rather than what is absolutely true in all situations (Cowan, 1964). In defining argumentation as a form of instrumental communication, we view the process as an audience-centered approach to the resolution of controversy. The goal of the practitioner of argumentation is to gain the assent of the audience regarding the issue under consideration. Argumentation is not an end in and of itself but a means to the end that results when consensus is achieved.

LEARNING ACTIVITIES

1. Discuss the advantages and disadvantages of using argumentation as a means of influencing the belief and behavior of others. How will the advantages of argumentation improve your ability to communicate your views in a controversy? How will you overcome the limitations of argumentation?
2. We have used commercials to illustrate the use of emotional responses and to discuss some of the differences between communication that is expressive and communication that is exclusively instrumental. To study these differences, find examples of advertisements in magazines or newspapers that seek an emotional response from the reader. For each example indicate the emotional response sought. Do any of these examples also make use of instrumental communication?
3. Find an example of argumentation that you perceive to be effective and respond to the following questions:

    A. Why is this an example of argumentation rather than persuasion? Or does it have elements of both instrumental and expressive communication?

    B. What evidence do you have that the author of the argument is fulfilling the ethical responsibilities of arguing?

4. Think about the opinions you most strongly hold. Upon what are these based? Examine the sources of these beliefs for evidence of reasoning, emotions, prejudices, tradition, or authority figures.

5. Develop a code of ethical standards for your argumentation class. In particular, the class should determine what social codes will be appropriate. What will you consider to be ethical and unethical behaviors?

SUGGESTED SUPPLEMENTARY READINGS

ANDERSON, J. M., AND DOVRE, P. J. (Eds.) *Readings in Argumentation.* Boston: Allyn & Bacon, 1968.

> This collection of essays offers views on argumentation ranging from the classical to the contemporary. We recommend the sections on the ethics of controversy and argumentation in society, and Sidney Hook's essay on the ground rules for controversy in a democracy, which may be used to formulate a standard of ethics for the argumentation class.

MARTEL, M. *Political Campaign Debates.* New York: Longman, 1983.

> Argumentation as practiced in presidential debates is this book's focus, and it provides a thorough treatment of the goals and strategies used in them. The author analyzes the 1980 Reagan-Carter debate and offers practical suggestions for candidate debates on political issues.

NILSEN, T. R. *Ethics of Speech Communication* (2nd Ed.). Indianapolis: Bobbs-Merrill, 1974.

> As the title suggests, the nature of ethics and the requirements for ethical communication are examined in depth. Particular emphasis is given to the speaker's obligation to offer the audience the opportunity to make an informed choice. An excellent work on ethics and persuasion.

RIVES, S. G. Ethical Argumentation. *Journal of the American Forensic Association*, 1964, *1*, 79-85.

> Rives describes the relationship between ethics and argumentation and focuses on the ethical responsibilities of arguers in terms of communication behaviors that regulate argumentation. He takes the perspective that an ideal democratic society would obligate communicators to operationalize three value standards: truth, human welfare, and rationality. These standards are explained in the context of academic argumentation.

2

WHAT DO I NEED TO KNOW BEFORE I CAN BEGIN TO ARGUE?

There are three commonly observed conventions of argumentation that are useful in determining the responsibilities concerning proof and reasoning for those who engage in argumentation. In both real-world and academic argumentation, those who advocate change and those who oppose change each have initial roles that assign responsibilities at the outset of the dispute. The **advocate** in argumentation is the person who communicates to encourage a change in the belief or behavior of others. The **opponent** is the person who acts to discourage the change supported by the advocate, fulfilling the role of spokesperson for the existing beliefs and behaviors of the audience targeted by the advocate. Using sports as an analogy, the advocate plays offense, the opponent plays defense. The conventions of presumption, burden of proof, and prima facie case development identify the playing field.

PRESUMPTION

All argumentation takes place over a piece of figurative ground occupied by existing belief, policy, or institutions. This figurative ground represents the way things are at present. **Presumption** is the term that specifies who occupies this ground at the beginning of the controversy. Historically, the concept of presumption has reflected two viewpoints: presumption is either artificial or natural. The concept of *artificial* presumption comes from the legal system. In the American legal system, every defendant is presumed innocent until the probability of his guilt can be demonstrated by the state, in the case of criminal law, or by the plaintiff in the case of civil law. This presumption of innocence is termed artificial because it is the result of argumentative ground being assigned arbitrarily as a result of a societally accepted convention. The French system of justice, for example, proceeds from the opposite assumption: The accused is guilty until he proves the probability of his innocence.

Natural presumption derives from the observation of the natural order in the world around us. When an advocate challenges a belief or behavior derived from existing institutions, practices, customs, values, or interpretations of reality, presumption automatically rests with the belief or behavior being challenged simply because it currently exists. Our understanding of natural presumption is drawn from the work of Anglican Archbishop Richard Whatley (1828/1963). In discussing presumption he used the analogy of a company of troops inside a fortress. Change would dictate that the company march forth to meet the enemy; presumption would dictate that the company remain secure within its fortress rather than venturing onto an unknown battlefield. Since natural presumption reflects the way things are in the world around us, the natural order of things would suggest that the troops not abandon a secure position in favor of an open field. It is up to the opposing force to attack their fortified position.

Pragmatically, presumption can serve as a decision rule for determining which viewpoint is acceptable if the advocate for change fails to make a good case. Whatley was particularly concerned that those who argue realize what presumption means in preparing an argumentative case. He urged that they begin by knowing where presumption lies and that in their arguments they point out whose is the burden of proving the argumentative position.

The importance of determining where presumption lies is emphasized when we consider that natural presumption resides in whatever point of view the audience of argumentation may hold. In addition to existing institutions, that for which the audience holds "deference" is identified by Whatley as a source of presumption. The persons, practices, ideas, or sources of information the audience accepts can be regarded as existing ground. A contemporary example illustrates how presumption may change depending upon the audience.

Suppose you are making a speech in favor of abortion to two audiences, one composed of members of a right-to-life group and the other composed of members of the National Organization of Women (NOW)—groups holding opposing views on the subject. The right-to-life supporters will not automatically grant that the Supreme Court decision allowing abortion, Roe

v. Wade, should stand until good and sufficient reasons come along to change it. They believe that good and sufficient reasons already exist. If you supported abortion, you would have to make a case for its continued existence, placing presumption with those who oppose existing practice. Before the NOW audience, the situation is reversed. Since this group favors freedom of choice in the matter of abortion, they will automatically grant that the existing practice is acceptable until good and sufficient reasons to change it are provided.

These two audiences hold diametrically opposed positions on the abortion issue and illustrate how presumption can shift given the audience. Not all audience beliefs will be as firmly held, however. The strength of any given presumption may vary from strong to weak depending upon the degree of importance the audience attaches to the subject. You might address these same groups on a different topic, such as social security benefits, and find they hold similar ideas about the existing institution of social security.

Realizing this audience-centered aspect of presumption can be very useful in practical applications of instrumental communication. Presumption is a communication convention with implications for audience analysis. Thus, a determination of audience beliefs is used to survey the figurative ground and help you decide what your responsibilities for proving arguments will include (Matlon, 1978; Sproule, 1976). Sproule (1976) suggests a method for determining presumption:

> The arguer is advised to ask such questions as: (1) to what groups do members of the audience belong? (2) to what sources of information (persons, books, groups) do audience members accord deference? (3) what is the popular and unpopular opinion on a particular subject? (4) what information on a subject might hold the advantage of novelty? Such queries would assist the advocate in selecting arguments and evidence best fitted to persuading persons on a given subject. (p. 128)

In addition to the view that presumption favors existing institutions and the view that presumption is found in audience attitudes, there is the view that presumption is a decision rule for determining who "wins" the argument. Usually applied in academic argumentation, the proposition for argumentation is a hypothesis that must be tested by the cases for and against its acceptance (Brydon, 1983; Patterson & Zarefsky, 1983; Vasilius, 1980; Zarefsky, 1972). The testing of the hypothesis occurs as advocate and opponent argue back and forth, with an evaluation made on the strength of their arguments, the quality of their proof, and the soundness of their reasoning. Hypothesis testing is a form of artificial presumption because academic argumentation usually accords presumption to the opponent and rests on the assumption that he or she who asserts a proposition must prove it.

We may, then, view presumption from three different perspectives:

1. Presumption identifies existing beliefs, policies, practices, or institutions.
2. Presumption is determined by prevailing beliefs of the audience.
3. Presumption is a decision rule that determines what the advocate must prove in testing the proposition as a hypothesis.

Which version of presumption should you use in preparing to argue? Decide by examining the context in which argumentation will take place. In interpersonal communication and certain public speaking contexts, analyzing your audience may be the best means of determining presumption. In a context where it is obvious that there seems to be universal agreement about what beliefs, policies, practices, or institutions exist, you may immediately recognize who or what occupies the figurative ground. In an academic setting, using presumption in the form of a decision rule may be more appropriate. Whichever version of presumption you have decided best fits your communication context, you will use the convention of presumption to identify the ground over which argumentation will take place.

Presumption grants possession to the person fulfilling the role of opponent. The opponent represents an existing belief, policy, or institution and gains a logical advantage. We assume that that which exists should be maintained unless good reasons exist to change it. Presumption simply describes what exists without making any kind of judgment about its worth or effectiveness. Consider the following description:

> The existing curriculum at Northern State University involves courses which are mostly worth four credit hours although a few one-, two-, and three-credit courses exist. Student schedules and faculty teaching loads are designed around the four-credit-hours-per-course system. Some members of the faculty and students would like to have the system converted to a three-credit standard.

In this case, presumption states that a system of four-credit courses exists and functions at Northern State University. Presumption does not suggest this is necessarily good for learning or teaching, just that it is present. Controversy over the credit-hour system would revolve around the efforts of advocates to present a series of good reasons for changing the system and the efforts of opponents who, using the logical advantage of presumption, might argue that the present four-credit system exists and functions and may be defended on the basis of its functioning.

In argumentation the importance of the convention of presumption lies in the responsibility it places upon the advocate. Since the advocate does not have the benefit of presumption, which favors no change, he must show good and sufficient reasons why we can no longer rely on those beliefs or behaviors that possess presumption because they presently exist. We may summarize presumption in the following principles:

1. The term *presumption* describes a situation that currently exists and points out a prevailing order—that the opponent presently occupies the figurative ground over which the argument will be contested.

2. Presumption only describes. It does not judge the value or lack of value of the existing beliefs, practices, policies, or institutions presently occupying the ground.

With these principles in mind, we can move to the second convention of argumentation, which logically derives from presumption.

BURDEN OF PROOF

Presumption describes the preoccupation of ground in argumentation by the opponent; the **burden of proof** is the obligation of the advocate to contest the ground by offering arguments that are logically sufficient to challenge presumption. The advocate of change has the responsibility of proving his position. To fully understand what the burden of proof involves, begin by recalling that presumption describes what exists without passing judgment on it.

The advocate, in fulfilling the burden of proof, both passes judgment on and criticizes present belief or behavior and recommends a new belief or behavior. He begins by specifying or naming what it is that should not continue—the existing belief or behavior awarded preoccupation of the ground by presumption. To fulfill his obligation of burden of proof, the advocate must demonstrate why whatever presently occupies the disputed figurative ground should not continue to do so. The content and scope of the burden of proof is specified by the statement of the proposition argued.

The burden of proof may also be described as the obligation of the complaining party in a dispute. In civil law, this obligation would be identified with the responsibility of the plaintiff to proceed first and make a case against the defendant, proving his complaint by a preponderance of evidence. If you were dissatisfied with an automobile you had purchased and decided to sue the dealership, as the plaintiff you would have to demonstrate through the introduction of evidence and testimony that you had been harmed or damaged in some way as a result of the dealer's actions. In criminal law, the State acts as advocate and must prove beyond reasonable doubt that the accused is guilty of the crime. This constitutes the State's burden of proof.

In a controversy, the burden of proof always falls upon the party who would lose if the complaint were rejected or if a settlement did not occur. In the case of your suing the auto dealer, as the person bringing the complaint you would lose if you could not demonstrate that you had been harmed or if you could not prove the harm was a consequence of the dealer's actions. In the example of criminal law, the presumption of innocence means that if the prosecution was unable to demonstrate the guilt of the accused at a sufficiently high level of probability, the State's case would be lost.

In some real-world applications, the requirements for the burden of proof may not always be as clear as they appear in legal argumentation. This is why audience analysis to determine presumption can be a good idea. It will help you discover exactly what your audience expects you to prove. If you were a student advocate addressing a Northern State University policy-making body made up of faculty and administrators, you might determine that their attitudes favored maintaining the four-credit-hour standard because faculty would be expected to undertake an additional course preparation and demand a salary increase for the extra work load. You would have to show that the greater good to students, obtained from changing to a three-credit-hour standard, would justify the salary increase or would offset the increased faculty work load.

Sometimes you have to make an educated guess regarding how much proof is sufficient to fulfill your burden to support change. An audience who already support the change will require a simple affirmation of their beliefs, and those who oppose the change become the ones who must provide good reasons to prevent it. An uncommitted audience may be open to the change but may require substantial reasoning and information to see that change is a good idea. An unbelieving audience may resist the change no matter what the proof but may sometimes be reached by your demonstrating that there are areas upon which agreement can be achieved. The latter is a common practice in labor-management negotiation and diplomatic relations. How many arguments are necessary and how much proof must support them depend upon such audience expectations and degrees of commitment.

In academic argumentation, the burden of proof is the logical opposite of presumption. The advocate has the responsibility of proving that the change is supported by good reasons. The opponent has the advantage of relying on existing belief or practice that will continue in the event the advocate fails to make a good case for change. We may summarize the burden of proof in the following principles:

1. The advocate has the responsibility to prove the argument. This is the burden of proof.
2. In fulfilling the burden of proof, present beliefs and behaviors described by presumption are judged and evaluated based on the available evidence, and an alternative pattern of thought or action is proposed.

How do you know when you have fulfilled this burden of proof? The third convention of argumentation provides the answer.

PRIMA FACIE CASE

To overcome the presumption that a belief or behavior should continue to exist, the advocate must present a fully developed case that would be strong enough to justify a change unless it was successfully challenged by some countering argument. Literally, a **prima facie case** is one that "at first sight" or "on the face of it" is sufficient to justify changing belief or behavior. A prima facie case causes us to suspend presumption either temporarily, if valid countering arguments are provided, or permanently, if the opponent is unable to establish a reasonable basis to maintain the original presumption.

Because he would lose the controversy if a prima facie case were not presented fulfilling the burden of proof and suspending presumption, the advocate normally initiates the argument by speaking or writing first. This initial presentation must be prima facie and sufficient to support his position concerning the proposition being argued. The legal system once again provides an example to clarify the concept. In order to establish the guilt of a person accused of a felony, the prosecution must present an indictment of this individual that suspends the artificial presumption of innocence. This presentation must constitute a prima facie case.

Suppose Ralph is accused of auto theft. A prima facie case would, at the very least, consist of evidence and testimony supporting the following arguments:

> An automobile was reported missing from the dealer's lot.
> Subsequent to receiving this report, the city police apprehended Ralph with the vehicle in question in his possession.
> Ralph's possession of the automobile was unlawful. He had not purchased it, nor had he received consent of any dealer representative to take it for a test drive.

Proving these three arguments would constitute a prima facie indictment of Ralph for grand theft–auto. The presumption of Ralph's innocence would be suspended until his attorney had mounted a successful defense. The defense attorney would have the responsibility of attempting to reestablish the presumption of Ralph's innocence by attacking the truth of one or more of these arguments, or by introducing argumentation demonstrating extenuating circumstances mitigating Ralph's guilt.

Since very few of you would confront the task of presenting a prima facie case on the proposition that Ralph is guilty of stealing an automobile, the question remains, how do you know when you have discharged your responsibilities as advocate regarding the burden of proof? Recall that the content and scope of the burden of proof is determined by the proposition being argued. In Chapter 1, we indicated how the Romans, in refining Greek rhetoric, developed a series of questions that were crucial in legal proceedings. These questions established the content and scope of the burden of proof for legal propositions. They are similar to the questions the prosecutor considered in preparing the case against Ralph. For fields of argument other than the law, similar sets of questions exist. They are commonly referred to as **stock issues,** the questions that listeners or readers want answered before they will accept the argument of either the advocate or the opponent. These questions focus the controversy and are naturally derived from the proposition being argued. In the next chapter we introduce several types of propositions about which people commonly argue. In later chapters, we identify the stock issues that pertain to each type of proposition.

Before we move on to discuss propositions, two other concepts pertaining to the prima facie case in academic argumentation require consideration. In addition to being logically adequate and offering sufficient proof, the advocate's proposal for changing a belief or behavior must fall within the bounds of the topic of the controversy and demonstrate inherency.

The advocate is responsible for developing a *topical* prima facie case. In academic argumentation, the advocate and his opponent agree to a proposition that identifies the broad, general topic to be argued. In ordinary conversations, and in some instances of real-world argumentation, it is easy to drift from topic to topic. When you want to make a specific case for or against some proposed change, that is not a desirable quality. Your sticking to the topic of argumentation prevents the audience from becoming confused about the issues and extends the same courtesy to others participating in the argumentative process. If you were going to argue about changing Northern State University's credit-hour system, the argumentative proposition might be stated thusly: Northern State University should adopt the three-credit-hour course as the university standard. In providing a prima facie case, the advocate would not be allowed to contest the amount a student pays per credit hour or the manner in which it is collected, since these issues are clearly outside the bounds of the topic. Tuition constitutes a different controversy requiring a different proposition and has as much relevance to a discussion of the credit-hour system at Northern as unpaid parking tickets would have to Ralph's guilt or innocence on the auto theft charge.

In addition to being topical, a prima facie case must demonstrate *inherency.* Argumentation is concerned with whether or not change is justified. To justify change, the advocate must examine both the problems in existing beliefs or behaviors, and the reason for the existence of these problems. The concept of inherency is concerned with the relationship between problems and the circumstances that produced them (La Grave, 1975). Inherency addresses questions such as: What is the cause of the problem? Is change necessary to overcome this cause? If we do not change, will the cause disappear and the problem correct itself?

Since it is generally assumed that if a problem's cause cannot be found we cannot determine how best to remedy it, this is a crucial part of an advocate's prima facie case. If the advocate fails to identify an inherent reason for a problem to exist, it will be impossible to determine if change will eliminate the problem. Inherency arguments establish the causal relationship between the absence of change and the continuation of a problem (Patterson & Zarefsky, 1983).

A problem's inherent nature is established by the presence of three elements: cause, permanence, and reform (La Grave, 1975). The advocate's case demonstrates inherency if it proves the presence of these elements. Cause establishes that the problem exists as a direct result of existing belief or behavior. If the cause is found in the beliefs of society, inherency is said to be "attitudinal." If the cause is found in behaviors which operationalize these beliefs, inherency is termed "structural." Permanence establishes that without intervention the problem will remain. Finally, reform establishes that only the change proposed by the advocate will eliminate the problem.

Attitudinal inherency results from beliefs, those opinions, feelings, or emotional reactions we have about things. To illustrate the power of belief as a cause, consider the following examples. The opinion that women are less capable of studying mathematics than men kept women from pursuing careers in many scientific fields. The feeling that college athletes are "dumb jocks" who receive preferential treatment can make them exiles in the classroom. Emotional reactions to the seeming unfairness of the tax system has led some to cheat on their taxes. Attitudes are often difficult to identify, but they play a powerful role in causing us to accept something as true or false, to value one thing over another, or to act or refuse to act in a certain way.

Structural inherency results when society adopts formal policies that operationalize a belief that is strong or widely held. Laws, institutions, and agreements form the fabric of our society. Structural inherency argues that a problem's cause is found in the behavior which formal policies require. In searching for the inherent causes of a problem, the advocate examines these policies, laws, institutions, and agreements to see if their presence or absence is what has produced the problem.

In our example of argumentation concerning Northern State University, if the principal reason we have for wanting to change Northern's credit-hour system is that the present system is (a) too restrictive of a student's options in choosing courses or (b) does not get maximum productivity from staff and facilities, we would be citing problems that are built-in features of the existing four-credit-hour system. Inherency in this case is structural; the problem is caused by the four-credit-hour policy. This policy has been in effect for a number of years, suggesting that the second element of inherency, permanence, is also characteristic of it. Faculty belief that a three-credit system would increase their work load also serves as an inherent barrier to change. If the faculty prefer the four-credit-hour system they have little or no inclination to change it, and the third element of inherency, reform, would be present. The problem could only be solved by implementing a change that the existing institution is ambivalent toward putting in place.

The role of faculty attitude in preventing reform also illustrates that it is possible for structural and attitudinal inherency to be present at the same time. It is a characteristic of controversy that there may be several explanations for a problem's cause. To remedy a problem, however, it is necessary to remove its prime cause. The advocate and opponent, in examining existing beliefs and behaviors, frequently disagree over whose explanation most clearly represents the probable truth. Conceptually, inherency is important to determining whether or not a prima facie case has been presented because it forces the arguers to examine the reasons why things exist and to explore whether they will correct themselves by the natural processes of change.

We view human beings as simultaneously in the state of being and the process of becoming. Some change in beliefs and behaviors is expected as a natural consequence of living and experiencing new situations. The same thing can be said regarding institutions. Inherency prevents us from arguing over trivia and things which would probably happen in the normal course of events. It is pointless to argue the proposition "The next century should be called the twenty-first century." At present, nothing prevents designating the years from 2000 to 2099 the twenty-first century. Arguing about calling that period something else would be trivial, unless good reasons were provided to justify some other title, but it would constitute an argument over something inherently precluded by present practices that are unlikely to change.

We may summarize the prima facie argument with the following principles:

1. The advocate has the responsibility of presenting a prima facie case, one that stands at face value and is consistent and complete.
2. The form and content of the argument determines its face value.
3. A prima facie case must be both topical and inherent.
4. Presentation of a prima facie case causes the suspension of presumption unless it is successfully challenged.

The following example demonstrates how the three conventions of argumentation discussed in this chapter come together in an argumentative message.

Proposition:

All students at this university should take a basic speech course as a requirement for graduation.

Presumption:

The existing state of affairs is that only some students are required to take a speech course. Presumption indicates that it is not necessary for all students to take a basic speech course and that the present system of graduation requirements should continue.

Figurative Ground Contested:

Graduation requirements for students seeking undergraduate degrees.

Burden of Proof:

The advocate of the proposition to change the present graduation requirements at this university has the burden of demonstrating a reasonable case for changing the present requirements.

Prima Facie Case:

The advocate seeks the suspension of presumption by presenting arguments, which are within the bounds of the topic and are inherent, and which a reasonable person would accept at face value. For example:

Argument 1

University students need a basic speech course. At present they are required to prepare and deliver oral assignments in many nonspeech courses. In History 101, Sociology 101, and Political Science 101, all general requirements at this university, students are required to make an oral presentation. Such requirements necessitate students having some basic speaking skills.

Argument 2

Some departments have already recognized the need for students to have such skills. The Departments of Business and Management, Accounting and Finance, and Criminal Justice, for example, have recognized this need and require their majors to take a basic speech course. This suggests that at present some departments believe that such a course should be required for graduation.

Argument 3

At present, making a basic speech course a requirement for graduation is extremely unlikely. Individual academic departments set their own requirements with the advice and consent of the academic senate. There is no sign that departments that do not presently require their majors to take a basic speech course for graduation will do so in the foreseeable future.

After hearing these arguments advocating a change in the university's general requirements for graduation, the opponent would have the opportunity to respond. She might explain why these arguments fail to justify a change in belief or behavior because of faulty evidence or logic. (The options and obligations of the opponent will become clearer as the responsibilities of the advocate and the evidentiary and logical requirements of sound argumentation are clarified in subsequent chapters.) At this point the opponent would be well advised to ask herself the following questions: (1) Is presumption properly placed? (2) Is the burden of proof assumed by the advocate? (3) Is a prima facie case presented so that presumption may be assumed to be temporarily suspended? If the answer to any of these questions is no, the opponent's job is greatly simplified. The logical advantages that presumption conferred on her at the outset still remain, and the advocate has lost his opportunity to alter belief or behavior.

This chapter has covered three critical concepts in argumentation— presumption, burden of proof, and prima facie argument. These concepts establish the boundaries of the playing field on which argumentation occurs and some of its rules. They require the advocate, as the party seeking a change in belief or behavior, to initiate discussion of the controversy and to perform certain tasks in getting argumentation started. These concepts confer upon the opponent certain advantages at the outset, advantages the advocate must overcome. Since the playing field of argumentation is further delineated by the propositions, or topics, about which people argue, the next chapter considers the nature of propositions.

LEARNING ACTIVITIES

1. Discuss what the three different views of presumption mean to the advocate and opponent in argumentation. Should we always assign the roles before determining presumption? In which communication contexts might you use the traditional view that presumption rests with existing institutions? In which would it be appropriate to determine the prevailing beliefs of an audience? Should we use the idea of hypothesis testing in other than academic contexts?
2. Choose an ongoing controversy such as smokers' versus nonsmokers' rights, abortion versus right to life, profreeze versus anti-freeze on nuclear weapons. Which side in the controversy has presumption? Which has the burden of proving that change should occur? What are the aspects of inherency in the controversy you have chosen?
3. Find an editorial from a current newspaper or magazine that you believe is intended to alter belief or behavior. Analyze it in terms of the following:
    A. What is the presumption that the editorial is trying to overcome, and with whom or what does that presumption lie?
    B. To what extent does the author of the editorial provide sufficient reasons and proof to overcome presumption? Is the argument prima facie?
    C. What do you see as the relationship between presumption, burden of proof, and the establishment of a prima facie argument in the editorial you selected?
4. Using the example on pages 26–27 as a model, construct an advocate's argument. Be sure to include the following:
    A. A statement of the proposition.
    B. A description of where presumption would lie.
    C. A delineation of the ground being contested.
    D. A statement of your responsibility regarding burden of proof.
    E. A prima facie case that would suspend presumption.
5. Exchange your assignment from activity 4 with a classmate. Examine the arguer's case in terms of the following:
    A. What is the locus of presumption?
    B. How does the arguer fulfill the burden of proof?
    C. In your opinion, has the arguer succeeded in creating a prima facie case?
    D. Assume that you will be the opponent for this case; indicate what you might argue in response.

SUGGESTED SUPPLEMENTARY READINGS

GOLDEN, J. L., BERQUIST, G. F., AND COLEMAN, W. E. *The Rhetoric of Western Thought* (3rd Ed.). Dubuque, Iowa: Kendall/Hunt, 1983.

This book surveys rhetorical theory from the Greeks to the present. We recommend you examine the portion of Chapter 9 relating to Richard Whatley and his development of the concepts of presumption and burden of proof. Also examine Chapter 21, "Rhetoric as a Way of Knowing: Stephen Toulmin and the Nature of Argument," which describes the philosophy behind the model and discusses the superiority of the Toulmin model as a means of generating understanding.

SPROULE, J. M. The Psychological Burden of Proof: On the Evolutionary Development of Richard Whatley's Theory of Presumption, *Communication Monographs*, 1976, *43*, 115-29.

A review of the development of the concept of presumption in Whatley's several revisions of his *Elements of Rhetoric*. Sproule concludes that Whatley felt presumption should be determined on the basis of audience beliefs and attitudes. He suggests how arguers might use the theory of presumption as a guide to audience analysis and argues that the psychological makeup of the audience should determine the responsibilities of advocate and opponent.

VASILIUS, J. Presumption, Presumption, Wherefore Art Thou Presumption? In D. Brownlee (Ed.), *Perspectives on Non-Policy Argument*, ERIC Document ED 192 382.

Originally presented at the 1980 Desert Argumentation Symposium at the University of Arizona, this paper offers ten justifications for using presumption to test hypotheses in value argumentation. Vasilius examines the problems faced by Cross Examination Debate Association (CEDA) debaters in determining the responsibilities of advocates and opponents. She explains how employing hypothesis testing as the philosophical basis for argument resolves this problem.

3

WHAT AM I GOING TO ARGUE ABOUT?

In Chapter 2 we said argumentation always take place over a figurative piece of ground, the limits of which are defined by a proposition stating a proposed change in belief or behavior. In this chapter, propositions are defined, three classifications of propositions presented, the relationship among propositions in the argumentative process explained, and guidelines for phrasing propositions offered.

THE NATURE OF PROPOSITIONS

The **proposition** is a statement that identifies the argumentative ground and points to a change in belief or behavior. Stating the proposition identifies the limits of the topic of argument, places the burden of proof with the advocate, and gives presumption to the opponent. Since controversies commonly arise over questions of "what happened," "what is," "what judgment shall I make in this situation," or "what is the best course of action to follow," the limits of controversy must be identified so the advocate and the opponent know the bounds of the argumentative ground. The proposition serves as the starting point for argument, setting the arguers on a particular path, and restricting them to it (Sproule, 1980).

The proposition defines the locus of disagreement and whether that disagreement is over some proposed change in belief or behavior. To argue effectively, in ways that will offer sound reasons to your audience, you must state the controversy in a way that readily identifies what the argument is about. By identifying the locus of disagreement in the form of a proposition, you will be able to fulfill three objectives in beginning and successfully pursuing argumentation.

Selecting Terms for Definition

The first objective is that arguers define the terms that describe the argumentative ground. By phrasing the locus of disagreement in the form of a proposition, important words or phrases that may need definition are made more obvious to both the arguers and their audience. One question frequently arises: what do the advocate and opponent mean when they use particular words or phrases? The proposition provides a semantic framework for argument and allows the advocate and opponent to offer interpretations of the important words and phrases contained in it.

For example, let's examine a possible proposition for argumentation: The federal government should significantly strengthen the regulation of mass media in the United States. This is a proposition for policy argumentation, but the same objective also applies to propositions for what is termed factual and value argumentation. Since the advocate must fulfill the burden of proof and open the argument, he must identify and define the terms in the proposition that the rational reader or listener must understand in order to follow the arguments justifying the change he seeks. In the example, three key phrases establish the figurative ground of the argument: (1) federal government, (2) significantly strengthen the regulation of, and (3) mass media. Only by determining the meaning of these terms can the advocate determine what proof and reasoning he must supply in order to fulfill his obligation to present a prima facie case.

Although the opponent doesn't begin the process of definition, she is not obligated, in all instances, to accept the definitions provided by the advocate in his initial presentation. In some instances, an early step in the argumentative process for the opponent involves arguing about the definition of specific terms in the proposition. Hence, the proposition is an important first step in clarifying the boundaries of argumentative ground.

The advocate for our proposition concerning federal regulation of mass media, for example, might choose to define one key phrase in this way: Mass media means films and video cassettes that depict explicit sexual acts between children under the age of twelve and adults of the opposite or same sex. The opponent may have the same uneasy feeling you just had, since she has now been cast in the role of defender of the right of pedophiles to obtain child pornography. Presumption is stripped away or even reversed by this definition of mass media, since it is difficult to conceive of many rational people accepting the notion that if child pornography exists, it should continue to do so in the future unless good and sufficient reasons are provided to show otherwise.

Our sample proposition is one for academic argumentation, about which more will be said shortly. In this instance, we see why an opponent might contest a definition, since failure to do so would place her at an extreme disadvantage. The opponent might suggest child pornography is not included in the argumentative ground, since it does not meet commonly accepted standards of what we define as mass media. Such an argument over the way a term has been defined would ask the audience to make a decision based on determining who has the most reasonable definition of the terms of the proposition. There is no established list of such decision rules, but the practices for defining terms described in this chapter offer many usable decision rules for definitions. One is in the mass media example: Common understanding of a term by most members of a society can be used to determine its definitions.

Specifying Direction of Change

The second objective in beginning argumentation, fulfilled by having a proposition, is that it identifies the alteration of belief or behavior sought by the advocate and resisted by the opponent. A proposition must specify the action to be taken or the belief to be altered. By identifying the change sought, the proposition identifies both the advocate's burden of proof and the presumption of the opponent's position against the change.

Taking our sample proposition once again, let us assume that the advocate has offered the following definitions:

> **federal government**—the Federal Communications Commission
> **significantly strengthen the regulation of**—impose a specific code of standards to govern the depiction of acts of violence
> **mass media**—all television programming broadcast by the three major networks, independent stations, and cable or pay television systems

The change sought involves increased regulation of the depiction of violence in television programming. Those of you who were reading carefully probably recognized that the way the proposition was defined directed change at both entertainment and news programming. The advocate has the burden to prove that such a change is necessary, desirable, and achievable. The opponent has the presumption of the present system of regulation by the Federal Communications Commission.

Even without definitions, the proposition pointed to the kind of change the advocate is expected to support. To state that the federal government should significantly strengthen the regulation of mass media in the United States is to point the advocate in the direction of supporting greater control. The proposition identifies the agency for change which the advocate must employ—the federal government. It identifies the type of change—significantly strengthened regulation. It points to the target of change—mass media in the United States.

Change is also specified in propositions of value and fact. Readers or listeners are asked to alter their beliefs regarding how something is to be valued or understood. In a value propositon such as "Preventing the sale and use of controlled substances on school property is more impotant than an individual student's right to privacy," the agency for change is the audience. They are asked to make a mental commitment to value safety over privacy. The advocate's burden to prove that change is necessary, desirable and achievable involves arguing one value's supremacy over the other. In a proposition of fact such as "The use of controlled substances on school property is increasing," the audience is asked to believe the relationship specified by the proposition, and the advocate's burden is to prove that relationship is true. Even before definitions were supplied, these propositions set general boundaries for argument that were flexible enough to afford both advocate and opponent the opportunity for interpretation.

This characteristic, flexibility, is usually found in propositions used in academic argumentation. We can distinguish these propositions from those found in real-world contexts. In everyday experience, the world of politics, or the legal system, controversy results when a very specific end or objective is sought. Real-world controversies are usually "associated with a real or imagined threat of people's needs, values, or purposes" (Windes & Hastings, 1965, p. 36).

In the legal process, the essence of a formal proposition is usually found in the statement of charges in criminal proceedings or in the plaintiff's complaint in civil proceedings (Mills, 1968). Defendant X has violated law or statute Y. If X is the owner of an adult bookstore and if Y is designed to prevent the production, distribution, sale, or exhibition of child pornography, then argumentation between prosecutor and defense attorney is joined over whether or not X is guilty of violating Y. The proposition being argued is specific and leaves fewer opportunities for interpretation than the academic proposition introduced earlier.

Fewer opportunities does not mean none. While we indicated that the opponent in academic controversy might object to the definition of mass media as child pornography, her real-world counterpart, the defense attorney, might employ a similar strategy. The presumption for child pornography is as weak in the real world as it is in the academic. Recognizing this, the defense attorney may attempt to redefine the proposition and put the law, rather than her client, on trial. Where presumption is found can be broadly interpreted. Rather than focusing on the specific act of selling pornographic materials, the defense attorney might turn to the law as a source of presumption. The First Amendment to the Constitution states "Congress shall make no law" regarding a number of institutions, one of which is the press. Since there is strong presumption for this document, the defense attorney might argue that the law under which her client is charged represents a greater threat to society than do the materials he is accused of producing, distributing, selling, or exhibiting because it violates the Constitution.

The clash of values in this example, and the feelings they evoke, are typical of real-world argumentation because it produces real consequences. Disputes over pornography usually take place over the figurative ground of which value is more important: freedom of the individual or public morality. Such examples of value conflict are common in real-world argumentation and may create paradoxes such as the American Civil Liberties Union defending the right of American Nazis to march in Skokie, Illinois, where a number of Holocaust survivors live. The point of considering this value conflict is that the direction of change specified in the proposition should be as clear as possible to avoid confusion. Identification of presumption may also require a definitional process to determine exactly what argumentative ground is at stake.

In your personal experiences with argumentation, the proposition may have been a declarative statement as simple as "I think we should go to a movie tonight" or as vexing as "if you really loved me, you'd prove it." This is not always the case. In naturally occurring argumentation, propositions are not always clearly stated at the outset of the controversy. The failure to state exactly what we are arguing about probably accounts for most of the instances of misunderstanding that occur in interpersonal controversy. Real-world propositions need not be clearly stated in advance; but when they are, they are narrow and open to fewer interpretations than propositions for academic argument.

Propositions for academic argumentation often seem easier to cope with than propositions for real-world argumentation because they are always clearly stated in advance. However, since academic argumentation exists solely for the purpose of developing skills and testing ideas, the disagreements are usually artificial or induced. To maintain interest in an academic exercise, it becomes necessary to have a proposition that is broad enough to allow interpretation and to provide sufficient intellectual challenge to the student who may have to work with it over a period of time. The seemingly unitary nature of many propositions in the real world is neither characteristic of, nor desirable for, propositions of academic argumentation.

In our example on regulation of mass media, controversy over what to regulate need not involve a discussion of television violence, since mass media include movies, newspapers, books, and magazines as well as television; neither is violence the only critical issue that might be considered. This is an example of a proposition that could be argued over an extended period of time, by a number of people, without becoming boring or repetitive. However, it shares one important characteristic with real-world propositions: It points toward some alteration of belief or behavior. If it did not, there would be nothing to argue; and misunderstanding and bypassing, which occurs in some real-world argumentation, might result. When the opponent in our earlier example of academic argumentation challenges the validity of the advocate's definition of mass media as child pornography, she is saying that the change in belief and behavior he supports points in a direction not reasonably suggested by the proposition they agreed to argue.

What are academic argumentative propositions about? Issues of social equality, the process of government, international relations, and economics are often topics for classroom argumentation. As a result, you may find yourself learning about past, present, and future events while you are developing and refining your skills.

Identifying Key Issues

The third, and final, objective fulfilled by a specifically worded proposition is the aid it provides in the identification of key issues. In subsequent chapters we devote specific attention to the analysis of propositions through the identification of intrinsic or stock issues; at this point it is sufficient to state that issues are central questions suggested by the specific wording of a proposition and its definition by the advocate. "An issue is an inherent and vital question within a proposition: inherent because it exists inseparably and inevitably within the proposition, and vital because it is crucial or essential to the meaning of the proposition" (Mills 1968, p. 96). Issues become the contested points in argumentation, the areas of disagreement between advocate and opponent. If the proposition can be said to define the potential boundaries of argument, the issues suggested by it provide the internal structure or framework for argumentation.

Issues grow directly from the definition of the proposition that the advocate provides, since this definition narrows and clarifies its meaning in academic argumentation. Earlier, we offered the following definitions:

> **federal government**—the Federal Communications Commission
> **significantly strengthen the regulation of**—impose a specific code of standards to govern the depiction of acts of violence
> **mass media**—television programming broadcast by the three major networks, independent stations, and cable or pay television systems

Our broad proposition has now come to mean something very specific: The Federal Communications Commission should crack down on television violence. If the opponent accepts these definitions as reasonable, argumentation can proceed on the issues.

What might these issues be? They are questions that a reasonable person, such as our advocate or opponent, might ask before accepting the change in the Federal Communications Commission's behavior required by the narrowed proposition.

Does something harmful occur because of the depiction of violence in television programming right now?

Would there be any advantage or benefit to be gained by further controlling the depiction of violence in television programming?

Is the way in which the Federal Communications Commission deals with the depiction of violence in television programming insufficient at present?

Is the Federal Communications Commission the best government agency to use for controlling the depiction of violence in television programming?

What might be the consequences of having the Federal Communications Commission try to control the depiction of violence in television programming?

These questions represent issues that give shape and structure to the process of argumentation over the figurative ground. By locating areas of disagreement, potential and real, the arguers specify for each other, and the listener or reader, the aspects of belief or behavior over which controversy exists. Issues, which sharpen the locus of disagreement, constitute the basis for determining whether to alter or maintain current interpretations of reality.

Those of you who were reading carefully enough earlier to notice that the definition of mass media includes both entertainment and news programming probably have two questions right now. First, exactly what does the advocate mean by violence, and does the use of the term depiction mean that while television could not show the act on the screen, it could show its consequences? Good question! In your role as opponent, listener, or reader you would probably get a sense of the answer to your question from the proof and supporting reasons the advocate provided in attempting to establish a prima facie case. That might not always be the case, and this points to a problem that can occur when we define a proposition. If we are not careful, all our definition accomplishes is to shift confusion from the meaning of terms in the proposition to the words and phrases we used in attempting to narrow and clarify its meaning.

Second, you might also be asking yourself what happened to First Amendment freedoms. If the lawyer defending the pornography merchant could try to get her client off the hook by claiming the law under which he was charged was unconstitutional, couldn't the opponent in this academic controversy invoke the same defense? After all, doesn't freedom of speech give us the right to watch Dan Rather bring us film of the latest deaths in Beirut or the right to watch the A-Team destroy motor vehicles? These are good questions that point to a particular feature of the academic proposition important in issue identification. We call your attention to a six-letter word in our sample proposition, *should*—a word that is common to many academic propositions.

One of the artifices of academic argumentation is that it frequently concerns itself with what ought to be rather than what will be. In a sense, we proceed from the assumption that if something should change, it can change, be it belief or behavior. We ignore the fact that in reality it might not, no matter how strong our proof or compelling our reasons. Before dismissing academic argumentation as a frivolous twentieth-century equivalent of the thirteenth-century disputation over how many angels can dance on the head of a pin and dropping your argumentation course, consider the following: The suspension of disbelief involved in argumentation is not dissimilar to what happens in the real world.

The government agency that passed the antismut law our hypothetical prosecutor used in attempting to bring our purveyor of child pornography to justice probably did exactly the same thing. The government representatives asked themselves whether something should be done, answered affirmatively, and passed the law. They may never have considered whether it violated the First Amendment. If they did, they decided either that it probably did not or, more probably, that it was a question for the courts. As a practitioner of argumentation in an academic context, you will find yourself doing the same thing, keeping in mind that your purpose is developing skills and testing of ideas.

Since argumentation in an academic setting often involves arguing both sides of a proposition or listening to the argumentation of classmates, you may find yourself arguing or listening to arguments about something you do not really believe in. You may find yourself believing that something is so distasteful, so wrong, that it could not happen in the real world because the courts, Congress, or the public would not allow it to happen. The same features of problem consideration exist in the real world. Some group or agency concludes that "something ought to be done," finds a course of action, and undertakes it. This sometimes produces decisions that are distasteful or harmful.

The internment of thousands of Americans of Japanese ancestry, and the confiscation of their property, during World War II is one of the more tragic episodes in our history. In the aftermath of Pearl Harbor, someone asked the question, should something be done? The courts, Congress, and the public allowed something very wrong to happen then. Farmers and community governments looked at the problem of insect and pest control and arrived at decisions to use highly toxic substances. The Justice Department decided that American Telephone and Telegraph operated in restraint of trade and ordered the company broken up; many think that was an unwise decision in the face of the resulting confusion over telephone services.

The perception that something should be done, that one value is more important than another, or that we must alter our understanding of something, carries no real-world guarantees that when a change is made, it will always turn out to be the most desirable one or that it will not have some unforeseen long-term consequences. Good argumentation in any context explores the extent of desirability and searches for potential drawbacks. As you examine propositions for argumentation in your class or in other contexts, you must practice the suspension of belief or disbelief in order to consider all aspects of the implied change. In sum, when you set out to discover what belief is best or what should be done, taking care in defining terms and examining all possible issues growing out of the proposition are important, albeit time-consuming, steps.

Summary of the Nature of Propositions

1. The proposition specifies the scope of the controversy, providing boundaries for argument. Defining selected terms of the proposition helps to clarify these boundaries.
2. The proposition expresses the advocate's goal, asserting the alteration in belief or behavior for which assent is sought.
3. The proposition delineates the advocate's responsibilities regarding the burden of proof and the opponent's opportunities that may result from identifying presumption, and it suggests potential issues that constitute the argumentative ground.

We have stressed choice, definition, and interpretation in reference to propositions. Before considering types of propositions, it would be useful to look at the rules of definition, the kinds of terms requiring definition, and some methods for providing definitions.

THE PROCESS OF DEFINITION

Since the definition of terms in the proposition may become a contested part of an advocate's argumentation, it is advisable for both advocate and opponent to be well versed in the process of definition. Note that disputes over definitions may arise regarding terms in a given issue as well as the terms of the proposition. This discussion of the process of definition is intended to help you in creating decision rules for defining the terms of a proposition. Arguers are obligated to make clear exactly what is meant when a particular word or phrase is used. To that end, we provide some general rules for defining terms, categories of terms that require definition, and suggestions for how to go about the process of definition.

Rules of Definition

The Inclusionary Rule.   Phrase definitions in such a way that they include everything that appropriately falls under the term. Recall the term *mass media* and the potential for including more in its definition than just television. To define mass media as television automatically rules out any argumentation over books, newspapers, radio, or magazines. You must take care not to narrow the proposition so sharply that an important issue is ruled out by the definition of the term. If both advocate and opponent agree that television is a suitable definition of mass media, there is no problem. However, the advocate should be prepared to defend his definition of mass media if it is questioned.

The Exclusionary Rule.   Phrase definitions in such a way as to exclude those things not appropriate to the term (just the opposite of the inclusionary rule). Your definition should not be so broad as to include things that do not properly fall into the category of the term. For instance, defining *mass media* as "all communication" would include communication between and within individuals, types of communication not aimed at a mass audience. Notice the problem in the following example. To define *man* as "a tool-using and tool-making animal" results in the inclusion of species of primates in the category *man*. Chimpanzees use objects as projectiles to be thrown or clubs to be swung and have been observed making tools to facilitate the harvesting of termites.

The Adaptation Rule.   Phrase definitions so that the meaning is appropriate to the context of the argument. Consider the needs of the audience before whom the argument is made. While it may be perfectly legitimate to define the Federal Communications Commission using the names of its members, it may not be appropriate to use such a definition if you are arguing about things it ought to regulate. Likewise, mass media might be defined in terms of technical specifications for the transmission of television and radio signals, but such a definition may not be appropriate to an argument whose figurative ground involves significantly strengthening federal regulation.

The Neutrality Rule.   Phrase definitions in such a way as to avoid unnecessary emotionality in language choice. It is inappropriate to use loaded language in defining terms. It would be inappropriate to define the *Federal Communication Commission* as "a group of nearsighted reactionaries more concerned with protecting network profits than promoting the public good" or to define a *teachers' union* as "an organization of socialist radicals undermining the quality of education." Definitions should be descriptive of the term defined, not of your feelings about it. In the context of issues, you will have ample opportunity to make those feelings understood and appreciated by your listeners or readers.

The Specificity Rule.   Phrase definitions so that the term itself is not a part of the definition. It may be true that "a rose is a rose is a rose," but to define a term using the term itself does not give the audience a clearer picture of its meaning. For example, what do you learn from the following definition? "The Federal Communications Commission is that commission in Washington, D.C., concerned with communications." Included in the need to be specific is the need to provide noncircular definitions. While it may be true that having money means not being poor, it scarcely improves our understanding to define *wealth* as "the absence of poverty" and *poverty* as "the absence of wealth."

   The Clarity Rule. Phrase definitions so that the definition will be understood more readily than the term it defines. To define *federal government* as "that central government, commonly known as the United States government, to which the fifty states have agreed to subordinate certain powers as specified in the United States Constitution," is unnecessary and fails to improve our understanding of the argumentative ground. Although the preceding is an extreme example, the problem of cloudy definitions is common, particularly on technical topics. If your proposition concerns computers, defining them in terms of RAMs and ROMs may not contribute to clarity in the controversy.

Terms Needing Definition

   Five categories of terms usually require definition if understanding, necessary for effective argumentation, is to be achieved. Since you are defining terms both for your opponent and for your audience, the meaning requirements of each must be considered. When you perceive a term to be equivocal, vague, technical, new, or coined, it should be defined.

   Equivocal terms have two or more equally correct meanings. Many common words in the English language have more than one standard meaning. Providing an opportunity for prayer in the public schools represents an ongoing controversy. Some schools provide a period of silent meditation. *Meditation* has become an equivocal term in the controversy surrounding public school prayer. Those schools using meditation have defined it as inner prayer, quiet reflection, or silent communion. However, for many people the term conjures up images of Eastern religions or transcendental meditation. Both are legitimate interpretations of the term; but for argumentation on the acceptability of school prayer to proceed, those arguing its value must agree on the meaning of meditation, lest they find themselves going off in distinctly different directions. Clearly, you cannot always rely on context to help establish the intended boundary for an equivocal term. Care must be exercised in making apparent the meaning you intend.

   Vague terms have shades of meaning; they lack clear-cut definitions, so that each listener or reader is free to supply his own meaning. Consider *freedom of speech*, which can have as many meanings as there are political views. Some terms, such as "democracy" can be both equivocal and vague. There are different versions of democracy such as a "democratic people's republic," and a "Jeffersonian democracy." At the same time, what constitutes the American version of democracy is subject to a great deal of interpretation. What does the term "good" or "inferior" mean to you? Value terms, terms of ideology and attitudes, are often vague. Because the term's meaning is open to so many interpretations, it must be defined clearly if the proposition's figurative ground is to make collective sense to the advocate, the opponent, and the audience.

Technical terms are jargon or specialized words belonging to a particular field or profession. Since many controversies involve the use of scientific or technical terminology, exact definition of terms such as "bioeugenics" is necessary if intelligent argument is to occur. Terms with a limited or specialized meaning should not be left undefined, since the reader or listener may not know their meaning but may supply one anyway. This is especially important when concepts are discussed in terms of their acronyms. An HMO is a health maintenance organization, a form of PPGP, prepaid group practice, not to be confused with HBO, which is a subscription television service, or PPG, the Pittsburgh Plate Glass Company.

New terms are brand new additions to the language, words or phrases that do not exist in the common vocabulary. Foreign policy and international relations can be the source of new terms as words are invented to describe policies. During the cold war, the terms *containment,* meaning "a policy aimed at checking the expansion of a hostile power or ideology by political, economic or military means" (Kohan, 1984, p. 42) and *brinksmanship,* meaning "a strategy in which a nation displays its willingness to risk war if an adversary does not back down," (Kohan, 1984, p. 42) were created to define new foreign policies. *Word processing, microprocessor,* and *microchip* are terms that have entered the language because of the computer revolution. The broadcasting industry has also added new terms to our vocabulary in the past few years—*satellite feed, earth station,* and *the dish.* Other examples of new terms in use are *condominium, burnout,* and *the nontraditional student.*

Coined terms are those invented when a convenient term does not already exist. Many coined terms are shorthand expressions for complex ideas. *Televangelism, kidvid,* and *Amtrak* are verbal shorthand for *television evangelists, children's television programming,* and *America's passenger railroad service.* Coined terms are also created to describe current developments in an evocative manner. *Petrodollars, the electronic church, user friendly, telectorate* (half television viewer and half voter), and *greenmailing* (the attempt to take over a company by buying enough stock to contol it) are contemporary examples. Coined terms can become standard English; consider that "television" was a coined term at one time.

How to Define Terms

Terms may be defined by using a **synonym** for the term, a more familiar word similar in both denotative and connotative meaning. This is how standard dictionaries typically define terms. For example, to be *nugatory* means to be "worthless or ineffectual." To provide a more specific definition for *reproduction*, in an argument about videotape recorders, you might use its synonyms: *copies, prints,* or *representations.*

Terms may be defined by the **function** an object, instrument, or organization performs. Some terms make more sense when described in terms of what they do. If you choose to define functionally, be sure that the explanation clarifies rather than obfuscates. To define *radial valve gear* as "a gear employing a combination of two right-angle motions for the purpose of cutting off the steam supply to the cylinder at an early stage in the piston's stroke" is to define both functionally and unclearly. People unfamiliar with steam locomotives will associate the word *gear* with the things in their car's transmission or their wristwatch, but there are no gears as such in the valve gear of a steam locomotive.

Terms may be defined by using **examples.** A common technique, employed in this and other textbooks, is to explain something by providing examples of it. This is the strategy used here. When you define by example, you attempt to clarify meaning by naming concrete, representative instances of the term. Suppose we were arguing the proposition "social science is the most important general requirement for graduation." If we do not know to what extent our audience shares our definition of *social science* we might define by example: "By social science, I mean the study of history, sociology, anthropology, political science, or economics."

Terms may be defined by referring to **authoritative definitions.** In a sense, your dictionary serves as an authority for the definition of words; but caution must be exercised in using standard dictionaries. The dictionary merely provides you with a list of all the ways in which users of words commonly define them. To discover just how equivocal many English words can be, consult an unabridged dictionary. Because specificity is a goal in defining, it is frequently useful to turn for a definition to a specialized dictionary, an encyclopedia particular to a field, or a recognized expert in the field. Medical dictionaries, legal dictionaries such as *Black's Law Dictionary,* or an encyclopedia such as *The Encyclopedia of Social Science,* can provide definitions when the precise meaning of a term in the clinical, jurisprudential, or sociological sense is required. It is also possible to derive an authoritative definition by turning to a respected source: "As explained by the chief justice, judicial review involves the Supreme Court's right to review any law passed by Congress in terms of its constitutionality."

Terms may be defined **operationally.** When we seek to clarify the meaning of a term by explaining it as the consequence of a single step, or series of steps, we employ an operational definition. Your stock broker tells you that "net income on this investment should be fifteen cents per share." You look puzzled and say, "I was sure that stock would pay more." Realizing you do not understand *net income* she defines it operationally: "If you take the total amount of income paid as dividends on the stock and deduct the amount paid in taxes and brokerage fees, the resulting figure will be the net income on the investment." In our mass media example, we might have operationally defined "significantly strengthen the regulation of" by specifying the new policy we are creating.

Terms may also be defined **behaviorally.** To define something that cannot be experienced directly, we may sometimes clarify the term by describing the behaviors commonly associated with it. It may be difficult to define *staff burnout* but relatively easy to describe the kinds of behavior associated with burnout cases: apathy toward change, absenteeism, and mistakes on the job. Behavioral definitions can be particularly useful in describing a theory or phenomenon such as intelligence. *Superior intellectual ability* may be defined in terms of a specified level of performance on the verbal and mathematical sections of the Scholastic Aptitude Test.

Finally, terms may be defined by **negation.** This type of definition indicates what the term does not mean. There are some terms whose definitions are best arrived at through negation. For example, someone who is single is "not married," someone who is insolvent is "not able to meet his financial obligations." Sometimes definition by negation is the best way to define a term: "A full-time undergraduate student is any individual enrolled for not less than twelve semester hours who has not previously received a baccalaureate degree from an accredited college or university."

Since the arguer's task is to locate the issues in a controversy, knowing the definitions being used to limit the controversy will assist both advocate and opponent in developing their arguments. Part of the process involves considering the type of proposition that lies before you. The next section of this chapter considers three classes of propositions.

THE CLASSIFICATION OF PROPOSITIONS

We classify propositions according to the ends sought by their advocates, a change in either belief or behavior, and have already referred to the three types of propositions commonly argued—*fact, value,* and *policy.* These correspond to the most common sources of controversy: (1) disputes over what happened, what is happening, or what will happen; (2) disputes asserting something to be good or bad, right or wrong, effective or ineffective; and (3) disputes over what should or should not be done. Remember that academic propositions are usually broad in scope, and we will be using many examples of academic propositions.

Propositions of Fact

Propositions of fact seek to alter our beliefs. They do so by asserting a relationship between two things, which is suggested to be the appropriate way to view reality. "Illegal immigration is detrimental to the United States," asserts a relationship between the presence of illegal aliens and some implied qualitative or quantitative harm. We may not accept the probable truth of this proposition without further clarification because we do not know what is implied by "detrimental." Proof of the asserted relationship would require identification of those areas in which the presence of illegal aliens in the United States causes harm.

Propositions of fact are further classified in terms of the change in belief that is sought—whether it is in the past, the present, or the future.

Past Fact

Life evolved naturally from existing conditions on Earth.

Few American presidents have enjoyed favorable press coverage while in office.

Present Fact

The American mass media is relatively free from government regulation.

Trade restrictions are necessary for the protection of American industry.

Future Fact

Computers will change the course of American education.

Most wildlife species will cease to exist outside of zoos in the next century.

In each of these factual propositions, the controversy concerns the relationship between things. To determine the truth of the relationship in the case of past or present fact propositions the process would be similar: Discover what would be required to establish the probable truth of the statement and proceed to verify it. Propositions of future fact depend upon discovering what the probability is that something will be the case. In Chapter 8 we explore in more detail what is necessary in proving propositions of fact.

Propositions of Value

Like the proposition of fact, the proposition of value attempts to alter belief in that it deals with our subjective reactions to things and our opinion of them. The proposition of value establishes a judgmental standard or set of standards and applies them. Any attempt to demonstrate something to be good, right, or effective ultimately depends upon the criteria defining goodness, rightness, or effectiveness. The advocate of a proposition of value normally applies his own criteria, especially if he believes them to be understood and accepted by either his opponent, his listener, or both. Notice the values involved in the following academic value propositions:

The rights of endangered animal species are more important than the rights of indigenous human populations.

American commercial broadcasters have sacrificed quality for entertainment.

Protection of the natural environment is a more important goal than the satisfaction of American energy demands.

"The military draft is an ineffective means of providing for the national defense." "This season's new television shows are the worst ever!" "Brand X popcorn is the best." All these are assertions of judgment based on subjective standards of ineffectiveness, "worstness", and "bestness" that the person making them has applied. All are propositions of value.

If propositions of fact may be verified by recourse to the data, then how may propositions of value be determined to be true? Once again, the concept of what is probable is important to keep in mind. Because they reflect the subjective judgments and tastes of the individuals who advance them, propositions of value can only approach the level of being probably true, but they cannot even approach this level unless we know the criteria on which they are based. Take the statement, "Brand X popcorn is best," for example. What makes something best? In the case of popcorn, is it price, nutritional value, flavor, the amount each kernel expands during popping, or the percentage of unpopped kernels?

Some of these criteria could be objectively verified, such as the percentage of unpopped kernels. We could test this standard of "bestness" as if we were trying to prove a proposition of fact. Other standards, such as flavor, are themselves judgmental. Knowing the criteria on which the judgment is made allows the listener to assess both their reasonableness as criteria and the extent to which the data show them to be probably true of the object of the value proposition. In Chapter 9, we discuss in more detail the development of cases for value argumentation.

Propositions of Policy

Unlike fact and value propositions, which are aimed at altering our beliefs, policy propositions seek a change in behavior. They suggest that something should be done. "The Food and Drug Administration should impose tougher standards on drug labeling" is an example of a policy proposition, as was our earlier example of federal regulation of mass media. They do more than attempt to alter our beliefs about the pharmaceutical industry and mass media. If we give our assent to these propositions, we are agreeing to a change in behaviors, ours or someone else's. The policy proposition calls for action to be taken.

The policy proposition is common in both political and academic argumentation. It is characterized by the word *should*, which only suggests something ought to be done, not that it necessarily will be done. The word *should* requires the advocate to indicate the specific change he supports and to prove it is *necessary, desirable,* and *viable*. It may have occurred to you that these latter words, necessary, desirable, and viable, are suggestive of a set of value propositions. That is one of the features of policy propositions— subpropositions of value, as well as fact, are frequently used in supporting them. This means that in argumentation the advocate seeking to alter behavior does so by first establishing a rationale for altering beliefs.

Policy propositions are sometimes more complex than propositions of fact or value. Proving a change is necessary, desirable, and viable may be more time consuming than proving the existence or worth of something, if for no other reason than the fact that demonstration of the probable truth of several value propositions is involved. Arguing a policy proposition calls for a more sophisticated and developed series of arguments. "The policy proposition involves facts and values, but extends into expediency, practicality, and action" (Mills, 1968, p. 80).

Let us examine some typical policy propositions used in academic argumentation to discover their complexity. What aspects of fact and value do you find? What actions are implied?

> The federal government should significantly strengthen the guarantee of consumer product safety required of manufacturers.
>
> The federal government should control the supply and utilization of energy in the United States.
>
> The United States should seek restoration of normal diplomatic relations with the government of Cuba.

These topics all deal with significant and highly complex political, economic, and social issues. How might you go about demonstrating that any of the changes suggested by them are necessary, desirable, and viable? Through examination of supporting factual and judgmental propositions. These policy propositions would be accepted only if arguments concerning certain subpropositions of fact and value were accepted. Therefore, the three types of propositions are related.

For example, to demonstrate why the alteration in behavior suggested by any of the policy propositions suggested here should be accepted, the advocate might begin by demonstrating that:

> a problem exists (fact proposition)
>
> because of this, people are harmed (fact and value propositions)
>
> despite people being harmed, the means of dealing with this problem is presently either inadequate or nonexistent (value and fact propositions)

Because acceptance of the alteration of behavior suggested by the policy proposition rests on a foundation of fact and value propositions, the concept of the probable is once again pertinent. In marshaling proof and good reasons to address the rationality of listener or reader in the attempt to precipitate change, the advocate supports what he believes to be the best course of action. Chapter 10 provides a complete discussion of the argumentation involved in policy propositions.

Summary of the Classification of Propositions

1. Propositions of fact assert a relationship between things, or between persons and things; they are proven to be probable by direct verification.
2. Propositions of value assert the worth or lack of worth of something; they are proven to be probable through criteria developed by the individual or discovered in society.
3. Propositions of policy assert that a course of action or behavior should be taken; they are proven to be probable through the establishment of supporting subpropositions of fact and value.

With the nature and classification of types of propositions firmly in mind, we can now conclude this chapter by discussing how to phrase argumentative propositions.

PHRASING THE PROPOSITION

Like defining terms, phrasing propositions concerns the nature of language, but in a slightly different sense. Phrasing has to do with choosing language that will establish the argumentative ground. The importance of choosing and wording a proposition for academic argumentation cannot be over-emphasized. Clear phrasing is needed to provide a meaningful basis for the process that follows. A failure in proposition wording is an invitation to misunderstanding and poor analysis of its component issues (Zeigelmuller & Dause, 1975).

First, the proposition should be phrased as a clear statement of the change in belief or behavior the advocate seeks. To do otherwise confuses the assignment of presumption and the scope of the burden of proof. Consider the proposition, "Something should be done about the possibility of a nuclear war." This proposition fails to meet the first rule for phrasing a good proposition. "Something" is vague, and determining burden of proof and presumption is very difficult. "Something" could involve increasing the number of weapons to bolster the nuclear deterrent, unilaterally freezing the development and production of weapons, creating an international organization to control such weapons, establishing a regular negotiation system among nations that possess nuclear weapons, and so on. If the idea of arguing this subject is to consider the viability of a nuclear freeze, a more appropriate wording for this proposition would be "The United States should freeze the further development and production of nuclear weapons."

The advocate knows he will have the burden of proving a freeze on nuclear weapons will accomplish something positive in regard to the possibility of avoiding a nuclear confrontation. Presumption is also more clearly specified in the revised proposition. The opponent may expect to defend a policy of deterrence or suggest an alternative to a unilateral freeze that might achieve the same goal. Both advocate and opponent have a better understanding of the argumentative ground in this proposition. As a result, the analysis both will undertake in preparing to argue it will benefit.

A second rule to observe in phrasing a proposition is that the proposition should contain only one central idea. Having improved our sample proposition by clarifying the change it seeks, let's see what happens when more than one central idea is introduced. "The United States should freeze the further development and production of nuclear weapons and significantly strengthen conventional foreign military commitments." This isn't really a single proposition. It now contains two separate and unrelated topics. They are related only to the extent that both deal with aspects of the defense policy. Further, the advocate is committed to affirm a reduction in one area and an expansion in another.

A proposition with more than one central idea saddles the advocate with separate burdens of proof for each idea—nuclear weapons freeze and increasing conventional military commitments—and the opponent now finds herself with two separate areas of presumption to defend. This introduces unnecessary complication into the argumentative process. Phrasing a proposition around only one central idea facilitates and improves the process of analysis. As an arguer breaks down a proposition into its component issues, he is looking for the questions that are central to it. If the proposition contains multiple ideas, the process of issue identification is made more difficult. For this sample proposition, both advocate and opponent may find it impossible to establish an internally consistent argumentative position because it calls for opposing changes in two distinct areas of defense policy.

For example, one reason an advocate might present for a freeze on nuclear weapons is that such weapons increase the probability of a war. If that is a good and sufficient reason for the freeze, it may also be a good and sufficient reason not to increase conventional military commitments since, like nuclear weapons, conventional forces may contribute to the escalation of armed conflict. It is better to phrase several separate propositions than to try to cram multiple central ideas into a single one.

A final rule for phrasing propositions is that they should be couched in neutral terms. The wording should favor neither side in the controversy. "Frequently, advocates of change are tempted to add colorful terminology to the proposition," (Zeigelmuller & Dause, 1975, p. 18). The advocate who falls prey to this temptation words a proposition with emotive language. "The United States should freeze the foolish development and production of weapons of the nuclear holocaust." Such value judgments should be saved for argumentation of the proposition. In academic argumentation, the idea of fair wording is stressed so that neither the advocate nor his opponent begin with an unfair advantage (Zeigelmuller & Dause, 1975).

Summary of Rules for Phrasing Propositions

1. Propositions should be phrased to indicate the direction of change in present belief or behavior that the advocate is responsible for supporting.
2. Propositions should be phrased as a single statement containing one central idea.
3. Propositions should be phrased in neutral language so that the cause of neither advocate nor opponent is favored at the outset.

Now you know what propositions are, how to define their terms, what the various types of propositions are, and how to go about phrasing propositions. Propositions are accepted or rejected by listeners or readers based on the arguments advanced by advocates and opponents. The way arguments are structured will add to or detract from the ease with which your audience comes to understand your proposition. The next chapter introduces the Toulmin model of argument and the parts of argument, basic building blocks that will help you structure your arguments more clearly.

LEARNING ACTIVITIES

1. Examine the following propositions. Identify the kinds of propositions—*fact, value,* and *policy*—represented. Be prepared to discuss how each example does or does not meet the rules for wording propositions suggested in this chapter.

ENERGY

A. Domestically produced energy sources are preferable to foreign imports.
B. By 1999 the United States will run short of fossil fuels.
C. The federal government should implement an accelerated program of conversion to domestically produced energy.

ECOLOGY

A. The present system of environmental protection creates toxic waste dumps.
B. The United States should significantly improve its environmental protection policy.
C. The protection of the national environment ought to take precedence over the expansion of industrial production.

LAW ENFORCEMENT

A. The judicial system should provide compensation to the victims of crimes against persons and property.

B. The victims of crimes against persons and property are seldom compensated for their losses.

C. The American judicial system unfairly favors the accused.

FOREIGN POLICY

A. United States foreign policy commitments often favor repressive anti-communist governments.

B. United States foreign policy commitments ought to reflect the American belief in the sanctity of human rights.

C. The United States should substantially reduce foreign aid to nations which fail to protect the rights of their citizens.

EDUCATION

A. The quality of education in American public schools ought to be the nation's first priority.

B. The education of teachers does not place sufficient emphasis on academic subjects.

C. The Department of Education should create and maintain certification standards for all public school teachers.

2. Go back to activity 1 and select one of the five topic areas. Examine the propositions and indicate which words in each proposition category require definition. Formulate your own definitions of these words or phrases. Be sure to include the following:
   A. What type of problem word or phrase is it?
   B. What rule of definition does your definition satisfy?
   C. What type of definition have you provided?

3. Taking the propositions in activity 1 that you did not work with in activity 2, pretend you are listening to an advocate's speech on each topic. As a member of the listening audience, identify which words or phrases in each proposition need to be defined.

4. Read the article "Creation Goes to Court" in *Newsweek*, December 21, 1981, p. 57. What is the policy proposition that the two sides are arguing? Which side has the role of advocate and which the role of opponent? What is the definition of the proposition offered by the advocate? Does the opponent's definition coincide with it? If not, what do the different definitions do to the burden of proof and presumption in this example?

5. Select three topic areas that you might like to investigate in greater depth in completing future assignments. Formulate specific fact, value, and policy propositions that these topic areas suggest to you.

SUGGESTED SUPPLEMENTARY READINGS

CRONKHITE, G. Propositions of Past and Future Fact and Value: A Proposed Classification, *Journal of the American Forensics Association*, 1966, 3, 11–16.

   Discusses how value propositions should be analyzed to determine the arguments that will focus attention on the value, the choice of criteria, and the facts that match the value object to the criteria. This article emphasizes that the choice of arguments will be based, in part, on how much time the arguer has to develop his position and what the audience is likely to accept without much argumentation.

MILLS, G. E. *Reason in Controversy* (2nd Ed.). Boston: Allyn & Bacon, 1968.

Although many of the examples are dated, this book offers a thorough discussion of propositions, analysis to determine issues, and a discussion of traditional policy argumentation. The appendix contains texts of debates and a discussion of debating by presidential candidates.

4

HOW DO I CONSTRUCT MY ARGUMENT?

Whether your interest in argumentation is motivated by a desire to learn how to construct a sound argument or by a desire to become a more perceptive consumer of argumentation, you will discover that arguments vary considerably in form and substance. In both academics and real life, people argue about all sorts of topics: which new car to buy, which hockey player is most adept, which candidate would make a more effective president, or which law is unfair. The possibilities for subjects of argumentation are limited only by the number of topics of interest or importance that people can discover.

The field in which argumentation takes place often influences the form and substance of individual arguments that make up a given instance of argumentation. An argumentative field may exist specific to a particular problem area, type of decision making, value structure, expert opinion, or type of argument used. We have discussed law, in previous chapters, as one field of argumentation that possesses features that make it unique, such as the artificial presumption of innocence. Other examples of fields of argument include business, religion, philosophy, the arts, the humanities, science, social science, and politics. Many of these fields can be divided into subfields. Science, for example, may be divided according to specific areas of inquiry: nuclear physics, biology, geology, meteorology, astronomy, and so on. Although a geologist and a criminal lawyer use different strategies in preparing and presenting their arguments, both need a structure to follow in building those arguments. The same is true when you begin to create your own specimens of argumentation. You will thoroughly investigate the field of your subject, but you will require a system for constructing each unit of argument that is transportable to any field.

Just as topics from fields of argumentation vary, so do the quality of individual arguments. You will find examples of argument as shallow as opinions on a bumper sticker or as complete as those found in political speeches. An argument may be based on overwhelming proof or limited to that which can be proven in only some instances. Despite these possible differences in an argument's form and substance, some common elements remain. In this chapter, we explore those elements common to the structure of all arguments. The specific reasons and evidence that fill in this structure are determined by the topic selected within a particular field of argumentation.

Whatever topic you choose to argue, your position as advocate or opponent emerges through a series of related subarguments, each employing the basic structure of claim, grounds, and warrant. The strengths or limitations of the argument you develop are explained through three additional elements: backing, qualifier, and rebuttal. This classification of the parts of argument was developed by British logician Stephen Toulmin (1958; and Toulmin, Rieke, & Janik, 1984).

THE PRIMARY TRIAD

Claim, Grounds, and *Warrant* make up the primary triad of parts of an argument. Since an argument is the movement from grounds, accepted by the listener or reader, through warrant to claim (Brockriede & Ehninger, 1960), the Toulmin model structures an argument in a way that corresponds to the rational processes people use in making decisions (Golden et al., 1983). Although the arguments you hear or read may not have all three elements clearly identified, the elements of the primary triad are basic to the structure of all argument. They represent the reasoning process invoked when someone makes a statement that requires support before another is willing to accept it as true or probable.

Claims

Argumentation begins when an advocate makes one or more claims. **Claims** are conclusions that do not stand alone. Claim statements look exactly like propositions and have many of the same properties. In Chapter 3 we said propositions establish the boundaries of argumentation and that several subpropositions are used in developing an argumentative position.

The proposition functions as a claim about the topic of argumentation and the subpropositions function as the subsidiary claims supporting it.

In argumentation, particularly academic argumentation, controversy over a proposition is disputed in terms of issues. Each issue defines a unit of thought related to the proposition and is represented by a claim. For example, earlier in your life you may have been involved in a controversy over the policy proposition, "You should eat your vegetables." Argumentation advocating this proposition probably included several subpropositions or units of argument: "Vegetables have vitamins and minerals." "Vitamins and minerals are vital to proper growth." "Vitamins and minerals are important to health." For the sake of clarity, such subpropositions are referred to as claims.

Claims require proof for a rational person to accept them as true or probable. A claim is something with which the listener or reader can ultimately agree or disagree. In this sense, claims both begin and end the process of argumentation. Claims begin the process by showing where an arguer has taken a stand about what must be proven. Claims also end the process, showing what the listener or reader is expected to accept as true or probable. In theory, claims are always capable of being supported by proof and reasoning, shown to be true or probable, untrue or improbable. The arguer's task in making a claim is to present a well-defined and supported position for the listener or reader to consider.

Like the propositions they resemble, claims also fall into categories, or types. There are four categories of claims, each of which performs a different function:

> **Factual Claims**—argue what was, is, or will be
> **Definitional Claims**—argue how something is to be defined or categorized
> **Value Claims**—argue evaluation or pass judgment on something
> **Policy Claims**—argue that something should be done

Factual claims resemble propositions of fact in that they are concerned with things that can be verified. They are concerned with past, present, or future fact. The arguer asserts that something did exist, now exists, or will exist in the future and then proceeds to offer whatever proof can be discovered to demonstrate it. Theoretically, the best proof of factual claims derives from direct observation and experimentation (Ehninger, 1974). Practically, most of us have to rely on printed sources of information for material to prove our factual claims. Where might you seek proof to back up each of the following factual claims?

> Failure to resolve the hostage crisis led to President Carter's defeat in 1980.
> Wayne Gretzky is the leading scorer in the National Hockey League.
> A cure for cancer will be discovered by the year 2000.

The second type of claim common to argumentation is the *definitional claim*. Such claims are used when the precise definition of a term becomes a contested issue. Definitional claims are concerned with how something is to be defined, as a particular type or category of act, individual, object, or idea. The following are examples of definitional claims:

> Mass media is commonly considered to be (is recognized as) television, radio, film, magazines, newspapers, and books.
>
> Computer literacy is (defined as) the basic knowledge needed to use computers.
>
> The USSR's occupation of Afghanistan in 1980 was (categorized as) a case of international aggression.

Like the value propositions they resemble, *value claims* show the arguer's evaluation or judgment. Value claims express an attitude toward something. They are identified by the use of evaluative language in the claim statement. The following are examples of value claims:

> "Return of the Jedi" has the best special effects of the three films in the Star Wars trilogy.
>
> The social security system is a poor substitute for effective retirement planning.
>
> Television advertising is more effective than newspaper advertising.

The *policy claim* is like the policy proposition, stating that an action should be taken, a behavior altered. Because policy claims advocate change, they always concern the future. The following are examples of policy claims:

> You should floss your teeth once a day.
>
> You should purchase United States savings bonds.
>
> You should register to vote.

Claims, regardless of type, are what arguments are about. Because they have so much in common with propositions, it is not surprising to discover that they assert relationships between people, things, and ideas or actions. For example, in advancing the claim, "The social security system is a poor substitute for retirement planning," the arguer seeks to relate an institution (the social security system) to a judgment about it (it is a poor substitute). Standing alone, this claim represents the arguer's opinion of the social security system. Opinion statements of this sort are usually insufficient to alter an audience's belief or behavior. More is required.

A final point about argumentative claims concerns how claim statements are worded. Since claims are frequently phrased as complete sentences, they have the properties of formal sentences. Claims may be phrased as simple statements, with one relationship asserted, or as complex statements, with multiple relationships asserted. All four types of claims may be phrased as simple statements:

Personal income tax fraud is increasing. (factual claim)
Personal income tax fraud is the willful evasion of one's obligation to pay assessed taxes on salaries and remunerations. (definitional claim)
Personal income tax fraud is harmful to the well-being of society. (value claim)
Tax law enforcement should be strengthened to prevent personal income tax evasion. (policy claim)

A complex claim statement differs in that it argues more than one relationship in its assertion. Compare the following examples of complex claim statements with their simple counterparts:

Personal income tax fraud is increasing and becoming more difficult to prosecute.
Personal income tax fraud is the willful evasion of one's assessed taxes and a violation of federal and state laws.
Personal income tax fraud is harmful both to United States citizens and to institutions.
Tax laws should be revised to more equitably distribute the tax burden and more stringently punish the tax evader.

Recall that in discussing propositions, we indicated it was unwise to have multiple ideas stated in a single proposition. In the case of propositions that delineate argumentation on the topic, this is true when the ideas are unrelated to each other. In wording claim statements that serve as subarguments, complex statements often serve the purpose of making argumentation more economical. By offering a single claim to argue that tax fraud harms two entities, individuals and institutions, the arguer saves time and keeps related ideas together in the listener or reader's mind. In addition, complex statements allow the arguer to set up patterns of reasoning through comparisons. A complex claim might be stated thus: "The seriousness of income tax evasion is demonstrated by the fact that tax fraud is increasing more rapidly than crimes against persons and property." The types of crime are unrelated, but the complex statement gives the audience a basis for comparison and a measure of the extent of tax fraud.

Grounds

Since a claim alone is insufficient to alter belief or behavior, you must consider the second major element of the Toulmin model—grounds. Grounding the claim provides the foundation on which an argument rests, the proof required for a rational person to accept the claim as true or probable. **Grounding** is that element in the argument given to the person addressed for his use in answering potential questions such as "what information supported this claim" or "upon what foundation is this claim based?" Common ground, that which the audience already knows and accepts, may exist in an argumentative situation. You may draw on common ground to support claims or you may add information to increase the probability of the audience's accepting your claim as true. A previously established argument may sometimes be used to ground a new claim. Grounds are those facts or opinions that support the probable truth of the claim.

We sometimes use the generic term *evidence* to classify all proof in the form of facts and opinions discovered through research and used to support claims. Since other parts of the Toulmin model may also utilize evidence, we identify this element of the primary triad and label it as the grounds for a claim. What kinds of things appear as grounds in an argument? Experimental observations, statistics, expert opinion, personal testimony, matters of common knowledge, or previously established claims make up the pool of material used as grounds in an argument. More specific information on the nature and application of evidence is provided in the next chapter. We discuss it here, as an element of the primary triad of argument, in terms of its relationship to claim statements.

Claims must always be supported by grounds, since claims alone are only tentative hypotheses until something supports their veracity. If we make the claim, "National Public Radio serves important needs for many Americans," your logical response might be "What needs?" or "How many American listeners?" The relationship of claims to grounds is such that "the claim under discussion can be no stronger than the grounds that provide its foundation" (Toulmin et al., 1984 p. 26).

Grounds used to support a claim are selected to provide specific information pertinent to that claim as distinct from all other possible claims. Grounds should always point toward the claim, leading the listener or reader directly toward the conclusion specified by it. It would be foolish for an arguer to attempt to prove "National Public Radio serves important needs for American listeners" by citing statistics on how many Americans subscribe to an arts channel on cable television. While both claim and grounds might refer to the specialized tastes of a certain segment of consumers of mass media, the grounds would not support the claim; they would be unrelated to it. As the next chapter suggests, you must learn to recognize what kinds of information serve as relevant supporting material for any given claim.

The second element of the primary triad in the Toulmin Model, grounds, strengthens an argument by providing the informational base upon which the claim is made. Consider the following example:

GROUND 1
Every week some 5 million
Americans tune to their
local NPR station for the
kinds of programs
commercial stations will
not and cannot provide.

CLAIM
National Public Radio
serves important needs
for many Americans.

GROUND 2
NPR offers the only
chance of hearing an
analysis of El Salvador,
an explanation of DNA,
Bella Bartok and Billie
Holliday, Richard II and
Sherlock Holmes, a
Congressional hearing or
presidential press
conference.

FIGURE 4.1

(Ronald Steel. "Turning off the Radio," Newsweek, 1981, p. 15 Copyright © 1981 by Newsweek, Inc. All Rights Reserved, Reprinted by Permission.)

Grounds tell us things, for instance how many people listen to National Public Radio and why they listen. However, the relationship between grounds and claim may not always be obvious to the listener or reader—Why are commercial stations unlikely to serve these needs? The third element of the primary triad in the Toulmin model is needed to resolve this problem.

Warrant

The third element in the primary triad is called the warrant. It shows why, if one accepts the grounds, one can also safely accept the claim. **Warrants** indicate how, given the available grounds, it is possible for the arguer to make a claim and aid the listener or reader in making the inferential leap from grounds to claim. "The assertor's task is normally to convince us not just that it was legitimate for him to adopt the initial claim for himself, but also that we should share it and so rely on it ourselves" (Toulmin et al., 1984, p. 46).

Warrants provide us with specific information about how the arguer reasons. By showing the relationship between grounds and claim, they demonstrate that making the mental leap from one to the other is rational. Warrants are found in things already accepted as true as a part of common knowlege, values, customs, and societal norms. In addition, natural laws,

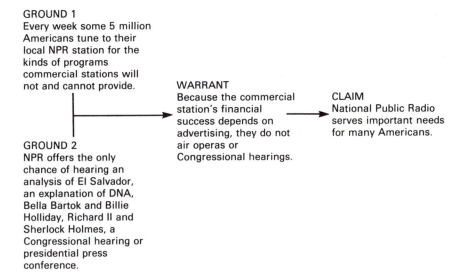

GROUND 1
Every week some 5 million Americans tune to their local NPR station for the kinds of programs commercial stations will not and cannot provide.

GROUND 2
NPR offers the only chance of hearing an analysis of El Salvador, an explanation of DNA, Bella Bartok and Billie Holliday, Richard II and Sherlock Holmes, a Congressional hearing or presidential press conference.

WARRANT
Because the commercial station's financial success depends on advertising, they do not air operas or Congressional hearings.

CLAIM
National Public Radio serves important needs for many Americans.

FIGURE 4.2

(Ronald Steel, "Turning off the Radio," *Newsweek*, April 27, 1981, p. 15 Copyright © 1981, by Newsweek, Inc. All Rights Reserved, Reprinted by Permission.)

legal principles, statutes, rules of thumb, or mathematical formulas may establish warrants. Warrants take the form of information that shows a relationship between a claim and the data used to support it. Consider Figure 4.2 as an example.

The warrant justifies movement from the grounds to the claim. Suppose the listener or reader failed to see the connection between the uniqueness of NPR's programming and the claim that it "serves important needs," saying to herself, in essence, "The leap I am asked to make from the grounds to the claim is unwarranted." The warrant demonstrates the logic of the connection. A rule of thumb is that commercial stations are in business to make money, and operas and congressional hearings do not attract a large enough audience to make the sale of commercial time highly profitable. National Public Radio's stations program in areas commercial broadcasters choose not to serve for financial reasons.

In the ebb and flow of everyday argument, warrants are often unstated. The listener or reader must discover them for herself. Very often, it is the warrant that defines the locus of controversy between advocate and opponent. We reason from claim to grounds or grounds to claim, and it is the warrant that specifies the reasoning. Thus, a claim stands or falls on the validity of the warrant. If you have ever confronted a claim and the grounds that purported to support it and felt, "This just doesn't make sense," it may have been because you were unable to find a warrant that reasonably linked the claim and grounds. For example:

JEANNE: Phil really isn't a very good student.
KATHY: Why?
JEANNE: Because he's on the football team.

Kathy probably wonders, "Why does being a football player automatically make Phil a poor student?" Her question arises because of the lack of a sensible warrant.

From this facetious example we can learn two things about the nature and use of warrants. First, warrants are a vital part of argumentation. If a clear link between grounds and claim is not provided, the reader's or listener's rationality may prevent her from accepting the claim. Warrants are the rational glue that links grounds to claim. Second, the arguer should always select a warrant which his intended audience is likely to understand and accept as rational. It "makes sense" that people seeking cultural experiences or political discussions might turn to NPR for those experiences and that such experiences are not necessarily commercial successes. It "makes no sense" that being on the football team is a sign of poor academic achievement. The warrant is essential in argument, but it is helpful only to the extent that it is understood by the intended audience.

Summary of the Elements of the Primary Triad

1. **Claim** is a conclusion that does not stand alone but requires further proof before the audience is willing to accept it as verified.
2. **Grounds** are information of fact or opinion used to provide verification for the claim; commonly known by the generic label *evidence*.
3. **Warrant** is the reasoning that justifies the mental leap from grounds to claim, certifying that given the grounds, the claim is true or probable.

Claim, grounds, and warrant do not always provide sufficient proof and reasoning to establish the argument. Because arguers face the need to be clear, accurate, and specific, it is sometimes necessary to build in additional support and qualification for the claim using the elements of the secondary triad of the Toulmin model.

THE SECONDARY TRIAD

Backing, Qualifier, and *Rebuttal* make up the secondary triad of elements of argument and constitute the things that show an argument's strength or force. These elements of the secondary triad need not always be used to build an effective argument, but we recommend that you use backing while you are learning argumentation skills.

Backing

The audience may require more information before they agree that given the grounds, and in light of the warrant, the claim is to be accepted. Warrants sometimes require clarification and additional information. What additional information might the arguer provide? Since "warrants are not self-validating" (Toulmin et al., 1984, p.62), the effective arguer demonstrates that the warrant he has supplied should be believed. **Backing** offers explicit information to establish the reliability of the warrant used in arguing the claim. "An argument will carry real weight and give its conclusions solid support only if the warrants relied on in the course of it are both sound and also to the point" (Toulmin et al., 1984, p. 63).

The type of information the arguer must use in providing backing may be either general or specific, depending on the requirements of the situation. As the warrant serves as justification for making the leap from evidence to claim, backing justifies belief in the warrant itself. Like the warrant, backing may be unstated, left to the imagination of the listener or reader. If the audience is knowledgeable on the subject being argued or familiar with the grounds used, backing, and even the warrant, may be an unnecessary distraction if included in the argument. However, in circumstances where the audience may not have much prior knowledge, the arguer is well advised to supply both warrant and backing to increase the believability of his position. Examine how backing works in the structure of the argument illustrated in Figure 4.3.

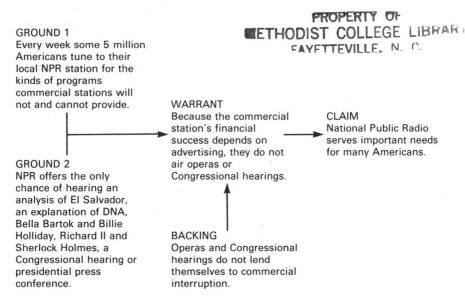

FIGURE 4.3

In this example, providing both warrant and backing is not argumentative overkill. Warrant and backing help the listener or reader understand the reasons why commercial stations differ from NPR and the kinds of programming implied when the claim "National Public Radio serves important needs for many Americans" is made. If after analyzing your audience you are undecided about whether or not to include warrant and backing, it is usually wisest to go ahead and include both. Claims seek to alter belief or behavior, and people are predisposed to resist change. The more proof you can provide, the greater your chances of success.

In addition, because warrants and their backing provide additional information, their use enhances your argument stylistically, taking it beyond the mere recitation of bits of evidence subsequent to making a claim. Warrants and backing help an audience to interpret and understand the factual basis upon which your claim rests, defining your frame of reference and instrumentally inviting them to participate in the process of argumentation.

Qualifiers

The second element of the secondary triad in the Toulmin model helps the arguer indicate the force or strength of his claim. Not all arguments have the same strength. **Qualifiers** show the degree of force the arguer believes his claim possesses. Not all claims must be qualified, because in some instances the arguer is certain of the correctness and strength of his claim. If in investigating a topic you discover exceptions or instances that disconfirm your claim, you will have to account for those exceptions in your argument. Consider the following examples of qualified and unqualified claims:

QUALIFIED: We should read all directions carefully before proceeding, except in those cases where we are already familiar with the product and its assembly.

UNQUALIFIED: We should read all directions carefully before proceeding.

The limitation of the first claim is suggested by the modal qualifier "except in those cases." Modal qualifiers are "phrases that show what kind and degree of reliance is to be placed on the conclusions, given the arguments available to support them" (Toulmin, et al., 1984, p. 85). Modal qualifiers typically take the form of adverbs, adverbial phrases, or prepositional phrases that modify the action suggested by the claim's verb. The following are examples of frequently used qualifiers:

presumably
necessarily
certainly
perhaps

maybe
in certain cases
at this point in time
with the exception of
in all probability

The use of such qualifying terms indicates the strength or limitation of your claim. Qualified claims provide the arguer with a means of advancing claims, reasoning, and developing an argument in circumstances where the reliability or applicability of the claim is not absolute or universal. The arguer using qualified claims is being honest in his communication, alerting the listener or reader to the fact that the claim is not valid in all instances or is not absolutely true. In practice, it is seldom the case that any position taken is 100 percent right or wrong. The use of a qualified claim does not necessarily signal that the argumentative position it supports is unsound, merely that it is not absolutely verified or verifiable.

If in our example we are not confident that our grounds, backing, and warrant absolutely confirm the claim that Americans need public radio, we would qualify it by stating, "*So it would seem,* National Public Radio serves important needs for many Americans."

Rebuttals

The final element of the secondary triad in the Toulmin model also provides a means of accomodating the limitations of claims. **Rebuttals** are added to claim statements that need to be limited to indicate the circumstances under which they may not be valid. Strategically, the use of a rebuttal anticipates objections to the claim and indicates the conditions under which it may not be true. Rebuttals help us avoid errors in reasoning and reflect that we are dealing with what is generally true, not absolutely true.

In our public radio example, attachment of a rebuttal might alter the qualified claim as follows: "So it would seem, National Public Radio serves important needs for many Americans, *except in areas where commercial stations provide such programming*" (see Figure 4.4).

You may feel using qualifiers and rebuttals is not a very good idea, since they seem to diminish the strength of arguments. The use of qualifiers and rebuttals acknowledges that argumentation is not an exact science and that human affairs are seldom discussable in absolute terms. There are two circumstances in which the use of rebuttals is particularly important if you are truly interested in addressing the rationality of your listeners or readers.

The first circumstance exists when grounds, warrant, and backing support the claim only under certain conditions. This occurs in our example regarding public radio, calling for the rebuttal statement we provide. The

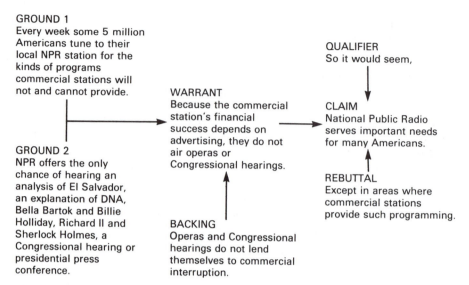

FIGURE 4.4

(Ronald Steel, "Turning off the Radio," Newsweek, April 27, 1981, p. 15 Copyright © 1981, by Newsweek, Inc. All Rights Reserved, Reprinted by Permission.)

second circumstance occurs when grounds, warrant, and backing provide only partial support for the claim. If you look at the claim statement itself, you will discover a rebuttal imbedded in it. The use of the term *many* limits the claim to what the available information will support. Without it, the claim "National Public Radio serves important needs for Americans," would imply that we believe the statement to be descriptive of *all* Americans, or Americans in general.

Summary of the Elements of the Secondary Triad

1. **Backing** provides the "credentials" that help establish the legitimacy of the inferential leap from grounds to claim.
2. **Qualifiers** show the amount, or degree, of force that a claim possesses.
3. **Rebuttals** limit claims, showing circumstances under which they may not be true and anticipating objections to the claim.

Knowing the structure of argument provides you with a method of arranging your thoughts into a pattern, but the resulting argument will be only as strong as the information that constitutes the grounds, warrant, and backing allows it to be. Since evidence is used to establish the basis upon which argumentative claims and propositions are ultimately affirmed or denied, its discovery and use is the bedrock on which argumentation rests. The next chapter assists you in developing skills relevant to the discovery and organization of evidence.

LEARNING ACTIVITIES

1. Select a topic with which you are familiar. Create four arguments for that topic corresponding to the four types of claims: fact, definition, value, and policy. For each unit of argument provide and label each of the following elements: grounds, warrant, backing and claim. When you have finished, examine your arguments. Do any of them require qualifiers or rebuttals? If so, provide and label appropriate qualifier or rebuttal statements. Concentrate on developing each part of the argument rather than on the use of evidence in establishing the grounds, warrant, and backing.
2. Find three examples of claims that use qualifiers. Develop a complete Toulmin model of each, being sure to label all parts of the argument.
3. Find three examples of claims that use rebuttals. Develop a complete Toulmin model of each, being sure to label all parts of the argument.
4. Select an argument such as an editorial, letter to the editor, or an opinion column. Complete the following:
    A. In a single sentence, state the proposition for argument.
    B. Identify the main arguments used in developing the proposition in terms of the claims advanced.
    C. Classify these claims as to type: fact, definition, value, or policy.
    D. Of the parts of argument, identify those which the author uses, those which are left to the reader to supply.
5. Classify the following claims as to type, and identify those claims that use qualifiers and/or rebuttals. Be sure to identify that part of the claim statement which serves as qualifier or rebuttal.
    A. Argumentation is the process of arriving at conviction through the use of reason.
    B. For good performance through a severe winter, front wheel drive vehicles are best.
    C. Restrictions on trade and imports will not solve America's economic problems.
    D. Discretion is the better part of valor.
    E. Evolution and Creation are opposing theories of the development of life on Earth.
    F. Professional football just isn't the same now that there are two separate seasons.
    G. If you want to develop confidence in your ability to communicate with others, take a public-speaking course.
    H. We should intervene in the affairs of Central American nations, since they are geographically close to the United States.
    I. Laughter is the best medicine.
    J. White tigers are a separate strain of Bengal tigers with recessive genetic characteristics that cause the white coat and blue eyes.
    K. In the absence of more equitable proposals, many Americans favor a policy of flat rate taxes.
    L. For those who would gain insights into the future, study the past.

SUGGESTED SUPPLEMENTARY READINGS

EHNINGER, D. *Influence, Belief, and Argument.* Glenview, Ill.: Scott, Foresman, 1974.

This book is full of excellent examples that have not become outdated. The fundamentals of argumentation are discussed in terms of the Toulmin model.

TOULMIN, S., RIEKE, R., AND JANIK, A. *An Introduction to Reasoning* (2nd Ed.). New York: MacMillan, 1984.

For the most comprehensive discussion of the Toulmin model, turn to the source, particularly Chapters 2 through 13. This book is clear and understandable for the beginner. It also examines several fields—law, science, the arts, and management—in depth.

5

HOW DO I PROVE MY ARGUMENT?

In some situations, proving your arguments will be a matter of drawing on your own information resources or those of your audience. In most situations, you will need to research the topic thoroughly. You will require proof and evidence, terms identified with argumentative grounds, discussed in the previous chapter. Generally, grounds are the element in an argument used as proof. In this chapter, we are concerned with the discovery of evidence and the assessment of its quality in a larger sense, because warrant and backing elements in argumentation also rely on evidence in many instances. By definition, **evidence** is information, taken from material of fact or opinion, used to establish the probable truth of a claim.

The kinds of information necessary to establish the grounds, warrant, or backing in your argument are determined by your discovery of the primary issues in your argumentative proposition. The standards to apply in determining the quality of proof required result from analyzing the prior knowledge and beliefs of the audience from whom you seek endorsement of your claims and in applying accepted tests of evidence. In Chapter 4 we indicated that the decision to use warrant and backing is made after you consider how much information you must provide for your audience to accept the rationality of your position. Since proof is the foundation of argument, you will need to learn how to discover and apply it. This chapter concerns types of evidence, standards for evaluating its quality, and techniques for finding it.

TYPES OF EVIDENCE

As our definition of evidence suggests, there are two general classes of evidence, *fact* and *opinion*. Equally, there are two sources of evidence, your own observations and the recorded observations of others. The most reliable source of evidence is personal observation and experimentation. Consider the experience of buying a new car. "Which car should I buy?" can be considered as a question that will ultimately lead to consideration of a policy proposition.

That proposition might be argued through a number of fact and value claims about the quantifiable performance and qualitative evaluations of a series of automobiles. The most reliable evidence would be obtained through your own road tests of these vehicles. However, even in something as personal as buying a new car, personal tests and observations are not always feasible or desirable. You may not have the time or ability to conduct as sophisticated a series of tests as those reported in *Car and Driver* or *Motor Trend*. Beyond saving time, reliance on printed sources relieves you of the need to be an expert in a number of fields. Additionally, in argumentation it is often advantageous to be able to add the authoritative weight of expert opinion or research to your own ideas. By using published facts and the opinions of sources "in the know," you strengthen your argument and increase the credibility of its rational appeal.

Evidence of Fact

Facts are those things that can be verified to be true or false. By verification we mean observation, either our own or that of someone whose ability to make such an observation we respect. **Factual evidence** is information obtained from direct or indirect observation. Factual evidence describes or reports what exists—events, objects, places, persons, phenomena. Factual evidence does not attempt to explain or evaluate; it merely reports what was observed. Direct factual evidence is observed by the arguer. Indirect factual evidence is that which is obtained from the reported observations of sources other than the arguer. In both academic and real-world argumentation, indirect evidence is used more frequently than direct evidence. Because we live in an age of relatively easy access to a variety of printed resources, using evidence obtained from the research of others has almost as much validity as evidence obtained through our own observations.

Examples and illustrations report or describe events and phenomena; they tell us what may be observed in a given situation. This type of evidence may be a brief statement or a detailed description. Compare the following:

Saturday mornings, after school, and even during prime time in certain weeks, children are shown half-hour animated programs based on products. On Saturday morning, between those fond old standbys *Tom and Jerry* and *Captain Kangaroo*, you'll find ABC's *Monchhichis* (a Japanese plush monkey), NBC's *Shirt Tales* (a Hallmark greeting card figure and doll), ABC's *Rubik the Amazing Cube*, and *Pac-Man*. (Cherubin, 1984, p. 31)

The stereotype's visual image is generally that of a Plains Indian. There are hundreds of tribes still in existence, each with its own housing style, language, religion, and other distinguishing cultural aspects. Yet the differences are obscured by the monotonous image ascribed to American Indians by television producers, directors, and writers. American Indians are all visualized as wearing beaded and fringed leather garb, hunting buffalo, living in tipis, and moving constantly. Those tribal groups who wore woven cotton garments, those who ate fish and acorns as their staple, those who resided in open-air or subterranean houses, along with those who moved only once a year or were sedentary are all obscured in the name of simplifying someone's concept of an American Indian for a television audience. (Morris, 1982, p. 189)

These two reports differ in degree of detail. The discussion of children's television programs based on products lists a series of brief specific instances. It amounts to a series of examples. The more detailed account of the basis of the Indian stereotype portrayed on television is longer and more informative. It possesses the characteristics of an illustration.

Statistics present descriptive and inferential information about people, events, or phenomena numerically. While an example often describes people, events, or phenomena in isolation, statistics can place such information in context. This gives the reader or listener a sense of the significance of that which is described. Compare the following statistical evidence to the series of examples of product-based programs in this regard. While details, program names, and character roles are omitted, the extent to which women and blacks do not represent society's powerful institutions is conveyed by the ratios between raw numbers.

Finally, we turn to the question of who represented the powerful institutions of society. The majority of characters were white males. During Saturday morning's programs no women or black males represented powerful institutions; in the afternoon programs there were 19 males and only 4 females; and in the evening there were eight males and only one female. Afternoon programs included 19 white representatives and four blacks, while evening viewers saw only two blacks representing powerful institutions. (Sandell & Ostroff, 1981, p. 57)

This is an example of a *descriptive statistic,* one in which the entire population of people, events, or phenomena of a particular kind are observed. The researchers looked at all television programing aimed at children, and their results describe what they found. Descriptive statistics can be reported in any number of ways. Averages or percentages are used to reduce raw numbers to more manageable form, and provide standards for comparing one group of people, events, or phenomena to another. The following example of statistical evidence provides both averages and percentages.

> Out of the 60 non-school half-hours (6:30–9:00am and 3:00 to 6:30pm) comprising the Monday-Friday period examined, Stratum 1 markets averaged 47.1 half-hours (79%) in which was available at least one program intended specifically for the two-to-11 age group (or some segment thereof). . . . In view of the relative concentration of children in the nation's largest television markets, the data for Stratum 1 are particularly significant. For, in the top 53 markets from which these 13 were selected, there reside 21.5 million children— some two-thirds (66.4%) of all two-to-11 year-olds in the U. S. population. . . . The 13 markets drawn from Stratum 2 averaged 40.6 half-hours of weekday childrens programming, or 68% of the morning and afternoon half-hours when children aren't in school. . . . The average Stratum 3 market offered 31.1 half-hours . . . 52% of total non-school time. . . . The average Stratum 4 market stood at just under 26 half-hours or 43% of weekday non-school time. (*The Availability of Children's Television: A 52-market Analysis of Weekday Programming, November, 1982*, "Children and Television," Hearings before the Subcommittee on Telecommunications, Consumer Protection, and Finance of the Committee on Energy and Commerce, House of Representatives, 98th Congress, First Session, March 16,1983, pp. 158–60)

This is an example of an *inferential statistic*, one in which data concerning a portion, or sample, of the entire population of people, events, or phenomena of a particular kind are observed. The researchers only looked at children's programming on 13 of the 53 stations in each of the four market strata, but their results infer that what is true of these stations is also true of the others. Besides demonstrating the use of averages and percentages, this example also demonstrates something that is important to remember when statistical information is used: For statistics to have meaning, they must be interpretable. This source aids our ability to interpret by including such phrases as "particularly significant" that call our attention to data the source feels should be given particular credence. In addition, the meaning of the term *averaged* is unambiguous because of the data that is reported. An odd number of observations (13) of phenomena that yield raw data expressed in whole numbers (the number of half-hours of programing) enables us to determine that the averages reported are means.

Statistical information can be deceiving, because when a source reports an *average* that number may represent the mean, median, or mode of a set of data. The mean is the arithmetic average of a set of numbers, the median is the middle score in that set, and the mode is the score that occurs most frequently. Given the following data, 98, 57, 23, 11, and 11, a source could report its *average* to be 40 (the mean), 23 (the median), or 11 (the mode). Be sure you understand what statisitcs your sources are using to avoid misleading your audience.

Scientific evidence reports the results of controlled experiments on the inferred effect of one variable on another. While it was probably reasonable for the authors of the study of the availability of children's programming to infer that what was true of the markets they sampled was true of all markets, it may have been unreasonable for them to infer that viewing is affected by availability. That conclusion would have to be supported by a *field experiment*. One variable, called the independent variable, has already been manipulated by the marketplace. Different amounts of programming are available to children in Stratum 1, 2, 3, and 4 markets. The experimenter would measure the dependent variable, viewership, by collecting viewing logs from a random sample of children in Stratum 1, 2, 3, and 4 markets, and confirm the probability of her hypothesis being true with an appropriate statistical test.

A *laboratory experiment* differs from a field experiment primarily in that its conduct affords the researcher greater control over the manipulation of the dependent variable, measurement of the independent variable, and the presence of nuisance variables. A simple laboratory experiment testing the effect of viewing violence on violent behavior might manipulate the dependent variable by making two videotapes, one high in violence the other low. These tapes could be shown to individual children to eliminate the nuisance variable of stress the child experiences by being in a group of strange children. The researcher could then unobtrusively observe the child's behavior at play after seeing the tape to measure the independent variable, and conduct the appropriate statistical test on the resulting data.

When it is quoted during argumentation, scientific evidence may not seem that different from other types of evidence of fact or opinion. Because it employs statistical tests of significance, scientific evidence differs from other types of evidence of fact in that its statements of direct or indirect observation carry with them an estimate of the probability that the inferred cause-effect relationship could have been produced by change or coincidence. Scientific evidence differs from evidence from opinion in that its credibility derives from the rigor of its method of observation, rather than the prestige of the person drawing conclusions about those observations.

Artifacts are actual exhibits of objects, audiotapes or videotapes, or photographs presented for verification by the audience. If you have ever watched a courtroom drama on television, you are familiar with the use of artifacts as evidence. In a courtroom, artifacts or exhibits constitute "real" evidence as distinguished from the testimony provided by witnesses. The use of artifacts as evidence enhances argumentation on certain topics. Consider how much easier it is to argue the merits of cotton over polyester if you have actual samples of both fabrics for your audience to feel.

Premises are factual evidence accepted because of uniform patterns of experience. There are some statements, which may technically be considered claims, that are so widely believed to be true that they are accepted as fact without further verification (Ehninger, 1974; Jensen, 1981; Ziegelmuller & Dause 1975). A premise is accepted because there are so many previously recorded or reported instances of its being true. Like other types of factual evidence, premises are discovered through observation or through consulting printed sources of information and opinion (Ziegelmuller & Dause, 1975).

Laws of nature, such as Water seeks its own lowest level, and rules of thumb, such as Better late than never, tend to be accepted. Because premises are predictions or projections based on experience, they can be verified like facts of other kinds. In theory, an audience could suspend belief until a premise is verified. In real-world argument, premises are used as proof to save time and effort and are seldom verified. When you can predict which premises an audience will accept, it becomes unnecessary to verify them. To do otherwise might insult the intelligence of your audience. Nevertheless, persons learning argumentation should verify premises by providing the warrant and its backing.

Evidence from Opinion

While factual evidence describes without judgment or evaluation, opinions are judgments and interpretations made on the basis of someone else's perception of the facts. Anyone may render an opinion, but in argumentation evidence from opinion usually refers to the use of the opinions of experts in the field you are arguing. **Opinion evidence** consists of the interpretive and evaluative statements made by an expert in a given field in regard to factual material pertinent to that field.

The opinions of authorities in a field provide arguer and audience with access to their expertise. If we are discussing the economy, we might turn to nationally known and respected economists like Milton Friedman and Paul Samuelson for their opinions. Not all experts, however, are nationally recognized. To find an expert, we seek persons with credentials in the field we are discussing.

Because opinions perform the function of evaluating and interpreting factual information, they often appear to be claim statements. The only real difference between a claim you might make in constructing an argument and the opinion of an expert is that the expertise of the source of the opinion is a kind of proof in and of itself. Consider the following statement by Daniel Boorstin; historian, Pulitzer Prize winner, a faculty member at the University of Chicago for 25 years, and presently head of the Library of Congress.

> People mistakenly assume that the new technology must displace the old. That's what I call "the displacive fallacy." Television did not abolish radio. That's not the way it usually works. Generally, new technology transforms the old, opening up unimagined uses for the old. Radio and television help us discover a new uniqueness and new uses for the book and all other printed matter. (Boorstin, 1980, p. 70)

The prestige of the source, or the isomorphism of his opinion with that of the listener or reader, can cause such opinions to be accepted at face value.

Mr. Boortsin makes a claim about the relationship between exposure to the new electronic media and the uses the public will have for the old print media. To the extent that we are willing to accept his expertise on the subject of books and their place is society's uses of media, we are likely to accept his opinion without demanding further verification. Examine, for instance, the following example of opinion evidence.

> Because it is done free and done by women, mother's work should not be devalued. But we know it is. Can our society ever respect a service freely given? Conditioned by unremunerated mothering at home, women are programed to accept less than adequate compensation for work outside the home as well. The depressing statistic that women earn only 60 cents for every dollar earned by men is by now all too familiar. The slogan "equal pay for equal work" remains, alas, just a slogan (Hechinger, 1981, p. 19).

To make a point, we purposely omitted mentioning the credentials of the individual offering this opinion. In the absence of credentials, opinion is accepted as proof only by a listener or reader whose opinions are not contrary to it. In essence, the opinion of an uncredentialed source functions as proof only when it is viewed as a premise by the audience.

This raises an interesting problem. In magazines such as *Time* or national newspapers such as the *Wall Street Journal* the credentials of the author are not provided. In some instances, the author is not even identified. Can you use such material as if it were an expert's opinion? Yes. In this instance, nationally recognized news sources such as those mentioned are acknowledged as reputable sources of information. The publication's own reputation becomes the credentials backing the opinion. However, news sources are not infallible. It is usually wise to check their opinions against those of acknowledged experts when you discover what you think might be a worthwhile specimen of opinion proof.

Often a news magazine or newspaper article with a named, or an unnamed, author will serve as a secondary source for the authoritative opinion of an expert, as in the following example:

> In *The Uses of Enchantment*, (Bruno) Bettelheim shows how irrelevant to the real needs of children the pro-social enterprise turns out to be. "Since the child at every moment of his life is exposed to the society in which he lives, he will certainly learn to cope with its conditions, provided his inner resources permit him to do so." In concentrating on mere outward behavior (cooperating, helping others), proponents of the pro-social neglect the child himself—the fearful, struggling child "with his immense anxieties about what will happen to him and his aspirations." The difficulties a child faces seem to him so great, his fears so immense, his sense of failure so complete, says Bettelheim, that without encouragement of the most powerful kind he is in constant danger of falling prey to despair, "of completely withdrawing into himself, away from the world." What children urgently need from children's stories are not lessons in cooperative living but the life-saving "assurance that one can succeed"— that monsters can be slain, injustice remedied, and all obstacles overcome on the hard road to adulthood. (Karp, 1984, p. 43)

In this instance, the credibility of the opinion derives as much, if not more, from the source Mr. Karp cited as it does from his own qualifications. While it would be best to read Bettleheim and quote him firsthand, the use of secondary-source material is acceptable.

In using opinion evidence as proof, remember that it does not provide facts but interprets or explains them. Expert or authoritative sources provide interpretations or judgments about facts and are always one step removed from the objects, statistics, and events that constitute their factual basis. Expert opinion is accepted by the listener or reader only when the expert is believed to be qualified to offer the interpretation or make the judgment.

Summary of Types of Evidence

1. **Examples and illustrations** describe or report events, phenomena that exist; examples are brief statements, illustrations are more detailed accounts.
2. **Statistics** represent information about people, events, and phenomena numerically; they may be expressed in raw numbers or summarized in percentages or averages.
3. **Scientific evidence** reports the results of field and laboratory experiments on the effect of one variable on another.
4. **Artifacts** are actual exhibits of such things as objects, audiotapes and videotapes, photographs, and diagrams.
5. **Premises** are factual claims that exist as evidence on the basis of their being accepted as uniform patterns of experience.
6. **Opinions** are interpretive and evaluative statements made by an expert in a field regarding factual information relevant to that field.

TESTS OF EVIDENCE

In addition to recognizing the types of evidence, you must be able to evaluate their reliability. There are specific tests that can be applied to each type of evidence and general tests of evidence with which the student of argumentation should be familiar. Tests of evidence give us the minimum requirements our proof must meet before it will be accepted as credible by our listeners and readers.

Tests of Facts

In testing evidence of fact, we are concerned with the accuracy and reliability of the observations being reported. In each of the categories—example and illustration, statistics, scientific evidence, artifacts, and premises—certain tests can be performed to determine their factual accuracy and reliability.

Tests of examples and illustrations concern the observations made by a reporter. These tests ask questions about the accuracy and reliability of the report.

Source Qualifications.   Was the observer capable of making the observation in terms of the necessary physical and mental ability? A blind witness, for example, may have difficulty describing an automobile accident but may be able to describe minute variation in the sound of an automobile engine. Did the observer have the training and experience to make the observation? Someone who has never driven a car, for instance, will have difficulty in describing the difference between an automatic and a standard transmission.

Data Accuracy.   Is the information reported in a straightforward manner or has it been manipulated to give it more or less importance? During the summer of 1983 and before the 1984 campaign, for example, both print and electronic news media were accused of making more of "Debategate," the story behind how the Reagan campaign gained possession of President Carter's debate briefing books, than was warranted by the facts, making it seem more serious than it actually was. Because information may be interpreted by the source reporting it, you must take care in checking the reliability of the interpretation.

Originality of Observation.   Is the information obtained from first-hand or second-hand data collection? It is possible to make observations on the basis of someone else's data, but more reliable reports of fact are obtained from first-hand observation. This does not mean that you should never rely on secondary information, since in some situations first-hand reports are impossible to obtain.

Recency of Observation.   In general, the more recent the information, the more reliable it will be. Some things remain relatively stable over time; however, many things do not. In using examples and illustrations taken from the reports of others, the recency with which the reporter made the observation can be very important. How easy is it for you to remember what happened last week or last month? The time that passes between when an observation is made and when it is reported serves as an additional filter through which a reporter's account must pass. Arguments dealing with economic matters are a classic example of the need for up-to-date information. One need only examine the economic history of the United States over the past decade to appreciate how much that which is observed may vary in a short period of time.

Attitude of the Observer.   Ideally, the best sources of factual reports should have a neutral attitude toward what is being observed. Since each person sees the world through a unique perceptual filter, prejudices, emotions, and ambitions may color the reporting of facts. Thus, a final test of examples and illustrations concerns the reporter's attitude toward what he is reporting. Try to find unbiased reports framed in relatively neutral language.

Tests of statistical evidence reflect our concern with verifying the reliability of our evidence. While statistics furnish us with an economical form of proof on a variety of subjects, at the same time they are more prone to distortion and misrepresentation than are other forms of proof. Statistical proof, you will recall, has a certain psychological appeal. The use of numbers seems somehow more credible, but you must take care that your statistics come from credible sources.

Source Reliability.   The first test of statistics is to identify the source of the information. Certain agencies and institutions are in the business of gathering statistics. The United States Bureau of the Census, for example, may be regarded as a highly credible source of demographic information about the United States. The Bureau of Labor Statistics might be regarded as a worthy source regarding information on employment. By comparison, the *TV Guide* is a less likely source of information on either population or employment, although it might be a source of information about America's television-viewing habits.

Statistical Accuracy.   In addition to knowing who collected the information, we also want to know how it was collected. Statistical information is frequently collected by sampling techniques. Did the counting procedure fairly select a representative sample? If a statistic claims to representatively sample the entire country, it should draw information from each state or region. Along with the process of data collection, accuracy is also influenced by the length of time during which data was collected. Conditions change, and it would be a gross misrepresentation to claim that inflation went down, based on statistics for December that report a drop in inflation, if inflation increased during the months January through November.

Comparable Units.   Since statistics frequently achieve their informative value through comparisons, it is important for the units being compared to be really comparable. Common sense tells us we cannot compare airplanes and microwave ovens because they don't have enough in common to render a comparison meaningful. The same caution is necessary when dealing in statistical comparisons because statistics can appear to have been gathered on comparable entities. If you want to argue about the use of technology in industrialized societies, for instance, before citing statistical information about the use of robotics in Canada, the United States, and West Germany, be sure the term *robotics* has been defined in the same way by the agencies that compile each nation's statistics.

Data Significance.   Statistics are often expressed in terms of means, modes, medians, percentages, or standard deviations, and data may be created, concealed, or distorted by the method by which it is reported. Stating that the price of a loaf of bread increased from fifty cents to one dollar and fifty cents in the last decade may not seem significant, but reporting a 200 percent increase in the cost of a loaf of bread in the last ten years does. Statistical measures can provide useful information, but that same data can yield different conclusions depending upon who interprets it.

Tests of Scientific Evidence are primarily concerned with the appropriateness of the methodology used in the experiment and possible effect of the laws of probability on its outcome. For that reason you should always understand the methodology of any scientific evidence you use, and be able to explain it to your listeners or readers. Three tests of scientific evidence should always be performed.

Generalizability of Setting and Subjects. Laboratory experiments offer researchers greater control over the variables of interest than do field experiments. Some, however, question the generalizability of laboratory findings to real-world settings. If a child behaves aggressively while alone in unfamiliar surroundings after viewing aggressive behavior on a specially prepared videotape, are we safe in inferring that same child would behave aggressively after seing an action-adventure series like *The A-Team* at home in the company of parents, siblings, or peers? In addition some experiments are performed on nonhuman subjects such as mice or monkeys for ethical reasons. However, if a certain food additive produces disease in a laboratory animal, are we safe in inferring it will produce the same disease in humans? Applying these tests does not mean you should exclude all scientific evidence from laboratory studies, or research using nonhuman subjects. Persons conducting such research often address these questions in describing their methodology and discussing the limitations of their study. Examine the arguments they present before dismissing their findings.

Variable Control and Manipulation. Whether in a laboratory or a field setting, a scientific researcher should take care to control as many of the variables that could confound their results as possible. If she has reason to believe that members of one sex may be naturally aggressive, or more easily influenced by television, the researcher should make sure that members of both sexes are assigned equally to each treatment condition of the independent variable. However, it is impossible to control all possible nuisance variables. Your own reading on a topic will give you insight into whether or not the reasearcher attempted to control the important nuisance variables. In addition, you should look at the independent variable and the way it is manipulated. Is it capable of influencing the dependent variable, and is it manipulated in a meaningful way? Is seeing a program on a nine-inch black and white set likely to produce different behavior than seeing that same program on a nineteen-inch color set? If a difference was found, does the researcher's methodology allow her to determine whether it was a consequence of size, color, or the interaction of size and color? Fortunately, much scientific research is published in refereed journals in which the editorial board, composed of top professionals in that field, screens and rejects methodologically flawed submissions. Know your source's editorial policy, and apply some common sense.

Consistency With Other Findings.   While external consistency is discussed under the general tests of evidence, it requires special attention in regard to scientific evidence. The conclusion of laboratory and field experiments rely on the application of statistical tests of significance to assess whether or not the independent variable may have had an impact on the dependent variable. When a researcher states that the effect of X on Y was significant at the .05 level, she is saying that there are less than 5 chances in 100 that a phenomena of the magnitude she observed could have occurred by chance or coincidence. However, her findings are tentative and conditional on others repeating her experiment and getting similar results. The ability to replicate is at the heart of the scientific method, and the need to do so is the reason why researchers publish their methodology along with their results. Even if the findings were true, probability theory suggests that if we replicated a study 100 times, randomly selecting a new set of subjects from the available population each time, our statistical test of the effect of X on Y might yield insignificant results on three or four occasions. If the conclusion of a piece of scientific evidence is inconsistent with other findings, you must be able to account for the difference. Was a different methodology used, or have relevant changes in the population from which samples were drawn taken place in the intervening time between when the studies were performed? If you are unable to find a reason for inconsistent findings, be extremely skeptical of them.

Tests of artifacts are usually performed by having the audience employ their own senses. There are only two tests of artifacts to consider.

Artifact Genuineness.   In an age when the ability to edit audiotapes and videotapes has benefitted from astonishing technological advances, the authentication of artifacts used as evidence is of some concern. Artifacts should be tested to determine their authenticity. Has a document or photograph been altered? The furor over the alleged Hitler diaries offers a clear indication of the importance of document authentication.

Artifact Representativeness.   Artifactual evidence is often used in value arguments concerning the worth of a product. Since it is usually impossible to examine all examples of a given item, a representative sample is used. When confronted by a large luscious hamburger in a television commercial, you probably ask yourself why it isn't typical of the burgers you get at the local fast-food emporium. What you are applying is a test of the representativeness of the video-burger as an artifact.

Tests of premises are difficult because our belief in a premise is based on the notion that things will continue in the future as they have in the past. Since premises are assumed to be valid because of the assumption that nothing will occur to invalidate them, you look for indications that circumstance, or our interpretation of them, will not change. The decision to inter thousands of Americans of Japanese ancestry after the bombing of Pearl Harbor was based on the premise that they represented a threat to the nation's security. The performance of Army units composed of the sons of these internees in the European Theater of World War II invalidated that premise. This example indicates the danger inherent in making policy on the basis of premises.

Summary of Tests of Factual Evidence

Examples and Illustrations

1. Was the report of fact made by a qualified source?
2. Was the information reported accurately?
3. Did the reporter make the original observation or is the report based on second hand information?
4. Was the report based on a recent observation of phenomena?
5. Was the reporter relatively unbiased toward the material being reported?

Statistics

1. Were the statistics collected by a reliable source?
2. Were the statistics accurately collected from a sufficiently large sample over a sufficiently long period of time.
3. Are comparable units used in statistical comparisons?
4. Is the method of reporting the data an unbiased and fair account of what was measured?

Scientific Evidence

1. Are the results of the study generalizable beyond the setting in which the research was conducted and the subjects who were invovled?
2. Are nuisance variables controlled and independent variables manipulated in a meaningful way?
3. Are the conclusions consistent with those of other studies conducted at roughly the same time using similar methodologies?

Artifacts

1. Is the artifact genuine or has it been altered in some way?
2. If the artifact is representative of a certain class of items, is it typical of that class of items?

Premises

1. Is there reason to believe that circumstances will not change in such a way as to invalidate the premise?

Tests of Opinion Evidence

Unlike facts, opinions are not directly verifiable. However, that does not mean that we cannot test opinion evidence. Opinion evidence can seldom be judged true or false in the same sense as factual evidence. Since an opinion is someone's belief about facts, it is subject to contradiction by someone else's opinion of those facts. Keep in mind that some of the best minds of the sixteenth century believed lead could be turned into gold given the right chemical formula.

Source Expertise.   In using opinion evidence, we are concerned with what the law refers to as the expert witness. While our opinions might all be of equal worth on some subjects, it is impossible for each of us to have the degree of experience necessary to make sound judgments about all the phenomena we encounter. If you want to know which automobile is most roadworthy, the opinion of a test driver for an independent consumer-testing agency might be more valuable than the opinion of your mother, who drives a twenty-year-old Ford. In testing the expertise of the source, we are concerned with the credentials that give this person the right to pass judgment on something. Investigate the training, background, and experience of the individual in her field of expertise. To the extent that your audience will accept those credentials, her opinion will have impact.

Source Bias.   As a general rule, seek the most unbiased source of opinion evidence. Although it is virtually impossible for experts to remain totally unbiased about their fields, the more objectively the opinion is stated, the more credible it will be. In instances where bias cannot be avoided, it should be forthrightly acknowledged so the listener or reader is aware of it.

Factual Basis of the Opinion.   As in the case of statistical information, the credibility of opinion evidence may be diminished if the opinion is based on second hand information. Although many opinions on historical occurrences must, of necessity, be rendered long after the fact, the most credible judgments are those made by an expert observer on the scene at the time something is happening.

Summary of Tests of Opinion Evidence

1. Is the source a qualified expert in the field by training, background, or experience?
2. Is the source relatively unbiased?
3. Is there a reliable factual basis for the opinion?

General Tests of Evidence

The **reliability of evidence** in assisting you in supporting your claims is the first general concern in selecting evidence for arguments. The audience determines the reliability of evidence based on its accuracy and recency.

Accuracy.   In considering tests of factual information, we stressed that the accurate representation of that which was observed was a key factor in choosing evidence. In particular, reports of statistical information and observations of events should represent them as closely as possible. If evidence is to be believed to be reliable, it must be as credible as possible. Evidence of both fact and opinion must be tested for accuracy.

To assure accuracy in your use of evidence: (1) When quoting directly, do not take facts, statistics, or opinion statements out of context. Make sure that you honestly portray what the source had to say. (2) When paraphrasing, make honest paraphrases. Sometimes, it is neither practical nor desirable to present a source's entire statement verbatim in your argument. When paraphrasing from books, speeches, or articles, do so honestly, in a manner accurately reflecting the author's intent or frame of reference. (3) When quoting or paraphrasing, accurately interpret your source; do not distort the information.

Recency.   Much real-world argumentation, and claim making of all kinds, is concerned with current events. Using recent sources of information will add potency to your argumentation. This does not mean you should not research the history of your topic carefully. Knowing what has happened in the past helps us to hypothesize about what will happen in the future. However, relying on out-of-date sources may cause you to miss recent developments.

The **quality of evidence** is also important. There is a temptation to confuse having a large quantity of evidence with having good evidence. Effective argumentation results more from having quality evidence than having great quantities of evidence. Quality results from choosing evidence that best helps the audience understand how you have arrived at the conclusions implied by your claim making. Quality evidence has the properties of being sufficient, representative, relevant, and clear.

Sufficiency.   Ideally, the best argumentation occurs when we have all the facts and opinions of experts on a given topic. Having all the evidence is seldom possible, however, particularly in our information-intensive society. Nevertheless, it is the arguer's responsibility to research the topic sufficiently to provide the support needed to make it possible for the audience to accept her claims.

Representativeness.   Is the evidence you have selected to support your claims representative of all available evidence? Just as we are concerned that statistical samples should represent available populations, the evidence of both the fact and opinion you choose to use should be representative of the available evidence on a given subject.

Relevance.   Is your evidence related to the claim it is supposed to support? In some cases, the relationship between grounds and claim in an argument is not always apparent. The reasoning process of the warrant, as discussed in the next chapter, can help make it more apparent; however, the use of additional evidence in backing the warrant may be necessary. The important thing to remember is that evidence that seems to have little bearing on the claim will be of little use in supporting that claim.

Clarity.   Will your evidence be readily understood by the audience? The advice on the importance of defining terms in such a way that they render a subject more understandable to the audience also pertains to the selection of evidence. Facts and opinions that are too technical, or in some way beyond an audience's level of understanding, may be unsuitable for that audience. Equally, vague or equivocal evidence will not contribute to the audience's understanding of the conclusions that your argumentation asks them to accept.

The **consistency of evidence** with itself, with other evidence on the same subject, or with normal human behavior contributes to grounding your claim making. Evidence that seems atypical, for whatever reason, is likely to cause the audience to disbelieve the claim it supports. Consistency is assessed on two levels.

Internal Consistency.   Does your evidence contradict itself? Evidence that comes from a single source, such as an expert, should not state contradictory positions. Except in instances where a simple explanation can be provided, a piece of information that reports both an increase and a decrease, or a positive and a negative result, may pose serious problems for the arguer who attempts to use it.

External Consistency.   Is your evidence consistent with other sources of information on the same subject. Allowing that new discoveries are being made constantly and that two equally respected authorities in a field may interpret the same event very differently, we generally expect that any piece of evidence should be consistent with others on the same subject. There is a natural tendency for a reader or listener to reject evidence that seems not to fit. A part of this need for external consistency is that we expect the evidence used in argument to be consistent with what we know about people in general. For example, because we expect the president of the United States to be supportive of American values and traditions, we might view skeptically a statement from the president condemning some instrinsic American value.

Audience acceptability is the last general test your evidence should meet. Will your listener or reader accept the evidence? There is little utility in having the best evidence if the audience will not accept it. Evidence must be selected with the audience in mind. This does not mean you should be dishonest or distort evidence in such a way that the audience will be forced to agree. It does mean that audience values, predispositions, knowledge of the subject, and technical expertise must be taken into account as you select the evidence to use.

Arguers have the responsibility of addressing the rationality of their listeners or readers. If you fail to consider the requirements and tests of evidence, your ability to affect an audience instrumentally through the process of argumentation may be seriously impaired. Always consider the possible available types of evidence and their tests as you prepare to argue.

Summary of General Tests of Evidence

1. Is the evidence accurate in its report of fact or statement of opinion?
2. Is the evidence a recent report of fact or opinion?
3. Is the evidence presented sufficient in amount to support the claim effectively?
4. Is the evidence representative of the available evidence on the subject?
5. Is the evidence relevant to the claim being made?
6. Is the evidence clearly presented?
7. Is the evidence internally consistent?
8. Is the evidence consistent with other available evidence on the subject?
9. Is the evidence adapted to the requirements of the particular audience?

THE DISCOVERY OF EVIDENCE

Now that you know the kinds of evidence to use in supporting an argument and how to determine the viability of evidence as a means of influencing belief or behavior, your next step is finding and recording the evidence. Your college library will probably be your best available source for locating facts and opinions. Get to know its organizational system and make the acquaintance of the reference librarian. A working knowledge of how your library is organized and the assistance the reference staff can give you will save time and frustration in your search for proof.

Begin with a devout belief in the premise, "The probable truth of any question is out there to be found" (Ziegelmuller & Dause, 1975, p. 56). It is up to you to go out and find it. The sources of information described in this section are available in most college libraries. The resources of the reference section can be discovered through guides that provide bibliographies of reference materials. *American Reference Books Annual* has been published yearly since 1970. It provides detailed explanations of such reference resources as dictionaries, general encyclopedias, specialty encyclopedias, foreign reference materials, selected government publications, abstracts, indexes, and some journals. It covers new editions of older references and annually describes references published in serial form. A second guide is *Introduction to Reference Work* by William A. Katz. It discusses the types of material common to the reference section of a library. If neither of these sources is available in your college library, consult the card catalog under the heading *reference bibliography*.

Books

Books, nonfiction unless you are arguing about literature, are a valuable source of evidence for argumentation. Your library's card catalog lists all books available in its collection. Card catalogs are usually arranged by title, author, and subject. Unless you are looking for the work of a specific author or know the title of the book you wish to locate, begin with the subject index. Do not be discouraged if you find nothing listed under the subject you choose. Those responsible for creating the subject headings may not have given your subject the heading you are using. You need to be a sleuth. Think of a variation of, or synonyms for, your heading. If all else fails, ask the reference librarian for assistance.

Books are useful because they usually provide a more comprehensive treatment of a subject than a periodical or newspaper has space to provide. Books provide historical background on a topic, but they have certain limitations as sources of information. First, books have the disadvantage of quickly becoming outdated sources of fact and opinion. The process of researching, writing, revising, and publishing a single volume may span several years. In that time, the factual basis of the book may become outdated, or superseded by new discoveries. Second, your library may have only a limited number of books on your topic, so you will be unable to find the quantity of information you had hoped. This does not mean that books are not good sources of information, only that they have limitations. If you require an abundance of up-to-the-minute information, you must seek it from other sources.

Periodicals

Periodicals offer access to current fact and opinion and may offer it in quantity. Because they are so numerous and varied, it is impossible to generalize about which periodicals will be of most value to you in preparing to argue. Consulting one of several excellent reference guides to periodicals will help you find the ones most pertinent to your topic. A good place to begin is *The Reader's Guide to Periodical Literature*, which indexes what are commonly termed popular periodicals—*Time, Newsweek,* and *U.S. News and World Reports,* for example. It indexes by subject heading, so the techniques you used in mastering the card catalog, if not the actual subject headings, can be applied to *The Reader's Guide*.

The Reader's Guide has one important limitation, however. It does not reference many scholarly journals or special-interest publications. If, for example, you are arguing about the unionization of public school teachers, finding out what is in *Newsweek* on this subject may be less valuable than finding out what is available in *The Journal of Collective Negotiation in the Public Sector*. Since the credibility of material from the latter is greater, you will need to examine specialty indexes. Most college libraries have the following indexes to scholarly or special-interest periodicals:

Agricultural Index
Applied Science and Technology Index
Business Periodical Index
Education Index
Human Resources Abstracts
Index to Legal Periodicals
International Index
Psychological Abstracts
Social Science Index
Sociological Abstracts

Once again, indexing is by subject. The difference between these indexes and *The Reader's Guide* is in what they do, not how they do it.

Newspapers

Not all college libraries offer current and back issues of a great variety of newspapers, but your library will certainly have one or more major newspapers from your state and some national newspapers such as *The New York Times*. The latter is an excellent source of material, not only because of its reputation but because it is indexed. This newspaper prints the text of major speeches, Supreme Court decisions, and documents such as the Pentagon papers. This is not to say that there aren't a number of other excellent newspapers, but they are not indexed.

In addition, a service known as *NewsBank* collects and reprints articles from fifty different papers. Although everything in a particular edition of a paper is not included, all material on a given topic, the 1984 elections for example, is available. *NewsBank* organizes by topic, so that if your topic coincides with a *NewsBank* category, the most recent information from a variety of papers across the country will be available to you.

A final note about newspapers in general and *NewsBank* in particular: Since most college libraries do not have unlimited space, newspapers are typically stored on microfilm or microfiche. Become familiar with how the equipment for reading film and fiche works.

Government Documents

If you are interested in nutrition, how to prepare an income tax return, or treaty restrictions on foreign trade, chances are that the government has published one or more documents on the subject. Texts of the hearings of major and minor Congressional committees, information bulletins, treaties and agreements, all proceedings of legislative bodies, court decisions, and the like are contained between the covers of government documents, indexed in the *Monthly Catalog of United States Government Publications*. This is the only available index to these documents, and its system of organization is unique in the art of indexing. It will take a little time to learn, but the rewards are well worth the effort.

The *Congressional Record* is a government document that is a particularly good source for topics on public policy. It is issued daily while Congress is in session and provides complete transcripts of congressional debates and presidential messages. It also includes an appendix containing a variety of materials—newspaper articles, resolutions, excerpted speeches, and anything else that might pertain to business before Congress.

Almanacs, Fact Books, and Other Resources

A variety of sources that compile statistics and other factual information is available in the reference section of your college library. What distinguishes them is that they compile information in condensed form and are organized for quick access. *The Statistical Abstract of the United States*, and *The World Almanac* provide statistical information on such subjects as population, demographic characteristics and change, transportation, agriculture, trade, mining, national and international banking, energy use, and more. They are updated annually. *Facts on File* provides a weekly summary of news from major United States newspapers and magazines.

Your library probably contains several sources of biographical information that can be used to discover the credentials of authorities and experts. A particularly good source is *Current Biography Yearbook*. In its fifth decade of publication, it provides biographical articles about living leaders in all fields, worldwide, which are updated yearly. If you wanted to discover more about Daniel Boorstin, you will find a three page biography in the 1985 edition.

While the text of important speeches, court cases, or announcements by public officials can be found in a variety of sources, *Historical Documents of (Year)* collects and publishes these important United States documents annually. First published in 1972, it contains texts of public affairs documents, court decisions, government reports, special studies, speeches, and statements by public officials on domestic and foreign policy. If you wanted the text of the speech in which Reagan's "Star Wars" defense proposal was first presented, you could find it in *Historical Documents of 1983*, Ronald Reagan's March 23, 1983 televised address, "Defense in Space."

A resource that treats topics in much the same way as arguers do, developing pro and con positions on a topic, is the *Reference Shelf.* A yearly publication, each volume is devoted to a single topic on a subject of public interest. This source contains reprints of articles, exerpts from books, and opinions of experts. It suffers the same limitations as all other books in terms of becoming dated, but it does provide a variety of sources of information. The series, which began in 1922, can be an excellent source of historical background information on how Americans have perceived many issues.

The foregoing is by no means a complete list of available reference sources, just some suggestions to get you started. To discover what else is available, browse through the reference section of your library or consult the librarian assigned to that section. As you become more experienced, you will find the process getting easier. We want to reemphasize that a good working knowledge of your library is the first step in the discovery of evidence.

RECORDING EVIDENCE

You should know how to record the material you research to render it most useful when the time comes to apply it in argument construction. It is one thing to discover information in the library; it is quite another to organize it so that it will be readily accessible in the future. You may be a person who functions quite efficiently with a notebook full of bits of information or a file folder crammed full of photocopied pages. Most of us are not that efficient, however. What follows is a workable system of note taking based on the premise that an organized system of note taking will make you a better arguer. Failure to have a good system for recording and organizing material is the most common problem experienced by beginning and seasoned arguers alike.

The first step in efficient research is to have a clear idea of the evidence needed. In the initial stages of working with a topic, attempt to discover what information is available by skimming summaries, prefaces, and opening paragraphs. Read for ideas as much as for examples, statistics, and opinion statements. Once you have surveyed the available information, look for specific things—a statistic grounding a relationship you want to claim, the opinion of an authority to back a warrant. Later you can become more concerned about the quality of the proof you are finding, but initially worry as much about quantity. The key concept to keep in mind is that you can be efficient in looking for proof only if you have a clear idea of the arguments you are trying to prove. Reading for ideas initially gives you a feeling for what can be proven with the resources available to you and keeps you from wasting time later looking for proof that may not exist.

Step two in the research process involves keeping an annotated bibliography and is performed in conjunction with step one. As you consider each source, record the title, author, publisher, date, and page numbers (where pertinent) on an index card; we recommend the four- by six-inch size. It is also a good idea to include the call numbers or reference numbers of all library materials so you can quickly find them again. In a few sentences, jot down the viewpoint of the author, a summary of what the source includes, and your personal evaluation of it. The purpose of this bibliography card is to give you a general idea of what a source contains. Make one card per source and have a system for keeping them in order, either alphabetically by author, chronologically by date, or conceptually by topic.

The third step in the research process involves excerpting specific facts and opinions in an organized system that will allow you to find what you need when you are ready to construct your argument. The mechanics of the system need not be complex. Again, we recommend the use of four- by six-inch index cards for recording each separate fact and opinion statement. Include the author, the author's qualifications, title, publication or publisher, date, and page number on the top of each card; then carefully record the fact or opinion. Accuracy is imperative. Omitting a word, punctuation mark, or phrase can seriously alter the meaning of the fact or opinion. Be especially careful in recording statistical information. In a moment of stress 3.6 million is less likely to be misread than 3,600,000. Also be sure the source stated million and not billion. It is easy to become confused when working with statistical information.

Once you have recorded information on a number of cards, you will have to arrange the cards in a fashion that will make it easy to find a particular piece of proof later on. If you require a particular opinion to back a warrant, you do not want to shuffle through sixty index cards to find it and then reshuffle through the same sixty cards to find the material to ground the next argument. An organizational system helps to avoid the paper chase. The fourth step in the research process involves developing a topical heading system to organize your index cards.

The system involves placing headings on each card that are brief, simple, and derived from the argument supported. The heading provides a two- or three-word summary of the information the card contains. Suppose you are arguing about drunk drivers. Some appropriate topical headings might be the following:

State laws—California
State laws—Nebraska
Deaths per year
Injuries per year
Proposed solution—ignition interlock
Proposed solution—random stop

These headings, commonly referred to as slugs, can help you organize large quantities of material into related categories and distinguish at a glance the cards pertaining to one category from all other cards. The important thing to remember about slugs is that they serve your purposes and should make sense to you. They reflect your impression of the contents of a particular card. Since you now have a lot of writing on a small card, confusion may be reduced somewhat if you record slugs in a different color of ink.

Because as a student of argumentation you may be required to both advocate and oppose the same proposition, it is possible that evidence suitable to one side of the proposition will become mixed with evidence suitable to the other side. Using different colors of index cards for advocacy and opposition can avoid this situation. If you cannot find different colors, using cards of different sizes serves the same purpose. If your argumentation course involves working with more than one topic area, the color or size trick can be used to keep evidence for one proposition from getting mixed up with evidence for another.

Although this may seem needlessly complicated, we assure you it is important. Because evidence is vital in establishing claims, it is at the nexus of effective argumentation. The more systematic your approach to the discovery and recording of materials of fact and opinion, and the creation of a means to facilitate its retrieval, the better you will be in building arguments.

Knowing the types of evidence used in building arguments, the tests it must meet, and the means of finding and recording information enables you to begin preparing arguments. You are now ready to begin using the skills of argumentation. The next chapter discusses how to turn your ideas into arguments by considering the relationship of grounds, claim, and warrant in the reasoning process.

LEARNING ACTIVITIES

1. Find two samples of each of the following types of factual evidence: example, illustration, and statistic. Explain how each of your samples meets the tests for its type of factual evidence.
2. Choose a topic with which you are familiar. Find three sources that provide authoritative opinion evidence on this topic. Explain why each source is credible in terms of the tests of opinion evidence.
3. Find five examples of evidence based on premises. Consider each premise in terms of how it came to be held as true without needing further proof. Is there any reason to believe these premises might become invalid?
4. Review the definitions of fact and opinion in this chapter. Decide which of the following statements are facts and which are opinions.
   A. The Supreme Court has decided that legal counsel will be provided for those who cannot afford to pay for it.
   B. Humans are primates descended from earlier forms of primates.
   C. The recession of the 1980s has finally come to an end.
   D. El Salvador will become another Vietnam.
   E. Many professional educators believe that studying a foreign language

will help students become more proficient in the structure and grammar of the English language.

F.　Railroads played an important part in the North's ability to win battles during the Civil War.

G.　Simply by visiting the Smithsonian, all may enjoy our nation's treasures.

H.　Natural-habitat zoos are more interesting than traditional caged-exhibit zoos.

5.　Begin researching the topic area you have selected for future assignments concerning propositions of fact, value, and policy. Your evidence file should meet the following criteria:

A.　All sources of information should be identified on bibliography cards.

B.　Each item of evidence should be classified as to type.

C.　Each item of evidence should be evaluated as to credibility—meeting the tests of evidence.

D.　Each piece of evidence should be slugged according to the topic you have selected.

SUGGESTED SUPPLEMENTARY READINGS

KIMBLE, G. A. *How to Use (and misuse) Statistics.* Englewood Cliffs, N.J.: Prentice-Hall, 1978.

Statistical and scientific evidence is used extensively in argumentation. This book provides useful insight into the scientific method and a thorough discussion of statistics, particularly the kinds used for significance testing in laboratory and field experiments. Its aim is the development of statistical literacy, rather than computational ability. We recommend it to students who foresee a specific need to develop greater understanding of this form of analytical thinking, or who are particularly interested in the use of statistical and scientific evidence.

WINDES, R. R., AND HASTINGS, A. *Argumentation and Advocacy.* New York: Random House, 1965.

Although this is an older text, it is still useful for its discussion of the place of argumentation in society and its excellent examples of famous historical American controversies. Of greatest use, however, is its thorough discussion of the types of evidence: historical, legal, scientific, and journalistic. Even though the evidence samples are sometimes dated, these principles and the techniques for discovering evidence remain valid.

6

HOW DOES THE REASONING PROCESS WORK?

Argumentation is a process of inferring for instrumental purposes. As you discover information on a topic, you make guesses about how it fits together, and how it might support or fail to support your own ideas about the topic. You become concerned with creating viable arguments. What makes an argument viable? In part an argument is viable because the evidence used to ground the claim has been tested for validity, but there is more to the viability of an argument than the validity of the evidence that supports it. The relationship between evidence and the claim it supports is established through reasoning. When you study the reasoning process, you are concerned with the logic of the inference drawn when you ground a claim with evidence. In chapter four we indicated that this inferential relationship is established by the warrant. A warrant can be tested for validity, and when it passes the test, we say that the argument is viable.

The reasoning process is based on recognizing common patterns of experience. Consider a not uncommon experience of dormitory life: You encounter Dennis and Paul. Dennis has an empty bucket and Paul is dripping wet. What goes on in your mind? Since you were not on the scene to observe first hand how Paul got wet, you probably inferred the cause of Paul's wetness. Experience suggests that the claim: "Dennis dumped a bucket of water on Paul," is viable. How reliably do the grounds, Paul's wetness and Dennis's empty bucket, support the claim? How do you know what really happened? You do not know with any degree of certainty based on the grounds and claim alone, but a warrant increases your certainty of the relationship between grounds and claim. This chapter is about the reasoning process, the warrant step in the Toulmin model of argument.

In using the Toulmin model to study argumentation, it is important to remember that it is an idealized blueprint for creating and testing arguments. It graphically depicts the process of reasoning from evidence to a conclusion. The form an argument takes in the model may not represent the best way to articulate it in a speech or an essay. The actual wording of an argument for presentation depends on such factors as communicator style, audience needs, and how individual arguments combine to shape your speech or essay. As we guide you through understanding how the reasoning process works, we will state some examples in Toulmin model form, but we will provide other examples that show how arguments are typically authored.

While you are learning about argumentation, we strongly suggest that you employ all four elements—grounds, warrant, backing, and claim—in creating your arguments. As you develop skill in argumentation, you may find it unnecessary to use all of them all of the time, and you will elect to use all of them only when your audience is likely to require them or want them supplied.

Reasoning is the inferential leap from grounds to claim made through the warrant in argumentation. In earlier chapters we noted that arguments may be taken or developed from many different fields. Although the subjects about which inferences are drawn may differ from field to field, the reasoning process does not change because it is based on patterns of common human experience. In this chapter we consider the forms of reasoning and the rules for testing the validity of warrants.

Six major forms of reasoning develop the relationship between data and claim: cause, sign, generalization, parallel case, analogy, and authority. In addition, two minor forms of reasoning are useful in certain circumstances: definition and dilemma. As you study these forms of reasoning, it is important to remember that reasoning, the warrant, is used to infer that "because these grounds exist, from this reason, therefore, believing this claim to be true or probable is justified."

ARGUMENT FROM CAUSE

Argument from cause is one of the most prevalent forms of reasoning in argumentation. When things are happening to us and around us, it is human nature to attempt to make connections between them. *As a form of reasoning, argument from cause suggests a temporal connection between phenomena.* We claim that an event or condition of one kind is the cause of an event or condition of another. Consider these phenomena:

Phenomenon 1—A student does not read his assignments.
Phenomenon 2—The student receives an *F* on an exam.

It is useful to conceptualize events as existing on a time line (Ehninger, 1974). Phenomena along it may be connected, and it may be traveled in either direction. A present effect may be said to be connected with a preceding cause; a presently existing cause may be identified to predict some future effect. Phenomenon 1 preceded phenomenon 2 and probably caused it.

Argument from cause is based on the premise that things occur in an orderly fashion. Since neither the affairs of humanity nor nature are random, we assume we can rely on the premise, "Everything has a cause." In an argument from cause, the grounds, warrant, and backing must validate the claim on the basis of temporal connection. If we are careful in researching phenomena, we can support claims that events or conditions of one kind are the cause of events or conditions of another.

As an illustration of how argument from cause works, let us consider some observable phenomena:

American public schools are judged to provide an inadequate education.
A shortage of math and science teachers exists.
Teachers are poorly trained.
At the secondary level, students are allowed to select courses from lists of electives rather than required to take a core of fundamental courses.

These phenomena may be organized into an argument from cause along the following lines:

GROUND₁   Teacher shortages exist in science and math.
GROUND₂   Teachers are poorly trained.
GROUND₃   In secondary schools, electives may be taken in place of fundamentals.
BACKING   The National Commission on Excellence in Education reported in May of 1983 that as a result of poorly trained teachers failure to emphasize fundamentals, and the shortage of teachers in key areas such as math and science, a "tide of mediocrity" has lowered the standard of American public education.
WARRANT   Because inadequacy is caused by a mediocre system of public education,
CLAIM   Education provided by American public schools is inadequate.

In this example, the reasoning revolves around linking a series of existing causes with the effect specified by the claim. The time line examines what came first, three causes listed as grounds, in conjunction with their consequence, an inadequate school system. The warrant identifies what produced these observable effects, the mediocracy of the educational system. If you were to encounter this particular argument in a speech or an editorial, its structure would probably not be stated in such detail. More likely, only the backing and claim would be presented as an argument from cause.

Let us examine an argument from cause where effects are known, but their cause is unknown and the subject of the claim.

BACKING   The Pacific current El Niño produces periodic variances in ocean temperature of the kind that cause extremes of rainfall and drought.

GROUNDS   India, Mexico, southern Africa, and the Philippines have experienced record droughts.

WARRANT   Since ocean temperature variation is said to cause unusual patterns in rainfall,

CLAIM   The drought in some portions of the globe is most likely the result of the El Niño current.

Notice that in this example the claim is qualified. Since weather forecasting is an inexact science, the claim is modified by the qualifier, "most likely." The evidence backing the warrant does not absolutely point to El Niño as the cause of the drought, but does suggest it is the most likely explanation of it.

Consider the following example of an argument from cause taken from an article by Professor George Comstock on television's effects on children:

When science is asked a question difficult or impossible to address directly, its solution is to address lesser approximations that are within its means. . . . For example, we might design an experiment comparing the behavior of young people who have just witnessed a violent television or film portrayal with the behavior of those who have not. This has been done dozens of times, and the results have been consistent: those who saw the violent portrayal subsequently expressed a greater degree of punitiveness or aggressiveness against another person than those who did not. We might also design an experiment in which we observe whether children imitate the acts they have just seen on television or film. This too has been done dozens of times, and the results also have been consistent: those who saw an example of violent behavior behaved more frequently in a manner just like what they had seen than those who did not see the violent portrayal. . . . While these experiments have shown that violent portrayal can influence behavior within the context of an experiment, they have not told us much about everyday behavior. After all, an experiment is an artificial experience, abnormal in time frame and setting. In an experiment a person might display behavior that he or she would suppress in real life. . . . The next question, then, is whether aggressiveness and viewing of violent programming tend to go together in real life. Scientists would reply by collecting data on the television viewing habits of teenagers through self-report and data on their aggressive behavior from their peers. This has been done a number of times, and in a majority of the instances there has been a significant positive correlation between the two. Teenagers who viewed greater amounts of violent television programming were in fact more aggressive in everyday behavior than those who did not. (Comstock, 1982, pp. 187–88)

Dr. Comstock offers an argument about the cause-effect relationship between viewing violence on television and subsequently engaging in violent behavior. At the same time, he gives you an insight into how laboratory and field experiments examine cause-effect relationships. While he does not specifically state his warrant, it is implied to be that the scientific method can reliably identify cause-effect relationships. See if you can identify his grounds, backing, and claim.

In arguing reasons based on causality, some precautions must be taken to ensure that our inferential leaps are justified. The most important question to ask is, are the grounds sufficient to bring about or cause the conditions specified in the claim? Focusing on the grounds is an important first step in testing the strength of the argument from cause. Examine your arguments from cause using the following questions as guidelines:

1. Are other grounds likely to lead to the effect?
2. Is the asserted relationship between grounds and effect consistent, or are there instances in which this effect has not followed from these grounds?

When using casual reasoning, you are generalizing about the relationship between phenomena along the time line: In the presence of phenomenon A (cause), we can always find evidence of phenomenon B (effect); or if we can find evidence of phenomenon B (effect), it is likely to have been the consequence of phenomenon A (cause). The regularity with which this generalization has been true in the past warrants speculation about causes or effects that are undocumented or undocumentable. This is particularly useful when arguing about things that have not yet happened, as in the case of weighing the costs and benefits of some proposed course of action. We take that course of action as a "cause" and speculate about the "effects," both good and bad, that it is likely to produce.

We also want to examine the generalizations produced by cause and effect reasoning to make sure they are really a cause and its effect, not simply two phenomena that happened to occur sequentially. Just because phenomenon A is followed by phenomenon B does not make A the cause of B. Many superstitions are based on this notion of false cause. A visit to Florida during the rainy season produced the following:

KARYN: (Raising umbrella in store) "I think I'll see if this works."
JANICE: "Putting up an umbrella indoors is bad luck."

Putting up an umbrella indoors only causes bad luck if you poke someone in the eye and that person sues you for all your worldly possessions.

Causality requires proof of more than chronological occurrence. When two things happen sequentially and you suspect a cause-effect relationship, consider whether or not the alleged cause is capable of producing the effect. Is the cause potentially strong enough to produce the effect? Two examples illustrate the danger of falling prey to believing false causes.

GROUNDS   In the 1968 presidential election, Karyn voted for Hubert Humphrey; in 1972, she voted for Eugene McCarthy; in 1976, she voted for Gerald Ford; and in 1980, she voted for Jimmy Carter.

WARRANT   Because Karyn has never voted for the winner, the candidate she votes for will lose.

BACKING   In every presidential election in which she has voted, Karyn has always voted for the loser.

CLAIM   Karyn's vote for Walter Mondale in 1984 cost him the presidential election.

That example may seem a bit foolish, so consider another from the 1980 presidential election.

GROUNDS   The hostages remained in Iran throughout the period of the 1980 campaign and election.

BACKING   Attempts at negotiations and the rescue attempt failed.

WARRANT   Because he was unable to bring the hostages home,

CLAIM   Jimmy Carter lost the election because of the hostage crisis.

Since the hostages were not released until Ronald Reagan had taken the oath of office, it is tempting to state that the hostage crisis cost Jimmy Carter the election.

Avoid being trapped by superficial connections between events by looking for alternative explanations of what happened. In both interpersonal and public relations, few things happen as the result of a single cause. The earlier argument on the inadequacy of the American public school system is a good example of the identification of multiple causalities. In the case of a presidential election, we can usually find several factors that contributed to one candidate triumphing over the other. For any given set of events, before placing too much faith in any single cause-effect relationship, look for possible alternative or multiple causes for the effect.

A cause may be discussed in terms of its being **necessary** and **sufficient.** A cause is said to be *necessary* if, without its presence, the effect will not occur. However, this cause may not be *sufficient* to bring about the effect all by itself. The easiest way to understand the difference between necessary and sufficient cause is to look at the traditional example of combustion (Ehninger, 1974). The presence of oxygen is a necessary cause of a fire's burning. If there is no oxygen, there is no fire. Oxygen alone, however, is not sufficient to produce burning. You must raise the temperature of a material above its point of combustion in the presence of oxygen to produce flame. A sufficient cause goes beyond that which is necessary to include all elements needed to produce the effect. In the case of fire, fuel, oxygen, and a spark are all part of the sufficient cause.

Why is this distinction important? In determining whether or not a cause produced an effect, sufficient causes can always be counted on to produce predictable effects. Recall the education example. Is a shortage of math and science teachers a sufficient cause for poor-quality education in America's public schools? Do more deficiencies have to be discovered before a sufficient cause for poor quality can be found? The distinction between causes that are necessary and causes that are sufficient helps to emphasize the importance of always looking for alternative and multiple causes.

Summary of Argument from Cause

1. Argument from cause suggests a temporal connection between events in which one produces the other.
2. When we can document effects, we may reason as to their cause; when we can document cause, we may reason as to their effect.
3. A necessary cause is a factor that must be present to bring about an effect, but it will not in and of itself produce the effect.
4. A sufficient cause includes all factors needed to produce a particular effect.
5. Causality involves more than chronological order and may be tested by asking the following questions:
   A. Is the cause capable of producing the effect?
   B. Is the effect produced by the cause or does the effect occur coincidentally with the cause?
   C. Are there other potential causes?
   D. Has this effect consistently followed from this cause?

ARGUMENT FROM SIGN

As arguments from cause link causes to effects, *arguments from sign connect phenomena with conditions that merely exist.* **Signs** are indicators—observable symptoms, conditions, or marks—that tell us what is the case. Would-be naturalists often study the behaviors of animals and connect those behaviors to other events. Consider the following examples of sign reasoning in which the sign has no causal connection to the events they are used to predict:

> A robin is the first sign of spring.
> When the squirrels store extra nuts, it means we're in for a hard winter.
> If the groundhog sees its shadow on February 2, spring is only six weeks away.

What kinds of things are signs? Events are often observed to be signs of attitudes or activities. We observe that a certain product is selling well and take this as sign evidence of the product's quality or the effectiveness of its advertising. Statistics are often interpreted with sign reasoning. High employment and low inflation are said to be signs of a healthy economy. Public opinion polls signify attitudes about policies, activities, and persons. Let us turn to an example of sign argument:

GROUNDS   52 percent of American military leaders describe themselves as Republican, 43 percent as independent, and only 4 percent as Democrats.

WARRANT   Describing one's party affiliation as Republican or Independent is a sign of politically conservative ideas.

BACKING   In the past, those who described themselves as Republican or Independents have tended to favor conservative policies; those who described themselves as Democrats tended to favor liberal policies.

CLAIM   American military leaders tend to hold conservative views.

The observable sign of political viewpoint used in this case is party affiliation: Republican, Democrat, or Independent.

Consider another example of this form of reasoning in an essay in which sex-role stereotyping in children's television is inferred on the basis of certain observable signs:

> Children's TV tends to reinforce traditional sex-role behaviors and personality traits extant in society. Thus, females are portrayed as being more passive in behavior and paying more attention to social relationships. They rate lower in aggression, and in self-concept and achievement-related behaviors—i.e., they seem less confident. They also display the virtues of unselfishness, kindness, and warmth, while being weaker, more peaceful, more dependent and more passive than males. These conclusions hold true for most females. The exceptions are female heroes . . . however, both female heroes and villains were rarely found. Out of 471 major dramatic characters, there were only 13 female heroes and six female villains. (Barcus, 1983, p. 61)

Mister Barcus lists several behavioral characteristics of female characters on television to ground the claim expressed in the first sentence. The warrant is implied rather than stated: The portrayal of passive behaviors and the small percentages of female heroes and villains are signs that television programs for children reinforce traditional sex-role stereotypes.

There are some cautions to observe in arguing on the basis of signs. The most important is to be sure the sign you are using is reliable. We have longed for spring months after the groundhog's first appearance. The problem with finding a reliable sign is that signs are only circumstantial evidence in many instances. We can never be absolutely sure that party affiliations are related to conservative or liberal attitudes. Both the Democratic and Republican parties have conservative and liberal elements. Things we observe to be signs may not really warrant any claim without backing.

A second caution regarding sign reasoning is that signs should not be confused with causes. A good rule to follow in attempting to distinguish sign from cause is this: *A sign tells what is the case, while a cause explains why it is the case.* Arguments from cause attempt to analyze events in terms of antecedents and their consequences. Arguments from sign do not concern themselves with what the sign will produce. They merely tell us what we can expect to observe as a result of having first observed the sign.

A final caution about sign reasoning is that we must be concerned with the strength of the sign. Sign arguments draw conclusions about what was, is, or will be. Signs are always presented as factual claims and must be tested the way we test any factual claim, by examining the grounds. We want to know if the grounds always or usually validate the conclusion drawn in the claim. Examination of the grounds might include asking if sufficient signs are present. After all, one robin does not constitute spring, but a flock of robins and other species, buds on trees, and the absence of snow may reliably lead us to conclude that spring is at hand.

Summary of Argument from Sign

1. Signs are observable symptoms, conditions, or marks used to prove that a certain state of affairs exists.
2. Signs should be reliable so that the grounds point to the conclusion drawn, not to some alternative conclusion.
3. Sign reasoning must not be confused with causal reasoning. Signs describe the situation; causes analyze the situation.
4. The strength of sign reasoning is assessed on the basis of there being a sufficient number of signs or the certainty of an individual sign's strength.

ARGUMENT FROM GENERALIZATION

Generalizations, based on sampling populations to draw conclusions about wholes, are very common. Much social science research studies a small sample of people or events and draws generalizations about the group they represent. A generalization states that what is true in some instances is true in all or most instances. *Generalizations are a form of inductive reasoning in which one looks at the details of examples, specific cases, situations, and occurrences and makes predictions about the entire class they represent.*

Generalizing may be the form of reasoning you have experienced most frequently in forming your attitudes, values, and beliefs. If you have had a negative experience with a course in Department X, you may reason that all courses offered by Department X aren't worth taking. Prejudices against people and nations are often formed on the basis of generalizations. This does not mean, however, that generalizations are not an effective and efficient form of reasoning.

What we see on commercial television is determined on the basis of reasoning from generalization. The Nielson ratings of the popularity of various television shows are based on sampling viewing habits in a few American homes and generalizing that what is true of the viewing habits of the sample is true of the viewing habits of all Americans. Consider another example of generalization regarding the effect of Music Television (MTV) on young children:

> Much of what they see is sexist, violent, or some mix of both. Educators and others worry about the effects such images have on impressionable young minds. . . . Action for Children's Television, a Boston-based watchdog group, has logged calls from pediatricians and child psychologists who reports kids unable to sleep after viewing Michael Jackson's horrific "Thriller" video. (Barol, Bailey, & Zabarsky, 1984, p. 48)

Generalizations may be restricted in nature, arguing from some to more, as in the example given. Notice the qualifier "much" in the opening statement. The arguer does not assert that all rock videos are sexist or violent; it is left to the reader to determine that all young minds are impressionable and, therefore, subject to harm. The use of qualifiers in claim statements facilitates generalization when the behavior of an entire population, or the qualities of an entire class of objects, cannot be validly predicted. You may have owned three cars made by The Motor Car Company, experiencing great dissatisfaction with each, but it would be unwarranted for you to generalize that "The Motor Car Company produces only lemons."

Generalizations may also be universal, arguing that what is true of some members of a group will be true of all members of that group. In making a universal generalization the arguer needs to be careful that the sample on which the generalization is based is sufficient to warrant the conclusion. Much of what was said in Chapter 5 about the verification of factual and statistical evidence applies to generalizations. There are four generic tests to apply to arguments from generalization. Applying them helps determine whether a generalization should be universal or restricted.

First, sufficient cases or instances should be cited as grounds to assure a reliable generalization. It would be unreasonable to argue on the basis of the experience of one state, that enforcement of laws to reduce drunk driving is inadequate nationwide. A sample composed of three or four states from each region might be needed to show a national trend. How large must the sample be? It must be large enough that the addition of more instances does not change the outcome of the generalization. Ultimately, the audience is the final arbiter of how many cases are needed to support the claim. The more familiar your audience is with the topic, the fewer the number of instances you will need to cite.

The second test of generalizations is sample representativeness. Do the individuals or items cited as grounds fairly represent the group or class about which the generalization is drawn? Items or individuals must be typical of a class if they are to represent it. One of the recurring criticisms of Nielson ratings is that they are not representative. In addition to being representative of items in a class, all items must actually come from the same class; and it makes a difference how you define the class. For example, generalizing about a class of objects called computers may be problematic if your definition allows the inclusion of both a pocket calculator and an IBM mainframe.

The third test of generalizations is that instances must be taken from random samples of populations. If in attempting to generalize about laws to control drunk driving you take all instances of state laws from states in one region of the country, distortion may occur. The region you have selected may have laws that are more or less stringent than those in other regions, and thus they will not accurately represent the national trend in law relating to driving while intoxicated.

The final test of generalizations asks if negative instances have been accounted for or explained. A generalization will not hold up if too many instances exist that contradict it. This is when the use of a rebuttal to modify the claim is necessary. If in preparing an argument on drunk driving laws you discover that one region has particularly stringent laws while the rest of the nation does not, you may use a rebuttal to account for the existence of stringent laws in a few states and their absence everywhere else.

Summary of Argument from Generalization

1. Generalizations argue that what is true of some members of a group will be true of more or all members of the same group.
2. Generalizations should be based on a sufficiently large sample of cases if a conclusion about an entire group is drawn.
3. Instances cited in making the generalization should be representative of all members of the group.
4. Instances should be randomly selected to avoid distortion.
5. Negative instances should be explained or accounted for.

ARGUMENT FROM PARALLEL CASE

Argument from parallel case is used when we have all the particulars about a given case and we reason from it, comparing the known case to a similar unknown case. *Arguments using parallel case involve reasoning on the basis of two or more similar events or cases.* Government policy makers and organizations such as universities often use argument from parallel case to frame their thinking. Those who set academic policies and regulations governing conduct may study what is happening at other similar schools, reasoning that what works at $college_1$, $college_2$, and $college_3$ should work at our college.

In arguments based on parallel case, grounds involve the case (or cases) that is in some critical way similar to the case about which the claim is made. The warrant, backed by additional evidence when necessary, explains how the case described in the grounds and the case identified in the claim are truly parallel cases. Consider this example.

GROUNDS   Cablevision of the North offers both Home Box Office (HBO) and
                    Cinemax to its subscribers.
BACKING   A consultant's recent analysis of these two systems has shown,
WARRANT   Westville's Cableprogram service is similar to Cablevision of the
                    North in terms of number of potential subscribers, cost of service,
                    and number of available satellite feeds.
CLAIM   We can anticipate that Westville's Cableprogram services will offer
                    HBO and Cinemax.

Another example of an argument reasoning from a parallel case is
found in this discussion of the Olympic Games, which makes a historical
comparison:

> Politics and professionalism may well destroy the modern Olympic movement,
> but the greater danger we must overcome is our willingness to delude ourselves.
> In our despair over the modern Games, we are holding history hostage; we like
> to think that once, long ago, the Olympics were somehow unspoiled and
> innocent.
>   In fact, the Games of the Greeks were just as flawed as our own. It was the
> Greek tyrant Pheidon of Argos who seized Olympia in the seventh century
> B.C. and presided over the games for the glorification of his strong-arm
> regime. Two neighboring city-states, Elis and Pisa, fought for generations
> over the right to control the Games and to collect their revenues. Sometimes
> such conflicts ended in an "An-Olympiad" or non-Olympics: the Games did
> not always go on.
>   Indeed, the ancient Greeks would be baffled by our belief in a bygone age of
> athletic innocence. Then, more so than now, winning was everything. If there
> were no shoe contracts or cereal endorsements, there were also no second- or
> third-place awards. The winner took all and it generally amounted to quite a
> fortune in victory benefits. Hundreds of inscriptions survive which were set
> up in honor of athletes, and from these we learn of free lunches for life and of
> professional "circuits" for runners and wrestlers. (Holt, 1984, p. 16)

The argument that historian Frank L. Holt developed about the Olympics
is based on examining the parallel cases of ancient and modern Olympiads.
To the extent that his readers perceived fundamental similarities between
them, the argument demonstrates his point.

There are two tests to apply to arguments from parallel case, and both
involve scrutinizing the similarities between the cases cited. First, ask
yourself, "How similar are the cases cited?" If we claim we can better
understand the modern Olympic Games by comparing them to those of
ancient Greece, we must be able to find enough similarities between them to
make the comparison hold up to the audience's scrutiny. The second test to
apply to arguments from parallel case is to ask, "Are the similarities cited
key factors?" In general, the more critical the factors common to both cases,
the more force the argument will have. In particular, the similarities cited
must have relevance to the claim being made in the argument. Holt claimed
that the Olympic ideal of ancient Greece should not serve as a standard for

modern Olympics because the ancient games were no less political than the modern ones. Notice the similarities he identified.

Summary of Argument from Parallel Case

1. Argument from parallel case reasons on the basis of two or more similar events or cases; because case A is similar to case B, we draw certain conclusions about what to expect.
2. For the argument to have rational force, the cases must not only be similar but the similarities must pertain to important rather than trivial factors.

ARGUMENT FROM ANALOGY

Analogies represent a special form of comparison in which cases are compared that do not have a sufficient degree of similarity to warrant argument from parallel case. *Arguments from analogy assume some fundamental sameness exists between the characteristics of dissimilar cases.* The argument proceeds much as it would if it were an argument from parallel case. A claim that is true of $case_1$ should be expected to be true of $case_2$ because both share a sufficient number of relevant characteristics. The essential difference between an analogy and an argument from parallel case is found in their relative forms of comparison. Analogies are figurative, often used as rhetorical devices to add style to an argument, while arguments from parallel case are literal.

Consider the following example derived from Douglas Ehninger's (1974) discussion of analogy:

GROUNDS	As everyone knows, the free and unimpaired circulation of the blood is essential to the health of the body.
WARRANT	Information is the life blood of society,
BACKING	Just as blood carries important "nourishment" to various parts of the body and assists in the elimination of impurities that would eventually poison it, information "nourishes" society and assists it in dealing with problems that would eventually poison it.
CLAIM	Therefore, the free flow of information is essential to the well-being of society.

Of course, if you were using this analogy in a speech or an essay, you would be more likely to phrase it like this: "Just as the free and unimpaired circulation of the blood is essential to the health of the body, so is the free and unimpaired flow of information essential to the well-being of society." (Ehninger, 1974, p. 69)

Comparisons in analogies are based on the function a thing performs. Blood and information have very few things in common. In the example given, the strength of the argument rests upon how similar their functions can be made to appear. The use of analogies can help listeners and readers better understand how something functions.

> No sane parent would present a child with a fire engine, snatch it away in 30 seconds, replace it with a set of blocks, snatch that away 30 seconds later, replace the blocks with clay, and then replace the clay with a toy car. Yet, in effect, a young child receives that kind of experience when he or she watches American television. (Singer & Singer, 1979, p. 56)

Because of its figurative nature, analogy has been classified as the weakest form of argument (Eisenberg & Ilardo, 1980; Toulmin et al., 1984; Ziegelmuller & Dause, 1975). It is said that the comparison of dissimilar cases is a rhetorical device and cannot actually warrant a claim. The analogy's usefulness is primarily confined to illustrating, clarifying, or making an argument seem more memorable or striking.

As Ehninger (1974) suggests, the position you ultimately adopt on the use of analogy will be determined by how you define argument and by the degree of probability you expect an asserted relationship to possess before you are willing to regard it as proven. If your definition of argument is restricted to instances where the relationship between grounds and claim produce conclusions that have a high probability of being true, you will probably not be satisfied with arguments from analogy.

Argument from analogy can be useful in instrumental communication. Since rendering the form of an argument understandable to the audience is a requirement for effective communication, there will be instances in which an analogy is the most appropriate argumentative choice. Analogy fulfills several critical functions in argumentation (Wilcox 1973). It helps organize and clarify thought by relating terms. It enables us to learn new information and adds style to our reasoning.

Should you choose to argue from analogy, there are two tests to apply to determine the viability of your analogy. First, the cases alleged to be similar must be sufficiently similar in function in all important ways. An analogy will not hold up if the compared functions are so dissimilar that to allege their similarity will make no sense to the audience. Second, the dissimilarities between the cases compared must not be so great as to adversely influence perception of implied similarities. Since analogies compare things that are essentially dissimilar, those dissimilarities must not overshadow the similarities.

If you decide to use this form of argument, search for analogies that will add force to your argument. While there is probably a point of diminishing returns in the use of analogy, it is possible to use more than one analogy to help your audience make connections between the available evidence and the claims you wish to advance.

1. An analogy is a comparison of fundamentally dissimilar cases that draws conclusions about the common functions they perform.
2. Analogies are commonly used as rhetorical devices, providing figurative rather than literal comparisons.
3. The dissimilarities of the cases should not be so great as to nullify the comparison being made.

ARGUMENT FROM AUTHORITY

In Chapter 5 we said arguers often use the opinions, and research of experts as evidence. Society has become so culturally and technologically complex that we are no longer confident of our own expertise on many subjects, so we rely on the knowledge of authorities. Textbooks, including this one, are examples of the reliance on authority to shape inferences about the nature of things. Watch the news on television, read an article in a magazine, or listen to the opinions of friends; it will not take you long to discover how reliant we are on authorities.

Who are these people we turn to for opinions and interpretations of fact? We label as an authority a person or group determined to possess expertise in a given field. Their expertise may come from education or experience, from having published in their field, or from being a well known professional—a scientist, physician, jurist, artist, or the like. In addition leaders, public figures, government officials, and spokespersons for well known institutions, groups, and organizations are acknowledged as authorities.

In an argument from authority, the inference is that the claim is justified because it is consistent with opinion, interpretation of fact, or research findings of an authority. *As a form of reasoning, argument from authority relies on the credibility and expertise of the source to warrant acceptance of a claim.* Since authorities use the same patterns of reasoning as the rest of us, an argument from authority may appear to be an argument from cause, sign, generalization, parallel case, analogy, definition or dilemma. What distinguishes argument from authority is that the warrant identifies why the audience should regard the authority as credible rather than drawing an inference about the relationship between grounds and claim.

Arguments from authority can be structured in one of two ways. In the first form, the arguer states his or her own opinion as the claim and reasons that accepting the claim is justified because an authority provides grounds for it. In a sense, this is the form nearly all arguments in academic argumentation take. Through research, you discover as much as you can about a topic, determine the opinions you hold on it, and how those opinions will be formed into claim statements. Then you find the appropriate evidence from credible sources to ground these claims. In the second form of argument from authority, the arguer takes an authority's view, restates its main point as the claim, and uses evidence taken from the authority's view as grounds for the claim. The warrant in either form of argument from authority is a statement that the authority should be considered credible, and backing applies one or more of the tests of argument from authority to establish that credibility.

Before turning to the tests used to establish the validity of an argument from authority, let us examine an example of this type of reasoning.

CLAIM	Membership in labor unions will continue to decline.
GROUND	Professor Greensmith states: My examination of the decline in union membership reveals that labor organizations have experienced an average decrease of 1.73 percent every year since 1974. Barring some revolutionary change in worker attitudes, there is no indication that this pattern will reverse itself.
WARRANT	We can believe Professor Greensmith's projection based on her expertise in the field of labor research.
BACKING	Professor Greensmith is an Associate Professor of Labor Relations in the Department of Management and Organizational Behavior at Northern State University and a consultant to the United States Bureau of Labor Statistics. Her findings are consistent with the membership declines reported by the American Federation of Labor-Congress of Industrial Organizations.

What makes our fictitious professor's opinion reliable is our willingness to accept her experience as a teacher and a consultant as establishing her expertise. The backing statement also indicates that her views are consistent with information from other sources. As you read the tests of argument from authority, notice how the backing statement met these tests.

Because argument from authority involves evidence that expresses an opinion, interprets fact, or reports research findings, many of the tests of evidence discussed in Chapter 5 may be appropriate. The specific tests of argument from authority seek answers to the question, Can the authority be regarded as credible?

The first test of argument from authority is to determine whether the source is a qualified expert in the field by reason of training, experience, or background. The academic degrees a person holds, the length of their experience, and the nature of their background are all ways of verifying that an alleged authority is indeed an expert. To be recognized as an authority, some demonstration of expertise must be made.

The second test of argument from authority examines the context in which the source offered an opinion or presented information. Is the statement made within the context of the alleged authority's area of expertise? Public figures express a variety of opinions that may not necessarily be within their field of expertise. For example, prominent members of the entertainment industry have expressed opinions about the development and production of nuclear weapons but are defense policy and international relations within the context of their field of expertise?

The third test of argument from authority examines the source's degree of involvement. Is the alleged authority relatively unbiased? The office or position a person holds may induce bias in a certain direction, and a person who is trying to protect tenure in an office or position will reflect such biases. We would expect the president of the American Medical Association to reflect some bias in expressing an opinion about government regulation of physicians' fees or the cost of malpractice insurance. While all authorities have a vested interest in their field, the important thing to look for in examining their biases are obvious conflicts of interest or self-serving statements.

The fourth test of argument from authority examines the source's statement in relation to those of acknowledged experts in the field. Does the alleged authority reflect a majority or minority view? In legal argument, each side may have its own expert witnesses, amply qualified, who express diametrically opposite views. Experts often disagree with each other on subjects inside and outside their field of expertise. Just because a view is different it is not automatically invalid. However, an alleged authority may also express a totally isolated point of view. While many accepted principles were once minority opinions, if you cite an authority whose view does not reflect majority opinion, be prepared to establish the credibility of that view by providing warrant and backing in your argument.

The fifth and final test of argument from authority examines the factual basis on which the source's statement rests. Is there a reliable factual basis for the alleged authority's opinion? Remember, it is not the image or stature of the alleged authority that grounds a claim, but the factual basis on which opinions are offered. When someone with prestige, office, or an academic reputation offers an opinion, we assume he has some basis for it. This may not be the case. He may be bluffing, expressing a point of view which is contradicted by the evidence, or speaking outside his field of expertise, relying on reputation alone to support his view (Wilson, 1980).

A final note of caution about argument from authority must be offered because of the special nature of this pattern of reasoning. Arguments from authority can be used to circumvent the reasoning process when authority is cited to prevent further consideration of a matter. In Chapter 7 this error in reasoning is discussed in more detail.

Someone is properly regarded as an expert because he possesses special knowledge, not because he is famous. The warrant in an argument from authority should reassure the listener or reader that the person cited is an expert because of special knowledge, not because of his status as a public figure. Backing is used to verify the basis of the alleged authority's expertise. It is important for you to include both steps in creating arguments from authority.

Summary of Argument from Authority

1. Argument from authority relies on the credibility of the source of information to warrant acceptance of the claim it grounds.
2. The source should be a qualified expert in the field by reason of training, experience, or background.
3. The statements of authorities are only credible within the context of their field of expertise.
4. The authority should not be unduly biased.
5. If the authority expresses an opinion at odds with those of the majority of experts in the field, the arguer should establish the credibility of that view.
6. The authority's opinion should have a basis in fact.

ARGUMENT FROM DEFINITION

A definition of terms is frequently offered within the structure of an argumentative case, and the arguer must justify its reliability. *An argument from definition specifies how something shall be defined or classified.* How something should be defined or classified may become a source of controversy. Dictionaries can be useful sources of definitions, however, in arguing the basis of a definition, how a term is used within an "entire communication environment" may be more satisfactory (Toulmin et al., 1984). Consider the following explanation of how the term *children's programming* should be understood.

WATCH [Washington Association for Television and Children] defines children's programing as including (1) those programs expressly designed for a child audience (the definition adopted by the FCC), (2) those programs watched by a large number of children, (3) those programs which have been made into cartoons such as *Mork and Mindy* and *Gilligan's Island*, and (4) those programs which generate lines of toys for marketing to children such as the *Dukes of Hazard*. WATCH also believes it is appropriate to define children as a wider group than the two- to eleven-year-old market. We would include adolescents in the wider group due to the fact their needs only partially overlap with those of an adult audience. WATCH sees childhood as a developmental continuum and we stress that arbitrary divisions into preschool, school age, and adolescent are convenient groupings rather than actual categories. (Washington Association for Television and Children, "Children and Television," Hearings before the Subcommittee on Telecommunications, Consumer Protection, and Finance of the Committee on Energy and Commerce, House of Representatives, 98th Congress, First Session, March 16, 1983, p. 199)

The important test of arguments from definition is that they must provide a clear explanation of the contested term and draw upon a common source of knowledge within the audience. In the sample definition, examples the listener or reader is likely to be familiar with are used extensively to add precision to the definition.

ARGUMENT FROM DILEMMA

This final type of reasoning deals with the problem of choice making. *An argument from dilemma forces a choice between two unacceptable alternatives.* Economic policies are common sources of arguments from dilemma. Consider the international financier's dilemma: which alternative causes the least amount of harm, renegotiating lower interest rates on loans to third world countries on the verge default or allowing them to default on billions of dollars in loans. During the Vietnam War, critics of the Johnson administration argued that the nation could not have both guns (the war) and butter (social welfare programs) without serious harm to the economy.

Regardless of the number of alternatives suggested in the argument, the validity of a dilemma depends upon its identification of a true either-or situation. The grounds presented must identify the options available; and these alternatives must indeed be different, mutually exclusive, choices. The goal of argument from dilemma is to point toward the one suitable, or least objectionable, choice or to place the opposing arguer in the position of having to decide which of two equally objectionable choices she is willing to accept.

> The First Amendment of the U. S. Constitution guarantees freedom of speech and of the press. This freedom has never been absolute, however. It is unlawful to speak or write so as to incite others to illegal acts, and communities may censor communications that are obscene or profane by their own standards. Those concerned about the effects of television on children have often threatened to use legal means (such as withholding a TV license renewal) to censor what they consider to be unacceptable content. Boycotting of advertisers, which has also been suggested at one time or another, may also be considered a form of censorship. Others, however, have expressed grave concern about placing *any* censoring function in the hands of a government agency or ideological group. These individuals say that the idea of generating lists of "approved" television programming for children frightens them more than anything they have seen so far on entertainment television. (Liebert, Sprafkin, & Davidson, 1982, p. 12)

In this example, the dilemma takes the form of a forced choice between freedom of speech and controlling programs aimed at children. The reasoning pattern that indicates this represents a true either-or situation is implied rather than stated. The reader is expected to recognize that a dilemma exists between unacceptable choices:

Reasoning makes the connection between claims and the evidence used to ground them. Although in actual argument the warrant and its backing are seldom stated, it is only through the presentation of the warrant that the arguer's reasoning is explicitly stated to her reader or listener. In your early attempts to frame arguments from dilemma, we suggest you include at least four elements of the Toulmin model—grounds, warrant, backing, and claim—as a means of developing facility with this technique of reasoning.

When you reason, you make an inference that establishes relationships between observed or known facts and the probable truth or validity of a claim. The purpose of reasoning is to assist in determining that probability. In the process, warrants are offered in the form of argument from cause, sign, generalization, parallel case, analogy, authority, definition, or dilemma. Each form has some specific tests associated with it that help determine the validity of the reasoning process. However, these tests do not identify all the potential errors in reasoning that can occur in argumentation. In the next chapter, these errors are discussed as we consider some of the common fallacies that can impair the quality of your arguments.

LEARNING ACTIVITIES

1. Conduct a discussion of argument from cause on one or more controversial topics such as gun control, abortion, euthanasia, or a campus controversy. What necessary and sufficient conditions establish cause in each case? Are these instances in which multiple causality may apply? What would be necessary to prove cause in each case?
2. Find examples of public opinion polls on a given issue such as the nuclear freeze, manditory seat belt legislation, or presidential popularity. Construct an argument from sign based on the statistical information. Explain the strengths and weaknesses of this sign in establishing the probable truth of your claim.
3. Conduct a discussion on the inferential leap that is made in going from grounds to claim. Why must this inferential leap be made? What are the assumptions we make in using each type of argument form (cause, sign, generalization, parallel case, analogy, authority, definition, and dilemma) to resolve concerns regarding the reasonableness of making this leap?
4. Examine the text of several speeches from a recent issue of *Vital Speeches,* or other similar source, for examples of the use of analogies. Share your examples in class. Which analogies succeed in creating comparisons that make the unknown more easily understood? Which seem to fail, and why do they fail? On the basis of this experience, are analogies a useful reasoning technique?
5. For each of the following (a) identify the kind of reasoning used and (b) apply the appropriate tests of reasoning.

    A. In a sense we have come to our nation's capital to cash a check. When the architects of our republic wrote the magnificent words of the Constitution and the Declaration of Independence, they were signing a promissory note to which every American was to fall heir. This note was a promise that all men, yes black men as well as white men, would be granted the unalienable rights of life, liberty, and the pursuit of happiness. It is obvious today that America has defaulted on this promissory note insofar as her citizens of color are concerned. Instead of honoring this sacred obligation, America has given the Negro people a bad check; which has come back marked "insufficient funds." But we refuse to believe that the bank of justice is bankrupt. We refuse to believe that there are insufficient funds in the great vaults of opportunity in this nation. So we have come to cash this check—a check that will give us upon demand the riches of freedom and the security of justice. (Martin Luther King, Jr., "I Have A Dream," 1963)

B.   The problem is a real lack of understanding of the balance of nature. Many Americans mindlessly oppose hunting, even in cases where animal populations are dangerously high. In some areas of Alaska wolves have become so prolific they are running out of hunting ground and prey heavily on moose, deer, and occasionally dogs. In the past, game managers curbed wolf populations by trapping and aerial hunting without wiping out the species. Still, whenever they propose to do this nowadays, they receive tens of thousands of letters of protest. Growing deer populations in parts of California threaten to starve themselves out. Sea otter colonies, burgeoning along the Pacific coast, are fast running out of fodder, too, as well as putting commercial fisherman out of business. (Morgan, 1979, p. 13)

C.   Perhaps more destructive is the general tendency of government to engage in patterns of spending that contribute to rising levels of inflation and progressively weakened purchasing power of the dollar. As parents are forced to spend more time in the work force in order to achieve minimal standards of living, there is less time to spend in family activities. As inflation and government regulation drive the price of private housing upward to where home ownership becomes a perquisite of the rich, the psychological benefits of ownership, such as the privacy and space, are lost. And when government attempts to fill its draining coffers through predatory taxation, it only makes matters worse. (Kellerman, 1981, p. 15)

D.   How many patients understand that "heart trouble" may refer to literally hundreds of different abnormalities ranging in severity from the trivial to the instantly fatal? How many know that the term "arthritis" may refer to dozens of different types of joint involvement? "Arthritis" may raise a vision of the appalling disease that made Aunt Eulalee a helpless invalid until her death years later; the next patient remembers Grandpa grumbling about the damned arthritis as he got up from his chair. Unfortunately, but understandably, most people's ideas about the implications of medical terms are based on what they have heard about a few cases. (Lipkin, 1979, p. 13)

E.   We watched the U.S. falsification of body counts, in fact the glorification of body counts. We listened while month after month we were told the back of the enemy was about to break. We fought using weapons against "oriental human beings," with quotation marks around that. We fought using weapons against those people which I do not believe this country would dream of using were we fighting in the European theater or let us say a nonthird-world people theater, and so we watched while men charged up hills because a general said that hill has to be taken, and after losing one platoon or two platoons they marched away to leave that high [ground] for the reoccupation by the North Vietnamese because we watched pride allow the most unimportant of battles to be blown into extravaganzas, because we couldn't lose and we couldn't retreat, and because it didn't matter how many American bodies were lost to prove that point. And so there were Hamburger Hills and Khe Sanhs and Hill 881's and Fire Base 6's and so many others. Now we are told that the men who fought there must watch quietly while American lives are lost so that we can exercise the incredible arrogance of Vietnamizing the Vietnamese. Each day—each day to facilitate the process by which the United States washes her hands of Vietnam someone has to give up his life so that the United States doesn't have to admit something that the entire world already knows, so that we can't say that we have made a mistake. Someone has to die so that President Nixon won't be, and these are his words, "the first President to lose a war." (John F. Kerry, "Vietnam Veterans Against the War," April 22, 1971)

F.   But when Militiades stood on the Plain of Marathon, he and his Athenian spearmen defended Greek civiization against barbarian invaders. As the Polish cavalry centuries later fell back before the German Panzer divisions, they fought to defend their land from the Nazi aggressor. And in most wars throughout history—for all their immortality and tragedy— their waste and cost and stupidity—there has been the essential distinction between the Athenians and the Persians—the Poles and the Nazis—the defender and the aggressor—the protector and the destroyed of international order. And to ignore that distinction is to deny the existence of a fundamental and moral choice—the distinction between the peaceful pedestrian and the thug who assaults him in the city street—between the thief and the sleeping householder. (Adlai E. Stevenson, "Foreign Policy: The Shades of Gray," June 1, 1965)

G.   It should not be difficult for you here in Europe to appreciate this. Your continent passed through a longer series of revolutionary upheavals, in which your age of feudal backwardness gave way to the new age of industrialization, true nationhood, democracy and rising living standards—the golden age for which men have striven for generations. Your age of revolution, stretching across all the years from the Eighteenth Century to our own, encompassed some of the bloodiest civil wars in all history. By comparison, the African revolution has swept across three quarters of the continent in less than a decade; its final completion is within sight of our generation. Again, by comparison with Europe, our African revolution—to our credit, is proving to be orderly, quick and comparatively bloodless. (Albert J. Luthuli, "Africa and Freedom," 1961)

H.   The ambassador says: "We have received continued assurances from the United States that they are committed to maintaining the sovereignty and independence of Lebanon." Oh? One cannot "maintain" what does not exist. Think of Lebanon as Connecticut (Lebanon is 20 percent smaller) with a government that, on a good day, controls part of Hartford. Imagine Connecticut with 45,000 Syrians, 12,000 Israelis, 6,000 U.N. troops behind Israeli lines, 16 militias and assorted Palestininans and Iranians. Now put 1,300 U.S. Marines at Hartford's airport and tell them to keep the peace. (Will, 1983, p. 100)

I.   It is harder and harder to live the good life in American cities today. The catalog of ills is long. There is the decay of the centers and the despoiling of the suburbs. There is not enough housing for our people or transportation for our traffic. Open land is vanishing and old landmarks are violated. Worst of all, expansion is eroding the precious and time honored values of community with neighbors and communion with nature. The loss of these values breeds loneliness and boredom and indifference. Our society will never be great until our cities are great. Today the frontier of imagination and innovation is inside those cities and not beyond their borders. New experiments are already going on. It will be the task of your generation to make the American city a place where future generations will come, not only to live, but to live the good life. (Lyndon B. Johnson, "The Great Society," 1964)

J.   No government or social system is so evil that its people must be considered as lacking in virtue. As Americans, we find Communism profoundly repugnant as a negation of personal freedom and dignity. But we can still hail the Russian people for their many achievements—in science and space, in economic and industrial growth, in culture, in acts of courage. Among the many traits the people of our two countries have in common, none is stronger than our mutual abhorrence of war. Almost unique among the major world powers, we have never been at war with each other. And no nation in the history of battle ever suffered more than the Soviet Union in the second world war. At least 20,000,000 lost their lives. Countless millions of homes and families were burned or sacked. A third of the nation's territory, including two-thirds of its industrial base, was turned into a wasteland—a loss equivalent to the destruction of this country east of Chicago. (John F. Kennedy, "The Strategy of Peace," June 10, 1963)

K.   But when television is bad, nothing is worse. I invite you to sit down in front of your television set when your station goes on the air and stay there without a book, magazine, profit-and-loss sheet or rating book to distract you—and keep your eyes glued to that set until the station signs off. I can assure you that you will observe a vast wasteland. You will see a procession of game shows, violence, audience participation shows, formula comedies about totally unbelievable families, blood and thunder, mayhem, violence, sadism, murder, Western badmen, Western good men, private eyes, gangsters, more violence and cartoons. And, endlessly commercials—many screaming, cajoling and offending. And most of all, boredom. True, you will see a few things you will enjoy. But they will be very, very few. And if you think I exaggerate, try it. (Newton N. Minnow, "Television: The Vast Wasteland," 1961)

L.   Great leaders are almost always great simplifiers, who cut through argument, debate, and doubt to offer a solution everybody can understand and remember. Churchill warned the British to expect "blood, toil, tears and sweat"; FDR told Americans that "the only thing we have to fear is fear itself"; Lenin promised the war-weary Russians peace, land, and bread. Straightforward but potent messages. (Korda, 1981, p. 7)

M.   To know how important the "art" of letter writing was, we have only to look at the accouterments our ancestors treasured and considered necessary: inkstands of silver, gold, or glass, crafted to occupy a prominent place on the writing table; hot wax for a personal seal; the seals themselves, sometimes ornately carved in silver; quills, and then fountain pens. These were not luxuries but necessities. (Wenzel, 1984, p. 14)

N.   In Regan's view, the scenario for World War III would become more like an arcade video game and less like a prime-time apocalypse. Insted of mushroom clouds springing up from charred landscapes and families being vaporized in their backyards or dying slow deaths from radiation sickness, the imagery would feature unmanned enemy projectiles being zapped and disintegrating high above the earth; the planet would remain out of harm's way. What is more, the U.S. would be able to protect itself without the threat of committing mass murder. Like Darth Vader spinning helplessly but harmlessly away from the doomed Death Star in his crippled TIE fighter, the Soviets would be mightly frustrated in their losing battle with American ingenuity, but they would not be incinerated. (Talbott, 1984, p. 81)

SUGGESTED SUPPLEMENTARY READINGS

BETTINGHAUS, E. P. *The Nature of Proof.* Indianapolis: Bobbs-Merrill, 1972.

The focus of this book is on making the message believable for the audience. It considers the use of evidence and reasoning and discusses the Toulmin model as a means of structuring thought. This is a useful book for examining the relationship between audiences and the arguments aimed at them.

KAHANE, H. *Logic and Contemporary Rhetoric* (4th Ed.). Belmont, Cal.: Wadsworth, 1984.

This book examines inductive and deductive reasoning and discusses how news media, advertising, and textbooks create distorted world views. It has three chapters on fallacies that offer extensive discussion and excellent examples of reasoning errors. The chapter on language fallacies is especially interesting in its treatment of the problem of "double speak."

MCDONALD, D. *The Language of Argument* (4th Ed.). New York: Harper & Row, Pub., 1983.

Although intended for composition courses, McDonald's discussion of reasoning techniques, which focuses on induction, deduction, and fallacies, can be adapted to speaking as well. He provides a good discussion of the uses and abuses of statistics. The bulk of the text is composed of examples that could serve as useful discussion material.

WALTER, O. M., & SCOTT, R. L. *Thinking and Speaking* (5th ed.). New York: Macmillan, 1984.

This is a popular public speaking text that focuses on persuasive theories used in creating and delivering speeches. Chapter 7, "Thinking and Speaking About Causes," provides extensive discussion of reasoning from cause. The historical basis for causal analysis, numerous examples of how cause-effect reasoning has been used and misused, and a thorough discussion of conditions influencing cause are highlights of this chapter.

7

WHAT SHOULD I AVOID?

The strength of your arguments is determined by the use of reliable evidence, sound reasoning, and adaptation to the audience. In the process of argumentation, it is sometimes possible to make a mistake. At this point, it is important to distinguish between things done deliberately to distort or deceive and things done in error. The message appears the same, whether the mistake is the product of intentional deception or the honest error of a novice arguer. These mistakes are generically termed **fallacies.**

For some (Crable, 1976; Sproule, 1980), fallacy is a litmus test for distinguishing a misrepresentation of the truth from a piece of sound reasoning. Ethical problems occur when argument is used to distort and deceive by falsifying, fabricating, or twisting the meaning of evidence, deliberately using specious meaning, or deceptively expressing the intent of your communication (Minnick, 1968).

Rather than identifying all possible ways in which deliberate distortion and deception can occur, focusing on some of the common errors arguers make will better serve your development as an arguer. Through the theme, "what should I avoid," we suggest in this chapter how you can improve your argumentative skills by becoming more aware of common fallacies.

Since most errors in logic result from faulty reasoning or problems in language choice, we want to emphasize the need to pay careful attention to the structure of arguments, the nature of the appeals they make, and the language used to phrase them. Consider these problems from the perspective that

> The study of fallacies can be thought of as a kind of sensitivity-training in reasoning. It should attune the student to the omnipresent dangers to which we are exposed as a consequence of imprecise expressions—vague, ambiguous, or misdefined terms—students should also be alert to unarticulated assumptions and presumptions. (Toulmin et al., 1984, p. 132)

FALLACIES IN REASONING

Hasty Generalization

When you make a hasty generalization, you have committed the error of jumping to conclusions. You will recall that in describing argument from generalization, two tests were that the generalization must be made on the basis of a sufficient number of cases and that the cases comprise a representative sample of all cases. The fallacy of hasty generalization occurs when the claim is not warranted, either because insufficient cases were used or because they constitute a nonrepresentative sample.

If you are arguing the claim "Dioxin contamination is a national problem" grounded on instances of dioxin spills in Michigan and Missouri, you have fallaciously based the claim on insufficient instances. The argument is salvageable, provided a warrant indicating that problems in Michigan and Missouri constitute "a national problem" can be backed. If backing cannot be found, or does not exist, the claim may be made, but it must be qualified as to its limitations. Since Michigan and Missouri are both Midwestern states, you could claim "Dioxin contamination is a problem in the Midwest."

Sometimes the generalization cannot be qualified. When you come across an atypical example and attempt to reason based on it alone, the generalization will be fallacious. Consider the following generalization:

GROUNDS   The Big Burger has "secret sauce."
WARRANT   Since it is typical of fast food,
   CLAIM   All fast food has "secret sauce."

In part, this example is fallacious because the warrant has no backing. It underscores the importance of our suggestion that arguers include all elements of the primary triad in the Toulmin model of argument and that they back their warrants. "If we are forced to spell out the warrants on which our arguments rely and the backing on which those warrants depend, it will usually become clear at once when our grounds are based on too small a sample of cases or on examples that are quite *untypical*" (Toulmin et al., 1984, p. 154).

A final potential for making fallacious generalizations lies in the temptation to try to squeeze more from a generalization than is actually warranted. This is similar to the problem of relying on insufficient cases in that the arguer makes an unqualified claim when only a qualified one is warranted. Consider the following example of overgeneralization:

GROUNDS   There are an estimated 350 synthetic organic chemicals in the nation's drinking water.

WARRANT   Because these chemicals can lead to an increase in the incidence of cancer,

BACKING   Dioxin, a synthetic chemical, was found leaking out of a dump at Niagara's Love Canal. Since then, the residents of the area have had a high percentage of birth defects, miscarriages, liver disorders, and various types of cancer.

CLAIM   There are a significant number of synthetic chemicals in our water that can cause cancer.

Because the claim is unqualified as to cause, we are asked to believe all 350 chemicals are capable of "causing" cancer. The warrant and its backing may not justify this conclusion. Recall the discussion of necessary and sufficient causes in the previous chapter. Before the medical community attributes cause, it conducts what are called epidemiological studies over a period of years using a large number of subjects. At best, the backing for this warrant justifies the use of *may* instead of *can* in the claim, and even that could possibly be an overgeneralization. Since generalization is one of the most frequently used forms of reasoning, you are well advised to examine carefully the generalizations you make and hear.

Transfer

Transfers extend reasoning beyond what is logically possible. There are three common types of transfer: *fallacy of composition, fallacy of division,* and *fallacy of refutation.*

Fallacies of composition occur when a claim asserts that what is true of a part is true of the whole. In the dioxin example, the degree of certainty we place in the causal connection between dioxin and cancer is unrelated to the degree of certainty we can place in that same relationship for the other 349 synthetic substances mentioned as grounds. When claims assert that what is true of a part is true of the whole, the warrant and its backing must be carefully examined, since they are what will justify the inferential leap from part to whole.

Fallacies of division are the opposite of fallacies of composition. The error arises from arguing that what is true of the whole will be true of its parts. When you break a whole into its parts and attempt to make claims about them, you may create an unwarranted transfer from the whole to its parts. "Speech courses are fun, and argumentation is a speech course; therefore, argumentation is fun." This argument may be true, it may be false; but the transfer from whole to part is not sufficiently warranted in this example. Consider a common example of this type of fallacy: "The Motor Car Company makes expensive cars. The windshield wiper blade is one part of those cars. Therefore, the windshield wiper blade on The Motor Car Company products are expensive." As with avoiding fallacies of composition, arguing that what is true of the whole will be true of its parts must be carefully warranted and backed.

The **fallacy of refutation** is the final transfer fallacy, also known as the *straw man* argument. It occurs when an arguer attempts to direct attention to the successful refutation of an argument that was never raised or to restate a strong argument in a way that makes it appear weaker. It is called a straw man argument because it focuses on an issue that is easy to overturn. It is a form of deception since it introduces a bogus claim, one that should not have been part of the argument, or misrepresents the original claim. Notice the creation of a straw man in the following:

> LISA: Our high schools are graduating a bunch of functional illiterates and mathematical incompetents. Why, achievement by seventeen-year-olds is down by over 4 percent in mathematics from what it was just five years ago; and besides, what you need to know to be competent today is a lot more extensive than what you needed then, and a lot less than you'll need to know five years from now.
>
> ANDREA: Wait a minute! Did those seventeen-year-olds graduate from high school? Maybe they dropped out. Aren't you assuming they didn't learn anything in their senior year? You can't say that the high schools are pumping out students who are incompetent unless you look at how they score when they graduate!

Fallacies of this sort are relatively easy to commit, even when you are not attempting to distort and deceive. Like Andrea, we often raise a series of questions, thinking they are sufficient responses to the arguments of another. When we are uninformed or ill-prepared, we unintentionally create straw man arguments because of our ignorance. If we do not carefully examine the degree of similarity or the number of cases used when we create comparisons, generalizations, and analogies, it is easy to shift argument accidentally in the wrong direction. However, responding to an argument perceived to be weak with a strong argument of our own does not automatically mean we are creating a straw man, since the quality of proof can vary from claim to claim, depending on both the competence of the arguers and the availability of evidence.

Irrelevant Arguments

An irrelevant argument is one that does not seem rational on the basis of the proof it offers. Such fallacies are also known as *non sequiturs*, Latin for "it does not necessarily follow." The critic of defense spending who argues that we should stop spending money on "star wars technology," since millions of Americans do not have adequate food and shelter may be making an unwarranted assumption about how federal monies are allocated, that funds that would have been spent on programs for the needy are being diverted to develop high-technology weapons. Unless proof is offered that such diversion actually takes place, the basic assumption of the argument is fallacious.

Circular Reasoning

Also known as begging the question, arguments that are circular support claims with reasons identical to the claims themselves.

CLAIM   Guns don't kill, people do.
WARRANT   Since the gun can't shoot by itself, a person must pull the trigger.
GROUNDS   A gun is an inanimate mechanical object.

In this example, the meaning of grounds and warrant are equivalent to the meaning of the claim itself. Strictly speaking, this is a nonargument, since it makes no inference from grounds through warrant to claim. It is an example of a fallacious attempt to support a claim by simply repeating the essential aspects of the claim.

Avoiding the Issue

Any attempt to shift attention away from the issue at hand is an error because it denies the integrity of the reasoning process and tries to replace it with something else. While we suspect that some avoidance behaviors are intentional, it is more likely that arguers pay insufficient attention to the task at hand. Monitor your own behavior and that of others for these common errors.

Simple evasion is the first type of avoidance. Changing the subject for no apparent reason, or bypassing a critical issue, diverts attention from the issues central to the argument. This error is most likely to occur when insufficient time has been spent determining which issues are inherent to the proposition.

Attacking the person not the argument is the second avoidance behavior. Known as an *ad hominem* argument, it shifts attention to the personality or appearance of the arguer, her ability to reason, the color of her skin, or the values she holds, all of which tell us nothing about the validity of her arguments. "She goes away to college for one semester, and now she's an expert on everything" is a parental response which ends some family discussions over Christmas break. While we may never become more than children in our parents' eyes in the familial context, it is essential that the worth of ideas behind claims be given primary consideration in the argumentative context.

Shifting ground is a third fallacy of avoidance. Shifts of ground occur when an arguer abandons his original position on a particular argument and adopts a new one. It is probably one of the easiest errors in reasoning to commit. In everyday social communication, most of us do not decide what we plan to say in advance. There is a tendency to adapt, to modify our thoughts and the manner of their expression to those around us. This becomes a real danger when we are involved in argumentation, because shifting ground gives the impression of evasiveness. We need to be careful to stick to our claims. This does not mean you can never change your mind or admit an error in argumentation. However, if you find it necessary to move away from your original claims, take special care to explain what has caused you to shift ground.

Seizing on a trivial point is the final error of avoidance. When you locate another's weak or indefensible argument and magnify it out of all proportion to discredit her entire position on the proposition, you have committed the fallacy of seizing on a trivial point. For example, she quotes an article from *Time*, September 31, 1981. You note that September has only thirty days. She argues that unemployment is running at about 8 percent. You concentrate your attack on the fact that unemployment is presently 7.92 percent. The accuracy of factual information is of great importance, but focusing all of your attention on some minor inaccuracy is not a sound argumentative technique.

Forcing a Dichotomy

A forced dichotomy is one in which the listener or reader is presented with an oversimplified either-or choice, phrased so as to force him to favor the arguer's preference between the options. The fallaciousness of the forced dichotomy rests on its failure to consider alternative choices fully. A popular bumper sticker of recent vintage provides an example of this error in reasoning: "America, love it or leave it." The only alternatives presented are unquestioning acceptance or absolute rejection.

The forced dichotomy is also known as the false dilemma. You may recall that in discussing dilemmas as a form of reasoning, we said that the either-or situation they create may force choosing the better of two options. The false dilemma, or forced dichotomy, is a fallacy in reasoning because the choice making that it forces is too simplistic. The argument "Either we unilaterally freeze the development and production of nuclear weapons or face a nuclear holocaust" appears to preclude other alternatives: multilateral treaty negotiations, or claims that development and production of more nuclear weapons may reduce the probability of their use. The either-or rhetoric of a forced dichotomy in this instance forestalls consideration of too many potential issues. In human affairs, it is seldom the case that choice amounts to selecting between two alternatives. Examine your own reasoning and that of others to avoid being trapped into arguing forced dichotomies.

Summary of Fallacies in Reasoning

1. *Hasty generalizations* offer conclusions based on insufficient information, basing reasoning on too few instances, atypical examples, or overstatements that claim more than is warranted.
2. *Transfer fallacies of composition* result from the unwarranted assumption that what is true of the part is true of the whole.
3. *Transfer fallacies of division* result from the unwarranted assumption that what is true of the whole is true of its parts.
4. *Irrelevant arguments, non sequiturs,* make assumptions which do not follow from the information provided.
5. *Circular reasoning* offers as warrants and data statements equivalent in meaning to the claims they are supposed to support.
6. *Avoiding the issue* is an error in reasoning that shifts attention from the issue under consideration. It commonly takes the form of a simple evasion of the issue, an attack on the arguer rather than the argument, a shift of ground, or seizing on a trivial point rather than the central issue.
7. *Forcing a dichotomy* puts the listener or reader in the position of having to choose between oversimplified either-or options.

FALLACIES OF APPEAL

When you construct an argument, you do not do so in a vacuum. You have an audience in mind and develop your arguments accordingly. This can lead to your committing a series of fallacies based on the appeals you decide to make. In particular we must be careful when appealing to emotion, rather than the ability to reason. There is nothing intrinsically wrong with emotional appeals, but problems can arise when you use these appeals to circumvent arguing the issues at hand. Appeals that bypass reason are usually based on the feelings, prejudices, or desires of the audience. The fallacies of appeal we shall discuss are some of the more commonly occurring lapses from rationality. Again, we emphasize that emotional appeals are an important part of the process of persuasion and caution that in argumentation emotion should not supplant reason.

Appeal to Ignorance

Appeals to ignorance, known by the Latin term *ad ignoratium,* ask the audience to accept the truth of a claim because no proof to the contrary exists. Something is true simply because it cannot be proven false. "Evidence does not exist to prove children are harmed by video games" does not demonstrate that video games do not harm children, only that evidence of harm cannot be found. Even more troublesome is the technique of claiming because we cannot prove that since something has not happened or does not exist it therefore must have happened or must exist. "The inability to disprove the existence of flying saucers and extraterrestrial visitation to earth confirms the existence of the former, and the occurrence of the latter."

Can you make nonfallacious claims about what the absence of proof may mean? Yes, to a certain extent. An absence of evidence suggests the possibility of a claim's validity. For example, drugs are tested for side effects and are presumed safe when none occur. The problem with using this type of reasoning is that backing for the warrant becomes the assertion that the lack of evidence is, in and of itself, evidence. This tends to trivialize the meaning of evidence as a concept (Toulmin et al., 1984).

There is one important exception: Artificial presumption may be assigned in such a way that failure to prove something leads to the conclusion that its logical opposite is true. When the prosecution fails to present a prima facie case against the accused, we conclude he must be innocent. In other cases, the absence of contrary evidence may strengthen a claim, but it in no way proves it. The absence of evidence may simply mean that research regarding the phenomenon has not been very thorough.

Appeal to the People

Also known as the bandwagon appeal, or an *ad populum argument*, appeals to the people address the audience's prejudices and feelings rather than the issues. When a claim is justified on the basis of its alleged popularity—we should do something because the majority of people are doing it—an appeal to the people is being made. For example, an advocate might argue for a change in laws governing the ownership of handguns because a majority of Americans are of the opinion that private ownership of handguns should be outlawed. In cases like this, the line between sound and unsound argument is blurred.

On the one hand, common sense suggests that when matters concerning "the people" are discussed, their will should be taken into account. In the case of a future law, this allows us to forecast whether or not it would likely be obeyed or violated. On the other hand, to make popular opinion the sole criterion of a claim's worth, and to appeal to this opinion so as to discourage consideration of pertinent facts, cannot help but result in less informed and less thoughtful decisions. In recent years, for example, voters in some states passed a series of tax reforms reflecting the popular belief that taxes were too high. After a few years of lower taxes, citizens in these same states are experiencing anguish over the loss of revenues for education. Critical consideration of the issues should take precedence over popular opinion.

Appeal to Emotions

As we suggested, the use of emotional appeals is not necessarily bad, nor is it possible to be entirely rational. Nevertheless, strong appeals to emotion are no substitute for careful reasoning. Any emotion may be a source of appeal; here, we will concentrate on the two used most frequently in poor argumentation: appeals to pity and fear.

Traditionally, the use of the appeal to pity was taught as a means of creating audience sympathy for an individual or group. Such appeals are common on topics that address the suffering of those unable to overcome misfortune without the aid of others. No fallacy is committed when such appeals are used in conjunction with sound reasoning. However, when pity is the only basis on which an alteration of belief or behavior is justified, argumentation has been abandoned in favor of persuasion. Consider the effect the following argument might have if it were not placed in the context of other issues:

GROUNDS   Amerasian children fathered by American servicemen, besides being social outcasts in Asian countries, have a high incidence of tuberculosis, malaria, and even a few cases of leprosy.

WARRANT   Because it would be cruel and heartless to turn our backs on children who should rightfully be American citizens when their condition is so desperate,

CLAIM   We must accept all Asian children who wish to seek refuge in this country who can prove American parentage.

The action ultimately taken, based solely on this criteria, might lack those qualities of administrative and economic feasibility that an effective remedy must possess. In a situation where an opponent was present to confront this advocate, some of these problems would certainly be addressed. However, in an argumentative situation in which a respondent for the other side of the question is not present, the arguer must place any appeals to pity in a context of sound proof and reasoning.

The appeal to fear is another form of emotion seeking, arousing concern over potential consequences. The opponent of our hypothetical advocate of the rights of Amerasian children would generate more heat than light if he succumbed to the temptation to counter the appeal to pity with the following appeal to fear.

GROUNDS   It is openly admitted that these people have dangerous, contagious diseases like tuberculosis, malaria, leprosy, and who knows what else.

WARRANT   Because we can't bring them into this country without bringing their afflictions right along with them,

CLAIM   Letting these children into this country will threaten the health and safety of your children.

As with appeals to pity, the use of an appeal to fear is a matter of appropriateness and balance. There are occasions when a little fear is needed to move people to action, but to appeal to fear alone may produce disastrous consequences. When fear dictates behavior, rash decisions, such as the blacklisting that destroyed careers during the McCarthy era or granting powers that deprived citizens of Japanese ancestry of their civil liberties, may result.

Appeal to Authority

An argument from authority that utilizes the opinions and testimony of experts is a legitimate form of reasoning. However, care must be exercised to ensure that the argument from authority does not become a fallacious appeal to authority. An appeal to authority is fallacious when a seemingly authoritative source of opinion either lacks real expertise or prevents a fair hearing for the opposition. Thus, instead of being used to ground a claim or back a warrant, the authority is characterized as infallible and is used to shut off further discussion of the issues. Abuses of authority commonly involve the Bible, the Constitution, revered persons, or testimonials by celebrities. We have become accustomed to this last form of appeal to authority. Tennis star John McEnroe promotes disposable razors, basketball player Ervin "Magic" Johnson tells us where to bank, and Roger Staubach endorses using antiacid tablets.

Are all testimonials fallacious? Not necessarily. The validity of the warrant in testimonials depends on the backing that establishes the authority's credentials. Consider the following:

GROUNDS   Life insurance is available from Veterans Life to any individual who is a U. S. military veteran.
WARRANT   Because Roger Staubach knows the needs of veterans,
BACKING   Since he graduated from Annapolis and served in the United States Navy before playing professional football,
CLAIM   They should buy this insurance which he endorses.

The audience is asked to accept the claim "you should buy this insurance" based on the testimony of someone who is a veteran first and a retired quarterback, who is therefore recognizable, second.

Be prepared to defend your choice of experts. Unknowingly, your choice may represent a fallacious use of authority if you cite someone outside his acknowledged field of expertise. While we might take John McEnroe's advice on tennis, is he likely to be an expert on shaving? Making this distinction is sometimes difficult because an individual may be an expert in more than one field. At one time, comedian Bill Cosby appeared in a series of computer commercials. We might acknowledge his expertise on issues of comedy or acting, but what about education, the major claim advanced in these commercials? In fact, Bill Cosby has advanced degrees in psychology and education, has produced several educational films, and has also lectured on race relations in education and student motivation. This illustrates why it is always important to provide information documenting the qualifications of those you cite.

Appeal to Tradition

We normally have strong ties to tradition, and learning the historical background of a topic is a good way to prepare to argue it. However, asking an audience to accept something because it is customary rather than because of the issues justifying it commits the fallacy of appeal to tradition. Before the issue was put to rest with the nomination of Geraldine Ferraro, it was typical to hear appeals to tradition that simultaneously begged the question, "A woman should not be on the ticket, because in the over-200-year history of American politics, no woman has had sufficient experience or national exposure to be the presidential or vice-presidential nominee of a major party."

Comparisons, which reference tradition, are not necessarily inappropriate. Value claims often involve matters of taste derived from tradition. A thorough analysis of the reasons behind a tradition provides a valid basis on which to argue its future violation or veneration. However, it is important to realize that arguing on behalf of a belief or behavior solely on the basis of tradition gives the audience insufficient understanding of the issues that justify opposing a proposed change in that belief or behavior.

Recalling our discussion of presumption, you may think something is amiss. Doesn't presumption favor *tradition,* that which is already in existence? Yes, and opponents in argumentation find themselves arguing on behalf of the benefits of continuing to believe or behave as we have in the past. However, when the opponent uses such argument, he must provide good and sufficient reasons to justify maintaining that tradition and not merely appeal to tradition alone.

Appeal to Humor

Appeals based on humor can be problematical for several reasons. The arguer who resorts to a series of jokes about women drivers to refute criticism of auto safety standards uses humor to entertain rather than enlighten. When humor is used to such an extent that it becomes the focal point of the discussion, the point of argumentation is lost. A series of commercials for a low-calorie beer features celebrities and retired sports figures. These commercials are so humorous that many viewers are unable to name the product being promoted but can recount the antics of the people promoting it.

Humor is also misused when it takes a claim to its most extreme and, therefore, absurd meaning. This is known as *reductio ad absurdum.* Reducing a claim to absurdity is a particularly troublesome kind of fallacy because it sometimes occurs in an effort to employ style but results mainly in decreasing the discussion's rationality. One of the premises of the National Rifle Association is frequently seen on bumper stickers: "I support the right to bear arms." This claim is reduced to the absurd by another bumper sticker: "I support the right to arm bears!" While such a turn of phrase may be humorous, it has the effect of trivializing a serious issue.

This is not to say that humor cannot be an effective device. Humor can have a positive effect, creating good will or lessening tensions in a heated situation. During the summer of 1980, President Carter had the unpleasant task of informing farmers in the southwest that desired economic aid would not be available. Just before his helicopter landed in the drought-stricken Dallas-Fort Worth area, there was a sudden rainfall. President Carter began an address to a group of farmers saying, "Well, you asked for either money or rain. I couldn't get the money so I brought the rain" (Boller, 1981, p. 346).

Summary of Fallacies of Appeal

1. *Appeals to ignorance* ask the audience to accept a claim because no proof exists to deny its validity.
2. *Appeals to the people* ask an audience to accept a claim because it is supported by majority opinion.
3. *Appeals to pity* arouse sympathy for individuals or groups to encourage the redress of some wrong or misfortune they have suffered.
4. *Appeals to fear* attempt to gain the audience's acceptance of a claim by arousing concern over the consequence it alleges.
5. *Appeals to authority* encourage reliance on some ultimate source of knowledge in place of reasoning as the basis of a claim.
6. *Appeals to tradition* ask an audience to accept a claim because it represents a customary belief or course of action.
7. *Appeals to humor* either fail to make a serious point or reduce another's claim to its most absurd level.

FALLACIES IN LANGUAGE

Since language is the vehicle of your argument's meaning, you must be concerned about how you use it in constructing arguments. We have already indicated some concerns about the way in which claims are phrased and stressed the importance of defining terms. We now discuss the care that must be exercised in choosing language appropriate to all aspects of argumentation. In any use of language, but especially in using it to alter belief or behavior, it is important to remember that meanings are in people, not in words. The meaning we attach to the words of others is a consequence of their passing through our own perceptual filters. Become aware of your own language habits and biases to avoid falling victim to the fallacies of language described here.

Ambiguity and Equivocation

The ambiguity of language interferes with effective argumentation when a term is used differently by both parties to the dispute. This "meanings are in people" problem may occur unintentionally, with the arguers operating on the basis of legitimate, but entirely different, meanings for a term. Consider the plight of the musician, the dentist, the billiards player, and the engineer engaged in an argument concerning the best way to use a *bridge*. This example may seem frivolous, but consider a real-world example. If you have ever handed in a paper and the professor, emulating Benjamin Disraeli, has told you, "I shall lose no time in reading this," you have experienced the uncertainty that ambiguity engenders.

Like the errors resulting from the ambiguity of language, errors of equivocation occur because words have multiple legitimate meanings. An error of equivocation occurs when a term appears to have two or more meanings within the arguments of one person. When you shift the meaning of a term in an argument, you are equivocating. The statements of candidates for public office frequently contain equivocations used intentionally to avoid offending part of the electorate. One candidate declares, "I stand for revenue sharing or an equalization of the tax burden," leaving uncertain whether the phrase following "or" restates the phrase preceding it or names an acceptable alternative. Another announces, "I favor appropriations adequate to ensure our national defense, which will not place an undue burden on the taxpayers of this nation."

Since the audience is a part of the process of argumentation, it will be impossible for you to avoid all instances of ambiguity. However, by exercising care in phrasing arguments and defining key terms, you can avoid many errors of equivocation. You should be cognizant of language in the arguments you construct and scrutinize the language used in the evidence these arguments contain, especially when it is opinion evidence.

Emotionally Loaded Language

The arguments of everyday life are frequently condensed to what fits on a picket sign carried at a march or rally, a bumper sticker, or a T-shirt. "War is unhealthy for children and other living things." "Abortion is killing." "A boy of quality is not threatened by a girl of equality." In addition to serving as a vehicle for the denotation of ideas, language is a powerful instrument for the expression of attitudes and feelings. Your choice of language can reveal your attitude toward a topic. One of our favorite illustrations of the connotative property of language is the following list of questions "for sexists only":

Why are forceful males referred to as charismatic while females are domineering?

When speaking about people who are talkative, why are men called articulate and women gabby?

Why are men who are forgetful called absentminded, when forgetful women are called scatterbrained?

Why are men who are interested in everything referred to as curious, but women of the same type are called nosy?

Why are angry men called outraged, while angry women are called hysterical?

Why are women who are ironic called bitter, while ironic men are called humorous?

Why are lighthearted men called easygoing, but the same type of women are called frivolous?

Why are devious men considered shrewd, when devious women are scheming?

Why are men who are thoughtful called considerate, while thoughtful women are called oversensitive?

Why are women who are dauntless considered brazen, when dauntless men are considered fearless?

Why is it that men of ordinary appearance are called pleasant looking, when ordinary women are called homely?

(Communication Research Associates, 1983, p. 107)

In various forms of imaginative or creative speaking and writing, language that fully expresses feeling or attitude is highly prized. Indeed, if language did not possess the power to express and elicit feelings, most of the world's great literature would not exist. In arguments, however, emotionally loaded language, which exceeds the natural warmth that marks a sincerely expressed belief and earnestness of purpose, becomes an impediment to rational decision making and represents a poor choice.

Technical Jargon

The use of the technical terminology of a field becomes a problem when it so confuses the listener that he loses sight of the issues or when it is used in place of reasoning on the issues. Beginning arguers can become so involved in the topic being argued that they forget that not everyone is as conversant with its jargon as they are. Technical terminology may be important to understanding the issues involved, but it is possible to send an audience into semantic shock if you ask them to deal with too many new terms at once.

When jargon replaces the real issues as the focus of the argument, an error has been committed. We would expect people arguing about education to be sufficiently informed to be able to discuss the advantages and disadvantages of *mainstreaming*. But if the argument centered on a disagreement over what should properly be included on a list of the different kinds of mainstreaming or the medical technicalities of the handicaps to be mainstreamed, we may, as an audience, lose sight of the real issues.

Summary of Fallacies of Language

1. *Ambiguity* occurs when a term is used in legitimate but different senses by two or more persons involved in argumentation.
2. *Equivocation* occurs when an individual uses a term in different ways in the context of the same argument.
3. *Emotionally loaded language* is a problem when we use terms that show more about our feelings on the issues than about the rational basis from which those feelings derive or when we use emotion as the sole means to alter the belief or behavior of others.
4. *Technical jargon* becomes a problem when the audience is overwhelmed with too many new terms or when it is used to impress the audience or replace sound reasoning.

The foregoing is a set of guidelines for constructing your own arguments and a yardstick for evaluating the arguments of others. You should now be able to construct patterns of proof and reasoning that are sufficient to support claims. You are ready to begin putting it all together. In the next chapter, we return to the idea of stock issues and consider how you go about building arguments advocating and opposing propositions of fact.

LEARNING ACTIVITIES

1. Each member of the class is to bring in an example of a fallacy of the type assigned by the instructor, one that has either been created by the student or discovered in a published source. Discuss what causes each example to be a fallacious use of reasoning or language.
2. Discuss current examples of advertising in the mass media. Which seem to have fallacies? What kinds of fallacies are they? Which examples of advertising, if any, employ sound reasoning according to the tests in Chapter 6?
3. Each of the following statements represents a fallacy of the types discussed in this chapter. Identify the type of fallacy in each statement and explain why the reasoning, appeal, or use of language is in error. Some statements contain more than one error, so be sure to identify all fallacies.
   A. In reference to high levels of defense and social spending, the government should have learned from the Vietnam experience that you can't have guns and butter at the same time.
   B. By definition, since a housewife is someone who doesn't work, it follows that all housewives are unemployed.
   C. When you've seen one zoo, you've seen them all.
   D. The Democratic party has always been the party of the working man and woman. It makes no sense for the AFL-CIO to endorse a Republican candidate.
   E. Obviously, the authors of this book want to make us schizophrenic. They want us to learn how to both advocate and oppose a proposition on the same topic.
   F. Your argument that drunk driving causes death and injury is very interesting, but what about all the people who weren't wearing their

seatbelts at the time of the accident? Aren't you assuming that every person involved in an automobile accident has been drinking? You can't really make that claim until you look at some of the other information.

G. We outlawed prayer in schools and look what happened! Within ten years of that sacrilegious Court's decision, the divorce rate is approaching 50 percent, students are becoming functionally illiterate, drug abuse abounds in our schools, and juvenile crime is increasing.

H. Cheating on exams must surely be acceptable. After all, most college students cheat on an exam at least once.

I. The advocate has obviously misanalyzed the situation. The Supreme Court ruled in favor of freedom of choice in the matter of abortions in 1973, not 1972.

J. The Motor Car Company's new Q-Body designs have had serious problems with their brake systems. I'd be suspicious of all their products.

K. Rolling Valley Vineyards must produce good wines. Their commercials state that they are the only American winery that doesn't use pesticides to control insect damages to the crop. We should all be concerned about pesticides in what we eat and drink.

L. The chairman of the rules committee says that our bylaws have been incorrectly developed. He ought to know. After all, he's the chairman of the rules committee.

M. Perhaps we shouldn't be as harsh with Marielitos who try to get back to Cuba by highjacking commercial airliners. They're just doing what any homesick person would do, finding a way home.

N. Professional athletics is a hotbed of drug abuse. Why just last week, more football three players were arrested for using cocaine.

4. Read the essay "A Mole Among the Gerbils?" in *Newsweek*, March 11, 1985, p. 14–15, and list the various fallacies it contains. You should be able to find more than just the one obvious one. Comment on how effective it is as a piece of argumentation, remembering the intended audience. Is this the most effective way to get the message across to this particular group?

5. In the essay "Reflections on a Hockey Helmet" in *Newsweek*, March 12, 1984, p. 13, the fallacies in reasoning, appeal, and use of language are less obvious. Read it and identify the fallacies it contains. To what type of audience do you believe this argument was addressed?

SUGGESTED SUPPLEMENTARY READINGS

FEARNSIDE, W. W., AND HOLTHER, W. B. *Fallacy: The Counterfeit of Argument.* Englewood Cliffs, N.J.: Prentice-Hall, 1959.

> This is one of the most comprehensive sources on the nature of fallacies. The authors provide an excellent classification system to cover fallacies of logic, emotional appeal, and language use. Despite its age, this book remains usable since most of the examples are taken from well known historical sources or common communication situations.

TOULMIN, S., RIEKE, R., AND JANIK, A. *An Introduction to Reasoning* (2nd Ed.). New York: MacMillan, 1984.

> Part IV, Chapters 14 through 20, examines what causes fallacies in reasoning in detail. It provides an excellent analysis of the warrant and how to avoid common reasoning errors in using it. The examples are varied, and the Toulmin model, of course, is used in many instances to show how reasoning has broken down.

8

HOW DO I ARGUE FACT PROPOSITIONS?

The goal of the advocate in factual argumentation is to win the listener's or reader's assent that the proposition of fact is probably true. Successfully gaining assent is accomplished by the presentation of a total "package" of proof and reasoning perceived as valid by its receivers. The process begins when advocate and opponent analyze the figurative ground over which the argument will be contested to discover the potential and real issues in the controversy. The advocate must develop a prima facie case through a series of arguments that marshall sufficient support to gain possession of the contested ground at least temporarily. The opponent responds by casting doubt on the existence of such a prima facie case. Although questions of fact, value, and policy are interrelated, we devote a chapter to factual argumentation alone because, in addition to being a goal in its own right, the ability to successfully argue propositions of fact lays the foundation for advocating and opposing both value and policy propositions.

You may already have had some experience in arguing factual propositions. If you have ever written a research paper or an essay in which you had to develop a point of view or take a position on a topic such as "The Vietnam War was an illegal war," "The Union blockade of Confederate ports was the decisive factor in the South's defeat," or "The Monroe Doctrine justifies U.S. intervention in Latin America," you have argued a factual proposition. The thesis sentence of the paper served as your proposition of fact and your subsequent development of ideas was intended to establish its probable truth. The research and thinking that you put into the paper were designed to fit your audience, the instructor whose favorable evaluation you sought.

In the real world, we encounter argumentation over fact in several different fields. Courts of law examine past fact, what is alleged to have happened. Lawyers, judges, and juries are concerned with determining the probable truth or falsity of questions such as "has some law been violated?" or "how should some law be interpreted in the given case?" In the field of politics, factual argumentation is involved as laws protecting or interpreting freedom of speech, press, and religion are considered. Although the main activity of legislative bodies is policy making, various agencies and committees engage in "fact-finding" investigations to determine the probability of something having been the case or to predict what will be the case in the future. Scientific disputes occur over the laws of nature—what biological specimens are, how flora and fauna are to be classified, or how life began. In the real world, factual propositions often arise subsequent to the discovery of information requiring interpretation or application.

In the context of academic argumentation, the proposition of fact also helps us to establish what was, is, or will be. To qualify as a proposition of fact, or an argument over fact, disputes must be limited to those questions that draw inferences about the past, present, and future (Ehninger & Brockriede, 1963) rather than those questions that may be resolved by consulting the appropriate source of information. "Abraham Lincoln was the first U.S. president to travel by rail," is not arguable because its probable truth can be determined by examining a book on presidential trivia (Andrew Jackson was the first president to travel by rail in 1833). "Forces of the marketplace presently determine the extent and quality of children's television" is not an arguable fact, since it can be confirmed by observation. It provides insufficient grounds for controversy, drawing no inference and not requiring argumentation to prove its probable validity. Contrast such nonarguable statements with examples of arguable propositions of fact:

> The "big bang," a massive cosmic explosion, created the universe.
>
> Allowing market forces to determine the extent and quality of children's television has resulted in the best children's shows being canceled.
>
> Granting tuition tax credits to the parents of children who attend private elementary and secondary schools will perpetuate segregation.

In this chapter we begin consideration of what constitutes the argumentative "package" in advocacy of, and opposition to, the proposition. Up to this point, we have focused on the elements contained in an argument, its logical structure, the kinds and tests of evidence, and possible patterns of reasoning. Now, we will put it all together in what is commonly referred to as **case development,** a process which begins with analysis of the proposition.

ANALYZING THE FACT PROPOSITION

The process of analysis is similar for propositions of fact, value, and policy. The ultimate goal of the process is to discover the issues to be argued by advocate and opponent within the proposition. Issues, the questions central to the controversy, are found through a four-step process of analysis: (1) locating the immediate cause of the controversy, (2) investigating the history of the topic, (3) determining which terms require definition, and (4) determining the issues in the controversy.

Locating the Immediate Cause

The causes of controversy are usually significant events, occurrences, or circumstances in the present or near past. To find them, arguers must ask themselves why the controversy is important at this time. The Supreme Court's affirmation of a woman's constitutional right to end her pregnancy, or its rejection of challenges to capital punishment statutes, may be the immediate cause of arguments over when life begins and when the state has the right to end it. A significant, usually harmful event will often be the immediate cause of controversy.

Analyzing the immediate controversy helps you discover why an issue is sufficiently important to justify argumentation. You will find indications of your topic's importance by studying recent history—is the controversy in the news? what are opinion leaders and respected sources saying about it? are there presently laws or programs that concern it? When you discover what is being said about the topic, examine the consequences attached to a given interpretation of fact. Is a serious problem evident in relationship to your topic? Immediate controversies point to causes and their effects that are deemed to be negative. Immediate controversies also raise the question of whether similar events, occurrences, or circumstances have occurred in the past. Analysis proceeds by investigating this question.

Investigating Historical Background

Investigating the contemporary and historical background of a topic provides the arguer with information pertinent to the proposition to be argued. Even in instances where the immediate cause of a controversy is obvious, discovery of historical episodes of dissatisfaction over the same questions provides important insight, especially if the investigation of historical background includes a thorough examination of past efforts to understand a body of factual information relevant to the controversy.

If you were involved in arguing the proposition, "Violence portrayed on television causes violence in the schools, the community, and the home," your background investigation might include examining social science research on the causes of violent behavior in children. You would discover that efforts to understand the impact of seeing violent entertainment on the receiver did not begin with the advent of television. Earlier in this century, educators, parents, and ministers were concerned about the effects of movies and comic books on children. You may find other historical connections to the present controversy, since the issue of violence and television is not a new one. Considering the proposition of fact in its historical context is important, since such propositions are often argued on the basis of trends growing out of past experience and extending into the future; an understanding of past beliefs about fact can be used to argue their propensity to continue in the future.

Finding the immediate causes and exploring the historical background of the controversy provides you with a frame of reference from which to argue the proposition. These two steps in the process of analysis also give you some clues to your audience's understanding of the argumentative proposition. To focus interpretation of the proposition, the third step in the process of analysis requires you to define its terms.

Defining Key Terms

In Chapter 3, we stressed the importance of defining terms in a proposition to identify the locus of disagreement within it. Recall that it is the advocate who initiates argumentation and has the responsibility of providing the initial definition of terms. Also recall the types of terms most likely to require definition: equivocal terms, vague terms, technical terms, new terms, and coined terms. Review Chapter 3 if you have forgotten the rules of definition and different methods of defining words.

Since the arguer's task is to locate the issues in the proposition, definitions can be used to identify and clarify key concepts. Defining which kinds of acts portrayed on television should be classified as violent has absorbed many researchers and resulted in different interpretations of what constitutes violence. Select the terms you believe need clarification in your proposition and formulate definitions. Identifying the key concepts, and deciding how you wish them to be interpreted, leads to the final step in the analytical process, determining issues in the controversy.

Determining the Issues

Thus far in the process of analysis you will have discovered the immediate cause of the controversy and examined its historical background. This will have provided you with the necessary information to determine the potential issues in the controversy. Not all the potential issues you uncover may, ultimately, be used in the preparation and presentation of your case. The issues that finally decide the controversy are those that are actually contested, for which the advocate or her opponent provides more convincing reasoning and proof.

The discovery of issues pertinent to the controversy, and the decision concerning which you will use in developing your argumentative position, is facilitated by the existence of certain stock issues—issues that exist in any argumentative situation. In Chapter 3, we stated that a proposition of fact infers a relationship between the subject and object in the propositional sentence. Propositions of fact are argued to determine whether or not this inference is probably true. The stock issues regarding factual argumentation focus attention on determining the means by which the inference may be verified and discovering if it is possible to employ these means to do so.

The stock issues related to arguments over propositions of fact focus the advocate's and opponent's attention on determining the answers to two questions:

1. What reasoning pattern is sufficient to establish the alleged relationship between the subject and object of the proposition?
2. Is proof sufficient to verify the alleged relationship?

These two stock issues are generic to all propositions of fact. The first suggests that the pattern of reasoning used must be appropriate to the inference made by the proposition, while the second suggests that evidence of fact and opinion must support such reasoning. If the proposition were "X caused Y," then causal reasoning would verify the inference. However, if evidence of causation could not be found, sign reasoning could be used to indicate that observable conditions suggest the probable truth of the inference "Y is a sign of the existence of X." Reasoning from generalization, parallel case, analogy, or authority could be used as well, with each suggesting a successively lower level of probable truth that X and Y are related.

While the specific issues contested will vary from one proposition to another, they "fill in the blanks" provided by the stock issues. The decision regarding which specific issues to include is also influenced by what you know about your audience and what aspects of the figurative ground you think are likely to be contested. If one issue seems most important to your audience, or one issue is isolable and particularly vulnerable to attack, that should be an issue to which you devote some attention. This, in conjunction with consideration of the questions raised by the stock issues, will enable you to determine the specific kinds of proof you will have to supply in the form of grounds and backing. It is at this level of analysis that the advocate's and opponent's cases begin to take shape.

In the next sections of this chapter, we discuss the use of these stock issues in advocating and opposing propositions of fact. Remember that regardless of whether you are arguing a proposition of fact, value, or policy, the process of analysis remains the same:

1. Discover the immediate causes of the controversy, a significant and usually harmful event that triggers interest in your topic.
2. Explore the background of the controversy, those events, beliefs, and circumstances in the past and present that provide information about it.
3. Select the key terms in the proposition and provide appropriate definitions for them.
4. Determine the issues and prepare arguments on those that will not be readily accepted by the audience, or which are likely to be contested by the other party to the controversy.

ADVOCATING PROPOSITIONS OF FACT

Construction of a prima facie case for a proposition of fact begins with analysis of the proposition. An advocate for the proposition, "Children's behavior is affected by watching television," may have discovered the following:

1. The immediate cause of controversy was the expressed concern of parents, educators, and television critics that children might be learning the wrong kinds of things from television.
2. Investigation of the historical background revealed studies, commentaries, and criticisms of television, and congressional hearings provided testimony that all pointed to one conclusion: People learn from television.
3. Consideration of the terms in the proposition led the advocate to decide *affected* was a vague term which should be understood to mean "the ability to influence." She defined *television*, because it might be ambiguous to include only "those programs specifically intended for the child audience and other programs viewed by children although not specifically intended for them."
4. As she researched the topic, the advocate found two questions being discussed: What kinds of things do children learn from television? and What are the consequences of this learning? The available evidence suggested that a case could be made for the fact that television teaches values, and that these values are expressed in the child's behavior.

Chapter 2 outlined the responsibilities of the advocate in constructing a prima facie case: Specify what is to be changed, interpret the proposition in a topical manner, address inherency, and present logically adequate arguments. With this in mind the advocate was ready to begin constructing her case.

Determining the Primary Inference

A prima facie case must be topical; it must stay within the bounds of the figurative ground of the proposition. The advocate interprets the proposition, clarifying the exact change in belief she seeks. This shows the audience what the advocate understands the proposition's boundaries to be and draws their attention to her unique interpretation of its primary inference.

How does the advocate determine the primary inference? Interpretation of the proposition combines aspects of the definition of terms with the issues isolated during research. Combining her definition of terms and the issues she discovered during analysis our advocate could state "those programs specifically intended for the child audience and other programs viewed by children, although not specifically intended for them, have the ability to teach the child values that are expressed in the child's behavior." She would refine this into a more succinctly stated primary inference: Children act in a manner consistent with the values they have learned from watching television. When she interprets the proposition in this way, her case satisfies the requirement of being topical. She properly places the primary inference, concerning the change she seeks, within the bounds of the proposition's figurative ground, television's influence on children.

Identifying the primary inference is a way of making a broadly worded academic proposition more specific. If our advocate was a member of an argumentation class, her classmates' analysis might yield different primary inferences such as:

Viewing violence on television causes violent behavior in children.
Television makes children fearful.
Children learn sex role stereotypes from television.

Building the Prima Facie Case

A prima facie case supporting the advocate's primary inference must answer two questions: What is currently believed about the primary inference? and What change in belief is sought? These questions require the advocate to consider inherency. She must decide what presumption exists about the belief she wishes to change.

In factual argumentation, inherency is sometimes difficult to argue. The advocate must *consider the audience relative to the proof needed to convince them of the probable truth of the primary inference.* If the advocate has selected a specific audience for her message, she discovers their present beliefs through audience analysis and determines if those beliefs come from deference to certain sources of information or reflect popular opinion. Whether the audience is well informed and has very specific opinions about the subject or is relatively uniformed with few if any opinions makes a difference in how inherency will be argued.

While an advocate in academic argumentation may analyze her audience to determine their beliefs, she should treat presumption as a decision rule and view the proposition as a hypothesis she must test by demonstrating that her inference about it is probably true. Whichever version of presumption determines the nature of her responsibilities in arguing inherency, the resulting argumentation will be the same. It will establish a cause-effect relationship.

Propositions of fact concern relationships alleged to be true of past, present, or future interpretations of fact. The proposition, "Children's behavior is affected by watching television," alleges present fact. When she interprets it to mean "Children act in a manner consistent with the values they have learned from watching television" the advocate's responsibility to demonstrate inherency becomes one of proving a relationship between watching television (cause) and learning values (effect).

This is all fine for propositions of past and present fact phrased to imply a causal relationship between the subject and object of the proposition, but what are the advocate's responsibilities concerning inherency and how does she fulfill them for propositions of future fact or propositions not stated in causal terms? The advocate is responsible for demonstrating inherency for any arguable proposition of past, present, or future fact. Suppose the proposition states, "Candidate X is losing his popular support." If the advocate and opponent agree that public opinion polls accurately measure popular support, the proposition is nonarguable. If they disagree about the accuracy of polling, to properly place presumption and burden of proof the proposition they should argue is "Public opinion polling is invalid." This proposition is phrased in terms of a sign, rather than a causal, relationship between the subject and the object of the proposition. Should the advocate rely exclusively on sign reasoning and argue the truth of the proposition based on a series of examples of invalid results? How many examples would she have to find to establish a prima facie case? Only two or three if she also demonstrated inherency on a theoretical level and explained what causes public opinion polling as a method to produce invalid results. In the absence of overwhelming sign evidence, failure to provide an inherent reason for polling's lack of validity would mean she had only proven "Some polls have produced invalid results."

Inherency is argued for future fact on the same basis as it is for past or present fact—what is probable. Even if an advocate for the proposition "Children's behavior is affected by watching television" relied solely on scientific evidence from laboratory and field experiments to ground her inherency arguments, she would only establish what is probable because these studies, which investigate causal relationships between dependent and independent variables, express results in terms of the probability that they did not occur by chance. This probability is always less than 100 percent. Because we cannot know the future with absolute certainty either, the concept of the probable applies equally to the advocate's arguments that demonstrate an inherent cause, as well as arguments which demonstrate its consequences. In arguing a proposition of future fact, the advocate wants her assessment to have the highest possible probability of being "true."

Inherency is an issue the advocate must argue for her case to be prima facie. She will have discovered inherency arguments through the application of stock issues in the analysis process. Recall that stock issues are not the same as the actual issues contested in argumentation. Stock issues are tools that help arguers discover the actual issues to raise in their cases. For inherency arguments, the first stock issue for propositions of fact is decided. Since inherency arguments are used to show cause-effect relationships, causal reasoning is the most appropriate pattern. The advocate would then apply the second stock issue—is proof sufficient to verify the alleged relationship—to establish the *factualness* of the belief that children learn values from watching television. If the advocate was unable to provide sufficient proof, she would still argue inherency but would do so using a pattern of reasoning other than causal reasoning.

Demonstrating inherent reasons for a belief is not the only requirement the advocate must fulfill in building a prima facie case. The advocate's analysis of the immediate causes and history of the controversy not only told her that children learn values in general, it identified specific values, how they are internalized, and how they are operationalized. Her primary inference suggests that signs of internalization and operationalization may be observed in the actions of children. In constructing her prima facie case, the advocate will make claims about these discoveries so that she can confirm her primary inference. The stock issues are once again employed to determine what pattern of reasoning would be appropriate—cause, sign, generalization, parallel case, analogy, authority, dilemma, or definition— and if sufficient evidence was available to ground these claims. How many claims the advocate will argue depends on what she discovered in analyzing the proposition, what she considers necessary to enable her audience to accept her primary inference, or what would be necessary to test the proposition as a hypothesis.

Preempting Opposing Arguments

Finally, the advocate is well advised to take a moment to *consider the proposition from the opponent's perspective.* What is the opponent likely to argue, and where are points of clash likely to occur? She should consider including **preemptive arguments** in her case, arguments that respond to the probable objections of the opponent in advance of their being raised. Prudent use of preemptive arguments keeps the discussion focused on the proposition and keeps presumption and burden of proof where they belong.

If the advocate uses the results of a public opinion poll as evidence, the opponent's strategy might be to concede that the poll contained the particular statistic the advocate cited, but to argue that it is meaningless because public opinion polls are invalid. The result is that the focus of the dispute shifts from the advocate's argument to a different one—"Polls are an invalid measure of public opinion." By anticipating this objection and building in a response, the advocate keeps attention focused on her interpretation of the proposition.

However, the advocate who chooses to preempt the arguments of her opponent must avoid excess, preempting everything but the kitchen sink, and creating a series of what might be unrelated arguments. Kitchen sink preempts are also a bad rhetorical strategy because they run the risk of weakening, rather than strengthening, the advocate's position in the minds of the audience. They create the impression that the advocate's position is weak if she can find so many objections to it herself.

Preparing the Argumentative Brief

Everything that has been said up to this point about advocating propositions of fact describes the thought processes involved. Determining the primary inference, assigning presumption to beliefs, discovering what is inherent about these beliefs, and discovering the actual issues to be argued may all be done mentally while researching the topic. To ensure that the speech or essay she produces is in fact prima facie, the advocate must now organize her materials and ideas in the form of a brief. The argumentative brief is an outline that is used to produce a speech, essay, term paper, or even something as lengthy as a book. *The brief outlines the essential elements of the advocate's or opponent's development of arguments on the proposition.* The advocate's brief should include the following:

1. A full statement of the proposition.
2. A definition of key terms.
3. A statement of the primary inference drawn about the proposition.
4. The claims and evidence that will make up the body of the case. Warrants and backing should be included when necessary.
5. The preemptive arguments the advocate has decided to advance.

As you gain experience in argumentation and become proficient at slugging the evidence you have collected, your brief may be nothing more than a stack of cards from which you mentally construct the other elements of your case. Realize that insofar as style is concerned, the actual presentation of the oral and written argument involves more in the way of style: An introduction or overview, explanation of arguments, transitions between arguments, and a conclusion. The following example represents an argumentative brief on a proposition of fact.

Argument in Action

PROPOSITION:	Children's behavior is affected by watching television.
DEFINITION OF TERMS:	Affected—the ability to influence. Television—those programs specifically intended for the child audience and other programs viewed by children although not specifically intended for them.

PRIMARY INFERENCE: Children act in a manner consistent with the values they have learned from television.

I. Television has the inherent potential to transmit values.

Significantly, through its potential to transmit the values of the culture, television becomes a meaningful agent in the socialization of the child alongside the family, the school, religious institutions, the peer group, and other community-based institutions. (Gordon L. Berry, UCLA Graduate School of Education, and Claudia Mitchell-Kernan, UCLA Center for Afro-American Studies, "Introduction." In Gordon L. Berry and Claudia Mitchell-Kernan, editors, *Television and the Socialization of the Minority Child.* New York: Academic Press, 1982, p. 2)*

II. One set of values transmitted by television relate to prosocial behavior.

Children can learn to be altruistic, friendly and self-controlled by looking at television programs depicting such behavior patterns. (National Institute of Mental Health, *Television and Behavior: Ten Years of Scientific Progress and Implications for the Eighties. Volume I, Summary Report.* Washington, D.C.: U.S. Department of Health and Human Services, 1982, p. 7)

III. Research proves that the values television transmits are reflected in children's behavior.

The clear and simple message derived from the research on prosocial behavior is that children learn from watching television and what they learn depends on what they watch. The programs they see on television change their behavior. If they look at violent or aggressive programs, they tend to become more aggressive and disobedient. But if they look at prosocial programs, they will more likely become more generous, friendly, and self-controlled. (National Institute of Mental Health, *Television and Behavior: Ten Years of Scientific Progress and Implications for the Eighties. Volume I, Summary Report.* Washington, D.C.: U.S. Department of Health and Human Services, 1982, p. 51)

IV. The effect is pronounced among poor children.

Adults need to arrange for children to watch prosocial programs such as "Mister Rogers' Neighborhood." Of special importance is the finding that increased cooperative play, nurturance, and verbalization of feelings were significantly greater among low-income children who viewed this program. (Alice Sterling Honig, Professor of Child and Family Studies, Syracuse University, "Television and Young Children," *Young Children*, May 1983, 38, p. 72)

V. The effect is pronounced among ethnic minority children.

More importantly, for those interested in the behavioral effects on ethnic minorities, particularly American Indian youngsters, it was found that

---

*References are fully cited only in the *Argument in Action* sections to show students the importance of fully documenting their evidence.

those children who were more reluctant to participate socially were even more positively affected by viewing sociable behavior on television. (Joann Sebastian Morris, American Indian Educational Commission, "Television Portrayal and the Socialization of the American Indian Child." In Gordon L. Berry and Claudia Mitchell-Kernan, editors, *Television and the Socialization of the Minority Child.* New York: Academic Press, 1982, p. 188)

VI.   Therefore, children's behavior is affected by watching television.

Before considering the manner in which propositions of fact may be opposed, reflect on this example for a moment. Notice that the advocate narrows the topic and discusses only one of the many behaviors that may be affected by television. She could have chosen to discuss several, such as violence and promiscuity. Had she done so, she would have had to make clear whether she considered it necessary to demonstrate that all those behaviors were affected or whether any one of them was, in and of itself, sufficient to warrant assent to the proposition of fact. After analyzing the proposition and going through the steps of case construction, the advocate decides how she will proceed. Her goal is to develop the best case she can in support of the proposition. Did she succeed in developing a prima facie case?

Summary of Fact Advocacy

1.   What is the primary inference identified in the proposition of fact?
   A.   Is the inference about past, present, or future fact?
   B.   What is the nature of probable truth concerning this proposition and how it should be argued?
2.   What do the stock issues lead you to discover about this proposition of fact?
   A.   What reasoning pattern is sufficient to establish each separate issue?
   B.   Is sufficient proof available to support this reasoning pattern?
   C.   What will audience expectations be in regard to proof and reasoning; should warrant and backing be included in establishing the pattern of reasoning?
3.   Have the requirements of a prima facie case been satisfied?
   A.   Are terms defined where necessary for clarity?
   B.   Is the interpretation of the proposition topical?
   C.   Has inherency been demonstrated?
   D.   Does the development of issues provide good and sufficient reasons for accepting the advocate's primary inference?
4.   Should preemptive arguments be used?
   A.   Is the opponent likely to be skeptical of the advocate's interpretation of the issues?
   B.   Will preemptive arguments focus argumentation or create confusion?

OPPOSING PROPOSITIONS OF FACT

Whether the proposition is one of fact, value, or policy, both advocate and opponent are obligated to follow certain rules. The advocate has the burden of proof and must develop claims that uphold it, the opponent initially possesses presumption. He may choose to question the validity of the advocate's allegations concerning fact in a number of ways. Determining exactly what to argue as an opponent is a matter of using the resources gained while analyzing the proposition and paying careful attention to what the advocate has argued.

The opponent begins construction of his case by examining the primary inference made by the advocate in interpreting the proposition. The inference established her unique way of describing the relationship between the subject and the object of the proposition. The opponent's task is to determine the strategies he will employ in disputing the probable truth of the advocate's primary inference.

Evaluating the Primary Inference

The opponent's first strategic decision is to determine whether or not to accept the advocate's primary inference as topical. The primary inference grows out of the advocate's definition of terms and the issues she discovered while analyzing the proposition. While the opponent is not obligated to dispute the manner in which the advocate has defined terms, it may be to his advantage to do so. If the advocate has defined terms in such a way that her primary inference represents an unreasonable interpretation of the proposition, the opponent may wish to argue for a different definition of terms. The opponent should consider whether or not the advocate has met her responsibility to develop a topical prima facie case.

What if the advocate defined *watching television* to mean "time spent by parents viewing television instead of interacting with their children," leading to a primary inference that "children deprived of parental interaction by television become juvenile delinquents." The opponent could argue that such a definition is not reasonably within the bounds of the proposition. He would argue that the advocate has improperly included parents and excluded children in defining *who* is watching television. In this instance, the first element in the opponent's case would be an overview in which he suggested how the relationship between the subject and the object of the proposition is best understood, and why his interpretation is more reasonable than the advocate's.

Using Presumption to Dispute the Primary Inference

Recall that presumption may be considered from a number of different perspectives. It may represent the audience's current beliefs, the sources of information to whom they defer in matters of judgment, or the view that the proposition is a hypothesis to be tested. Presumption lies with the opponent at the outset of argumentation since he nominally represents the interpretation of fact the advocate wishes to change. The opponent's second strategic consideration is to decide how, or if, he will use presumption.

The opponent has the option of using presumption to argue in favor of existing beliefs. If the audience was previously skeptical of television's ability to affect the behavior of children, the opponent could offer authoritative arguments, sign arguments, whatever pattern of reasoning he deems best, that suggest their previous interpretation of fact was a correct one. This may be a weak strategic position for the opponent. If the advocate has presented a prima facie case, the presumption of previously existing beliefs he is celebrating has been at best suspended, or at worst reversed.

A stronger strategic position is created when the opponent contrasts the presumption against the advocate's primary inference to the inherency arguments she offered on its behalf. Recall that inherency arguments establish the probability of a cause-effect relationship being true, and cannot reach a level of absolute certainty. The opponent should assess how probable the relationship actually is. How does the opponent do this? Since inherency arguments are causal arguments, the opponent should apply the tests of causal reasoning discussed in Chapter 6. In addition, he should make sure that the advocate has not committed one of the fallacies of reasoning described in Chapter 7. If the advocate's inherency claim is grounded on the testimony of experts, does her argument reason from authority, or has she committed the fallacy of appealing to authority? If the advocate's inherency claim is grounded on a series of examples or illustrations, does her argument reason from sign or cause, or has she committed the fallacy of over generalization? If presumption was being used as a decision rule, the opponent would be arguing that the advocate's interpretation of the proposition should be rejected as a hypothesis because the probability of its being "true" is unacceptably low.

Arguments celebrating presumption may be offered in an overview, tangential to what the advocate has argued, and standing apart from the opponent's other attacks on her argumentative position. However, presumption arguments that question the probability of the advocate's inherency arguments should be addressed directly to the advocate's case, and integrated with whatever other arguments the opponent offers that examine the patterns of proof and reasoning she has used.

Refuting by Denial and Extenuation

Having examined the advocate's primary inference to assess its topicality, and her inherency arguments in light of presumption, the third strategic decision that the opponent makes concerns how he will respond to the remainder of her arguments. The opponent must determine whether the strategies of denial and extenuation can be used to refute these arguments. The opponent makes his decision after examining how well the advocate's arguments satisfy the requirements of the stock issues of factual argumentation

First, the advocate will have selected a particular pattern of reasoning to use in constructing arguments substantiating the proposition. The opponent should make sure that this pattern is sufficient to demonstrate the probable truth of the inference she has made about the proposition. Second, the opponent may elect to challenge the sufficiency of the proof offered by the advocate. In essence, this strategy asserts that while the advocate's claims in and of themselves would be sufficient to establish the probability of the inference, those claims are not grounded in proof and reasoning sufficient to warrant our assent. The two strategies commonly used by opponents to refute the advocate's arguments are denial and extenuation.

In employing a strategy of **denial,** the opponent argues not that the advocate has knowingly engaged in distortion or deception but that her arguments are nonetheless fallacious because she has:

1. misanalyzed the situation, and the analysis provided by the opponent is proper;
2. overlooked certain important facts, which the opponent provides along with an explanation of the significance of their having been overlooked;
3. given undue significance to certain facts, and the opponent explains why they lack significance; or
4. drawn unwarranted conclusions from the proof, and the opponent provides the proper conclusion.

Those who disputed the conclusions of the Warren Commission, that Lee Harvey Oswald, acting alone, assassinated President Kennedy, based their arguments on the strategy of denial. Oswald was not that good a marksman, the rifle he was alleged to have used could not be fired rapidly enough to inflict all the wounds, evidence suggested that the shots came from more than one direction, and so on. Denial is a form of refutation in which the opponent argues that the advocate has either failed to determine what proof would be sufficient to establish the inferred relationship or has failed to provide sufficient proof to establish it.

Extenuation is the other strategy commonly used to oppose the advocate of a proposition of fact. Arguments of extenuation focus on the circumstances surrounding the facts about which the inference is to be made. In this type of refutation, the opponent argues that the relationship inferred by the advocate is based on a limited understanding of the circumstances surrounding those facts, and that a more complete understanding of those circumstances would lead to a different inference. Extenuating or unusual circumstances warrant a conclusion other than the one normally drawn when these facts are present. The defense team for John Hinkley, Jr. may have conceded that he fired the shots that hit President Reagan, but it did not concede the criminality of the act. Extenuating circumstances, in this case insanity, lead to another inference—a proposition of fact advanced by the nominal opponent. John Hinkley, Jr., was not guilty of shooting the president of the United States by reason of insanity.

Responding to Preemptive Arguments

The final strategic choice the opponent must make concerns what to do if the advocate presents preemptive arguments. Is he obligated to respond to them? No. The opponent has as much right to determine his own strategy and select the arguments he will advance in refutation of the proposition as the advocate has in advancing the proposition itself. The opponent must examine the advocate's preempts carefully. Although they may represent a sincere and ethical attempt to keep argumentation focused, they may be nothing more than a collection of straw man arguments cynically and unethically introduced to gain an advantage.

Preparing the Argumentative Brief

Like the advocate, the opponent is ready to construct his argumentative brief only after analyzing the proposition thoroughly. In reality, he must proceed tentatively, since he opposes that which the advocate presents. Because he may not know exactly what that will be until he hears or reads it, the opponent must be flexible; he must be prepared to adapt his arguments to hers. His job is facilitated if he did a judicious job of slugging his evidence. He can also prepare some "generic arguments" in advance. On the topic of television's effect on behavior, he may anticipate that the advocate might present arguments on violence and prepare some possible responses. However, if the advocate does not cooperate but argues that television causes prosocial behavior instead, the opponent must adapt, for he would commit a *non sequitur* fallacy by saying, "Yes, but it doesn't cause violence." Consider the following example of argumentation opposing the proposition of fact advocated earlier in the chapter.

Argument in Action

PROPOSITION: Children's behavior is not affected by watching televsion.

I. Television's potential to transmit values has not been shown to be inherent. The advocate's evidence asserts television's potential to transmit values without explaining how or why. Therefore, the advocate commits the fallacy of appealing to authority.

II. The effect of prosocial television is limited.

> There are a number of studies that indicate that *Mister Rogers' Neighbor-hood* and *Sesame Street's* prosocial episodes can have prosocial effects, but that the influence is limited to situations that are quite similar to those presented on the program. In addition, while a single exposure to a prosocial segment of *Sesame Street* apparently produces immediate effects, these do not even last for a day. (Robert M. Liebert, Professor of Psychology, State University of New York (SUNY) Stony Brook, Joyce N. Sprafkin, Director of the Laboratory of Communication, SUNY Stony Brook, and Emily S. Davidson, Associate Professor of Psychology, Texas A & M

University, *The Early Window: Effects of Television on Children and Youth* (2nd Ed.). New York: Pergamon Press, 1982, p. 209)

III.   Whatever limited effect occurs is a consequence of adult intervention.

Friedrich and Stein also found gains in three to five-year-old children's imagination after exposure to *Mr. Rogers'* program. The experimental condition involving prosocial television *(Mr. Rogers')* related play materials and teacher training and involvement produced the most consistent effects on both positive social interaction with peers and imaginative play. (Dorothy G. Singer, Professor of Psychology, University of Bridgeport, and Jerome L. Singer, Professor of Psychology, Yale University, "Television and the Developing Imagination of the Child," *Journal of Broadcasting*, Fall 1981, 25, No. 4, p. 384)

IV.   People, not television, affect children's behavior.

Television can never take the place of the school, the church, the home, or any of the other social institutions that rely on interpersonal contact to help children grow emotionally and intellectually. (John Blessington, Vice President, Personnel, CBS/Broadcast Group, "Children and Television," Hearings before the Subcommittee on Telecommunications, Consumer Protection, and Finance of the Committee on Energy and Commerce, House of Representatives, 98th Congress, First Session, March 16,1983, p. 149)

V.   Therefore, television does not affect children's behavior.

Notice that in addition to questioning the probable inherency of the advocate's primary inference the opponent uses both the strategy of denial and the strategy of extenuation in contesting the advocate's claims. The dispute might not end at this point. Depending on the rules to which the advocate and opponent had agreed, discussion might continue with a rebuttal by the advocate. Regardless of how long the dispute would continue, it would remain focused on the question of whether or not prosocial television affects behavior, with the issues of the inherency and significance of television's effect on children's behavior serving as the decision rules to determine the victor.

Summary of Fact Opposition

1.   Will the advocate's definition of terms be challenged or accepted?
     A.   Does the advocate's definition of terms stay within the bounds of the proposition's figurative ground?
     B.   What definition of terms does the opponent offer, and why is it a more reasonable interpretation of the proposition?
2.   Will the opponent support presumption?
     A.   Are there existing interpretations of fact that the advocate has overlooked that the opponent wishes to argue?
     B.   What is the level of probability that the advocate's inherency arguments prove a cause-effect relationship? Is that level of probability greater than the level of probability associated with presumption?

3. How will the advocate's argumentation of stock issues be opposed?
   A. Will denial arguments be used to argue that the advocate has misanalyzed the situation, overlooked important facts, given undue significance to certain facts, or drawn unwarranted conclusions?
   B. Will extenuation arguments be used to argue that special conditions or circumstances result in interpretations of fact other than those made by the advocate?
4. If the advocate has presented preemptive arguments, how will they be addressed?
   A. Are such arguments truly representative of the opponent's point of view or are they straw man arguments?
   B. Do preemptive arguments reveal flaws in the advocate's interpretation of the proposition?

Propositions of fact attempt to establish what has been, is, or will be. The process by which they are analyzed by advocates and opponents may be used to gain an understanding of value and policy propositions as well. The stock issues suggest a series of questions about the proposition that must be answered before listeners or readers feel their assent to the proposition is warranted. An understanding of the manner in which propositions of fact are advocated and opposed provides important insights into the argumentation of propositions of value, the subject of the next chapter.

LEARNING ACTIVITIES

1. Examine the text of a landmark Supreme Court decision such as Marbury v Madison (1803), Brown v the Board of Education of Topeka (1954), or Roe v Wade (1973). What issues seemed most important in the Court's decision? What interpretations of law were made in deciding the case? What factual inferences form the bases of the decision?
2. How would you discover probable truth for the following propositions?
   A. One of the two major political parties will nominate a woman for the presidency by the end of this century.
   B. The international monetary system will collapse under the weight of third world loan defaults.
   C. Nuclear arms will be brought under international control.
   D. Computer literacy will soon be a requirement for graduation at most four year colleges and universities.
   E. The number of narrow-cast services on cable television will continue to expand.
3. Written or Oral Assignment:
   A. Frame your own proposition of fact. Prepare a prima facie case from the advocate's position.
   B. Respond in opposition to the advocate's proposition of fact that you developed, or to that of one of your classmates.
4. Read Keith Barron's essay, "Not Too Much Pepper, Thank You" in *Newsweek*, April 9, 1984, p. 18. The author argues the factual proposition: "Some of nature's own foodstuffs are more toxic than the manmade chemicals we eat." What is the inferred fact? What is done to prove the probability of the

alleged fact? Is the argumentation sufficient to warrant your assent? Why or why not?

5. Read the essay, "Don't Close Our Borders" by Julian Simon in *Newsweek*, February 27, 1984, p. 11. The author uses the strategies of opposition in providing refutation for five "myths" about illegal immigration. What strategies of opposition are used? How does the author support his claims? Do you find his argumentation convincing? Why or why not?

SUGGESTED SUPPLEMENTARY READINGS

SPROULE, J. M. *Argument: Language and It's Influence.* New York: McGraw-Hill, 1980.

This is a book for the more advanced student, but it provides extensive discussion of argumentation in the larger context of persuasion. Of particular interest here is Chapter 4, "Descriptions: Arguments That Draw Issues of Fact," in which Sproule considers the use of examples, statistics, and testimony as the basis for grounding factual arguments. The chapter features an interesting extended example of argumentation on the existance of UFOs.

9

HOW DO I ARGUE VALUE PROPOSITIONS?

Propositions of fact attempt to determine what is most probably true of a past, present, or future relationship inferred by the proposition. Value propositions differ in that they attempt to establish what is the most acceptable application of judgment to a particular person, place, event, policy, or idea. In value argumentation, the controversy centers around which of two or more opposing evaluations is the most credible.

THE NATURE OF VALUES

We begin discussion of value argumentation by indicating the range of meanings applied to the term. Consider how a number of scholars have tried to fix the meaning of something that is a psychological and sociological process:

> Values are intangibles . . . things of the mind that have to do with the vision people have of "the good life" for themselves and their fellows. (Rescher, 1969, p. 4).
> A value is a general conception of what is a good end state or a good mode of behavior. (Rieke & Sillars, 1984, p. 125)
> A *value* is an enduring belief that a specific mode of conduct or end-state of existence is personally or socially preferable to an opposite or converse mode of

conduct or end-state of existence. A *value system* is an enduring organization of beliefs concerning preferable modes of conduct or end-states of existence along a continuum of relative importance. (Rokeach, 1973, p. 5)

Values may be defined as concepts that express what people believe is right or wrong, important or unimportant, wise or foolish, good or bad, just or unjust, great or mean, beautiful or ugly, and true or false, and that, therefore underlie all choices. (Walter & Scott, 1984, p. 224)

From these definitions, we can begin to perceive what the arguer grapples with in a controversy involving values. Values are deeply rooted mental states and are formed early in life. They predispose us to categorize something as existing somewhere along a mental continuum ranging from highly positive to highly negative. A value, which may be held by an individual or a group, may not be verbalized or discussed until it comes into conflict with some other value about which judgment is going to be made. Because no two people possess exactly the same life experiences, the potential for value conflict is present when people begin to make judgments. Lastly, values do not exist independent of each other. They exist in a hierarchy, with some values being deemed more important than others in a given set of circumstances.

Locus of Value Conflict

Where do we find examples of value argumentation? Almost any statement, lengthy or brief, can contain a value judgment. How we describe something or someone will necessarily be colored by our feelings toward that which we have described. Throughout this textbook, both implicit and explicit claims are made about the worth of studying and practicing argumentation—they are value judgments. Value argumentation communicates our feelings about something or someone and the standards of judgment from which those feelings derive. The ubiquity of value propositions is that they can exist about any subject and are characterized by the use of intrinsic or extrinsic judgmental criteria.

There are some fields of endeavor that deal almost exclusively in value argumentation. Religion and philosophy are both concerned with right and wrong, moral and immoral, and ethical and unethical behavior. Both fields seek to determine standards of socially or doctrinally acceptable behavior. A theologian examines behavior in terms of whether it measures up to a moral code expressed in sacred texts. The philosopher may speculate on the existence of several alternatives for ethical and unethical behavior.

The arts—film, theater, music, sculpture, photography, painting, and dance—concern themselves, in part, with judging that which is produced against a set of critical standards to determine what is "good art." The critics continually seek and revise these sets of standards to keep pace with trends and changes. We rely on the opinions of the professional critic to help us determine what we will patronize and accept. You have a chance to observe how critical standards for evaluating film are developed and applied through value argumentation by watching shows such as "Sneak Previews" on the Public Broadcasting System, and "At the Movies" on the Chicago independent station WGN.

Other fields also engage in value argumentation, particularly regarding standards of ethical behavior. Medicine, law, business, education, and almost any other field you can name are concerned with determining acceptable behaviors for their practitioners. Is prescribing a certain drug to certain categories of patients ethical? Is a certain sales technique an ethical business practice? Is a certain behavior appropriate for a professional educator? Often, professional organizations draw up codes of behavior, such as the American Bar Association's code for legal ethics. Such codes provoke extensive value and policy argumentation as individuals and groups seek to interpret and apply them.

The locus of value argumentation in real-world contexts is as varied as the groups and individuals who are concerned with standards of excellence and codes of conduct. In academic argumentation, you may be asked to develop argumentative cases about the quality or lack of quality of some institution or practice, the appropriateness of the actions of certain groups of people, or whether something is in the best interests of the nation in general.

Processes of Value Change

All the definitions of value, and examples of value argumentation, suggest that values are mental sets, or frames of reference, the individual is predisposed to keep. Recall that argumentation involves asking the reader or listener to alter his belief about how something should be valued. How you advocate and oppose such changes in values or value systems is the focus of this chapter. Nicholas Rescher's (1969) discussion of the process by which values change suggests that values are seldom accepted or abandoned absolutely, except in the rare circumstances of religious or ideological conversions. Instead, values are changed through processes of redistribution, emphasis or deemphasis, rescaling, redeployment, restandardization, and retargeting.

When **value redistribution** occurs, society adopts the value of a minority group that has successfully promoted a different way of attributing importance to that value. In the past two decades, some insurance companies have promoted "women's work," or "housework," as being equally valuable as the work of wage earners and, therefore, worthy of insurance coverage against the possibility that the homemaker might die or become incapacitated. This places a new connotation on the value of housework by putting it in an insurable category of labor.

Environmental change can cause **value emphasis or deemphasis.** Some deeply entrenched value, perhaps one that is not even openly stated, is suddenly threatened by a change in the physiological or psychological environment and takes on a different level of importance relative to other values. In the analysis of a value topic, emphasis or deemphasis may be part of what has produced the immediate controversy. A toxic waste accident can suddenly make the protection of the community or the right to feel secure in your own home seem extremely important, while 500 miles away people in an area of high unemployment are excited about the jobs that will be created by the opening of a toxic waste dump outside their city limits.

You may be familiar with the phrases "standard of living" and "quality of life"; both refer to a system of defining that which is attained. One means of changing values is through a **value restandardization**. Societal goals are particularly subject to social, economic, and technological change. John Naisbett's book *Megatrends* (1982) suggests ten areas that will produce change, among them technological innovations that will in turn change what we view as a good life. In the past, a good job was a white collar position in an air-conditioned office. In the future, the good job will be the one that allows you to work at home, linked to the office by your home computer. "Telecommuting" will restandardize quality of life values.

All of us have goals that operationalize enduring values. Since a goal does not always help us to maximize attainment of a particular value, we find ourselves engaging in **value implementation retargeting.** In this case, the value itself does not undergo change; what changes is the manner in which we pursue the value. Most people in our society place good health high on their value hierarchies. Government and private medical plans reflect the high value we place on good health. This value has not changed substantially, but the manner in which it is pursued has. Instead of focusing on the treatment of disease, medical care has shifted toward the prevention of disease—the "wellness" concept.

Factors That Promote Change

Rescher (1969) also discusses shifting societal values in terms of those factors that bring about change: changes of information; ideological and political change; erosion of values through boredom, disillusionment, and reaction; and changes in the operating environment of a society.

The value system of a society can change when **new information** is introduced. Consider the impact that the discovery of antibiotics or vaccines against polio and measles had on health or the way in which the development of the birth control pill influenced moral standards. Many of today's changes are brought about by scientific discovery. One of the great unanswered questions that may produce a significant value change if it can be resolved is the determination of the point at which life begins. While it has sometimes been said that there is nothing new under the sun, new discoveries about old things happen with some regularity. As you seek to change an audience's value hierarchy, your analysis should consider new discoveries in the field of your subject.

A second way in which society is altered is through **political and ideological change.** These can be revolutionary changes as in Iran in 1978. In that situation, both political and ideological changes took place as a monarchy was replaced with a theocracy. Such change is not necessarily abrupt; "it can take the gradualistic form of conditioning, advertising, propaganda, and promotion" (Rescher, 1969, p. 117). For instance, consider the ways in which television commercials and programs articulate what is to be valued.

The third way in which societal values change is through their **erosion,** which occurs when large numbers of people resist acting in accordance with a value. This was what happened during the 1960s when thousands of young men refused registration for the military draft. Erosion can also occur as a society experiences gradual change over time and, as a result, a value loses much of its importance. In an age when leisure pursuits are strongly encouraged and widely "sold" by the mass media, the value of work and the Puritan work ethic has less importance attached to it. Society may also become disillusioned with a value. In the early part of this century, sobriety was so highly valued that in 1920 a constitutional amendment prohibiting the manufacture and sale of alcoholic beverages was adopted. Disillusionment over the Eighteenth Amendment was such that it was repealed by the Twenty-first Amendment just thirteen years later.

The final way in which value changes occur is through a **change in the operating environment** of the society, the "whole range of social, cultural, demographic, economic, and technological factors that comprise the way of life in that society" (Rescher, 1969, p. 117). Some of the demographic changes that have influenced society in recent years include the entry of more women into the workplace and the coming of age of the "baby boom" generation. These are the same people who will cause another change at the beginning of the next century as they reach retirement age. Among the technological changes that have brought about value changes are the widespread availability of television, the continued development and spread of nuclear weapons, and the increasing use of robots in the workplace.

It is in this last category of value change that you will most frequently find material related to value argumentation. Social, cultural, demographic, economic, and technological factors that influence values also cause them to come into conflict with one another. Two important values may have to be placed in a hierarchical relationship to each other to resolve this conflict, as is the case in the controversy over whether a clean environment or a healthy economy should be our priority. Value conflict forces a reconfiguring of the value hierarchies, the task of the arguer in a value proposition. The process of argumentation engages us in an examination of the relative merits of retaining old values versus the costs of changing value structures, and the utility of maintaining a particular value system.

CHARACTERISTICS OF VALUE PROPOSITIONS

In value propositions, controversy exists over opposing evaluations of a person, object, event, or idea. The purpose of argumentation is to decide how we should judge something—a political candidate, a product, a federal program, an artistic performance, or a moral standard. Advocacy of a value proposition rests on a series of fact and value claims. The advocate's role in arguing a proposition of value is to provide good and sufficient reasons, a prima facie case, for the audience to evaluate the object of the proposition in the same way as she does. The opponent's role in value argumentation is to examine the soundness of the arguments and to examine the present value attributed to the proposition's object.

Value propositions always have a particular form that aids the arguers in establishing responsibilities for proof and reasoning. The proposition contains a **value object,** some idea, person, action, agency, tradition, practice, or custom that exists or is proposed, and a **value judgment,** a general assignment of value—good-bad, fair-unfair, safe-harmful, effective-ineffective—to the object. The value judgment sets forth the criteria by which the value object is said to be measured.

In Chapter 3 we said the proposition should always be phrased in such a way that change is implied, and so that the advocate supports a change in the judgment normally assigned to the value object. This is important because in some instances, the value proposition reflects two equally prized objects and the advocate's task is to argue the primacy of one over the other:

> The freedom to publish or read anything is more important than the moral objections that its content may raise.
>
> A strong national defense is more important than a balanced federal budget.

Notice that both propositions could be reversed and argued from the opposite perspective. They are worded in such a way as to specify the argumentative ground to be disputed by the advocate and opponent.

In other propositions, the value object and the value judgment are unitary in nature:

> The portrayal of violence on television is extremely harmful to young viewers.
>
> Ronald Reagan will be remembered as the greatest president of the twentieth century.

Even though only one value object and judgment is supplied in these propositions, there are still ample opportunities for disagreement. You discover what values may be in conflict through analysis of the proposition.

ANALYZING THE VALUE PROPOSITION

When we argue value propositions, we are arguing both the criteria on which judgment should be based and the extent to which the object of the proposition conforms to these criteria. In order to achieve this, we have to discover as much as possible about the value object and the value judgment. Thorough analysis of the field specified by the proposition will help you discover this information. The four stages of analysis of propositions of fact discussed in Chapter 8 are appropriate in value argumentation as well.

Locating the Immediate Cause

In value argumentation, analyzing the immediate cause of the controversy seeks to discover why the value object and the proposed value judgment are salient at this time. Is something happening that causes concern? What explains the need for society to reorder its value structure? You should seek information that reveals how the value object is presently seen, what status it is accorded in society, and what criteria are used to evaluate it.

Immediate controversy analysis is necessary to help you discover the values presently in conflict. If the question is one of freedom versus morality, do societal attitudes seem to favor morality at the expense of freedom or vice versa? Is freedom regarded from a politically liberal or conservative perspective by the nation's lawmakers and opinion leaders? What are respected authorities saying about how the object of the proposition ought to be valued? Do these authorities offer standards by which the value object may be judged?

Search the field of your proposition. Has there been an important discovery that has led to a value controversy? Has a significant event taken place that has focused national or international attention on the value object? Do experts in the field agree or disagree? Are their views compatible with those of the society at large? These questions will lead you to discover the probable cause of the immediate controversy over the value object and judgment. The key questions are, Why has this judgment of the value object emerged at this time? What standards of judgment are attached to it?

Investigating Historical Background

Because values are for the most part slow to change, in value argumentation you must extensively examine the background of a topic. Advocates and opponents must study the artifacts that reflect the society's structure and values (Warnick, 1981). Artifacts include such documents as the Constitution, Supreme Court and other decisions interpreting the

Constitution, the Declaration of Independence, and laws. If, for example, you are engaged in an argument about abortion, artifacts might include the Supreme Court decision in Roe v Wade and the Bible. The artifacts germane to the value object and judgment may vary considerably with the topic, but some, such as the Constitution, are basic to most controversies.

You may also find relevant artifacts in a particular field of argument. Does the proposition suggest a field such as science, politics, economics, or law? Does the proposition suggest a particular ethical system or code of conduct such as an economic system, the Judeo-Christian moral code, a political system, or a professional code of conduct? The importance of placing the proposition in its appropriate field is that the field may suggest criteria appropriate to judging the value object.

Historical American value systems are of particular importance to your analysis of a value proposition. There are certain dominant patterns of valuing that can help you identify societal value hierarchies. Rieke and Sillars (1984) offer the following examples of dominant value patterns in the American society:

Puritan Work Ethic—obligations to God and society to work hard at one's job or profession.

Enlightenment Value System—belief that reason must be free and the role of the government is to protect individual rights.

Progressive Value System—belief that movement of a society should always be forward, ever-increasing development and productivity.

Transcendental Value System—belief that self knowledge is best, the individual should turn inward for the meaning of life.

Personal Success Value System—belief that one's individual achievements are what is most important.

Collectivist Value System—belief that society's excesses must be controlled through law and order, the importance of team work in accomplishing goals.

Above all, in examining the background of your topic, search for predominating societal values and identify conflicts among them. Such conflicts may be current or longstanding. Sproule (1980) identifies certain values that frequently appear in juxtaposition with each other—freedom, equality, morality, safety, and privacy.

We can determine criteria for standards of value through an investigation of the topic's backgound. The examination of common sources of value is a good starting point, followed by careful consideration of the field in which the value proposition might exist. Some useful questions that can help to find value criteria include the following: What are cultural values or norms that pertain to the value object? What are the particular standards of value that have been historically established for this value object? Why is this particular value object perceived as it is?

Defining Key Terms

Both the value object and judgment may require definition. In particular, value judgments often have connotative implications; they must be defined to provide the criteria by which they are to be validated. *Desirable, effective, beneficial, injurious, disadvantageous,* or *harmful,* for example, must be defined. The criteria specified identify for the reader or listener the standard of judgment to be applied to the value object. What must occur for us to deem an effect serious or adverse? What renders a policy beneficial? Criteria specify the attributes something must possess to be evaluated in a certain way, and they serve to clarify the nature of the figurative ground over which arguments concerning propositions of value take place.

Value-laden terms should be defined in such a way that they suggest a series of statements capable of being supported with proof and reasoning. If you are arguing about the effectiveness of U.S. foreign policy, ideally your criteria would set observable standards by which effectiveness could be determined. Some possible criteria might be these: (1) An effective foreign policy keeps us out of wars, (2) an effective foreign policy makes us more friends than enemies, (3) an effective foreign policy prevents the spread of communist influence, and (4) an effective foreign policy treats all nations equally.

The definition of terms in a value proposition is of special importance, since the way you define value terms shapes the argumentative ground. In addition to setting the criteria for judging the value object, how you define terms will shape the issues of your value argumentation.

Determining the Issues

Issue identification for value propositions proceeds in the same way as for propositions of fact. Issues take the form of vital questions that must be answered if the arguer's case is to be accepted. Issues shape into an argumentative case the material discovered in investigating the immediate controversy, its background, and the definition of terms. Once again, the availability of stock issues facilitates the process. The three stock issues that shape value advocacy and opposition are identified in the following questions:

1. By what value hierarchy is the object of the proposition best understood?
2. By what criteria is the value object to be located within this hierarchy?
3. Do indicators of the effect, extent, and inherency of the value object show that it conforms to this criteria?

These questions help you determine the nature of the dispute, the judgmental criteria to be used to resolve it, and the kinds of arguments used to measure the value object by these criteria.

Once the appropriate hierarchy and criteria for judging values have been established, the central question in arguing a value proposition becomes, does the value object meet the criteria for evaluation? If only a single criterion has been advanced, it is obviously deemed sufficient to allow a proper evaluation to be made. However, if multiple criteria are advanced, they are not all automatically considered necessary. The advocate advancing these criteria may not require the value object to meet them all in order to be judged in the manner described by the proposition of value. If this is the case, the criteria will be applied independently, and demonstrating that the value object meets any one of them will be sufficient to warrant the judgment specified by the proposition.

The decision to employ single or multiple criteria, which are either necessary or sufficient, is one of the strategic choices the advocate makes in deciding how best to advance her value proposition. These choices reflect the advocate's consideration of the information the reader or listener may legitimately require in order to assent to the value proposition. As was the case with propositions of fact, claims in support of value propositions should be worded so that argument over them provides information relevant to the stock issues. This is accomplished through the use of factual claims with their attendant proof and reasoning.

ADVOCATING VALUE PROPOSITIONS

Construction of a prima facie case for value advocacy is a four-step process that begins with defining terms and proceeds through value hierarchy consideration, criteria identification, and application of the criteria to the value object. Successful case construction depends on thorough analysis of the proposition beforehand.

Define the Value Object

Defining the value object is the first step in the process. In some instances, the value object may be instantly recognizable and may not require lengthy definition. If the advocate was arguing that television has had great positive impact on the electoral process, she would not feel compelled to provide extensive technical definitions in order to clarify the nature of the value object. Such is not always the case. If the value proposition involves an assessment of the quality of children's television, it would be necessary to specify what is included in the category called children's television. Providing examples of the value object is one way of specifying meaning. Recall an example in Chapter 6 for instance: WATCH used examples in order to specify what *children's television* meant. Of course, examples are not the only way to define terms. The advocate may choose a functional definition, a definition from an authoritative source, or some other method. Just remember that definitions should clarify the value object's meaning for the audience.

Identify the Hierarchy

Value hierarchy identification is the second step in case construction for the advocate. In analyzing the topic, the advocate may have found that one or more field provides value standards that are potential sources of criteria for judging the value object. Which field will she use—legal, moral, ethical, political, economic, scientific? The value hierarchy that is most appropriate to her approach to arguing the proposition must be determined during case construction. Even if she adopts a well-known value standard, she must still identify its field to avoid confusion.

While this step in case construction identifies a value hierarchy, in reality a field has no value hierarchy until the advocate begins to examine issues regarding the value object. Until she knows the status of the value object, where presumption resides, she does not know what controversy exists. Value argumentation attempts to resolve questions regarding an object's appropriate place in the value hierarchy. The political field has placed "don't discriminate" relatively high in its value hierarchy on the basis of significant political pressure. This value ordering has translated into law and policy on affirmative action in the business field. Force from one field created issues in a second, placing "don't discriminate" above "seniority and tenure" to guide hiring, firing, and promotion practices. In working out the hierarchy of values in a field, the advocate starts with the notion of what standards are appropriate for this field. Application of these standards suggests when a particular value should be considered ahead of all others.

At this stage of case construction, the advocate's responsibilities are to identify the field from which value standards are drawn and to locate the value object in a value hierarchy. The appropriateness of the advocate's repositioning of the value object within the hierarchy can be verified by arguments which (1) prove the superiority of the advocate's interpretation of the value object relative to all other possible interpretations, (2) offer the testimony of "admirable people" who support valuing the object of the proposition in this way, and (3) identify signs demonstrating that this interpretation best fits the existing societal value hierarchy.

Conflicting values are framed by value propositions, and value argumentation is aimed at resolving this conflict. The advocate attempts to resolve the conflict in her favor by creating a decision rule: (1) proving the advocate's value maximizes another agreed-upon value, (2) proving the advocate's value subsumes opposing values, (3) proving the advocate's value has more desirable consequences, or (4) arguing from definition in which the advocate's value is the defining property of the opposing value, (Zarefsky, 1976). This initiates argumentation on the first stock issue, what value hierarchy should be used to measure the value object.

Specify the Criteria

Statement of the criteria for evaluation is the third step in the advocate's case construction. Description of the criteria for evaluation occurs first as the advocate states what criteria will be used. Because the criteria defining values lie at the heart of argumentation over these propositions, the two approaches that can be taken in identifying and applying them need to be considered, the *criteria discovery case* and the *criteria development case.*

The **criteria discovery case** uses an existing framework of values—one already understood, and generally accepted—as a standard by which phenomena may be evaluated. These criteria may be set forth in a general statement, but because they are so commonly accepted, advocate and opponent focus all argumentation on the appropriateness of judging the value object as a member of the class of phenomena to which this evaluation is commonly applied. Consider the general outline of a case using criteria discovery:

Value Proposition:

Drug XYZ is an effective treatment for cancer.

Criteria as Discovered from the Medical Field:

The effectiveness of a drug rests on its ability to cure, contain, or prevent a disease, without producing adverse side effects.

Inference:

If drug XYZ can safely cure and contain cancer without producing serious side effects, it can be considered an effective treatment.

Claims:

Drug XYZ can cure cancer.
Drug XYZ can contain cancer.
Drug XYZ has no adverse side effects.

In this instance, the decision to adopt discovered criteria is reasonable. Most listeners and readers would consider a substance with purported medicinal properties to be effective if it had curative powers. Three criteria, the ability to cure cancer, the ability to contain cancer, and the absence of adverse side effects are applied.

The **criteria development case** is used in situations where the advocate finds the criteria by which value may be determined either do not exist or are not commonly understood and, therefore, require explanation. This approach may also be used in situations where the criteria may be understood but are not readily accepted and, therefore, require substantiation. If upon analyzing the proposition the advocate decides to combine value standards from different fields or to use a relatively unknown value standard, the criteria development case will be her best approach to case construction. In criteria development cases, the locus of controversy may include the stock issues of hierarchy and criteria as well as the issue of whether or not the value object is appropriately measured by them. A prima facie case is established only if proof and reasoning relevant to all three stock issues are presented.

In arguing value propositions, a reasonable question to ask is "Should I use discovered criteria or should I develop them?" There are some practical considerations that affect the answer to this question. Sometimes, a controversy over values has its genesis in a misunderstanding of the value term. A "good" sandwich may be tasty to you, economical to me, and nutritious to someone else. For this reason, criteria development may be the best approach because it has the potential of better assuring clarity of focus in argumentation rather than assuming it will occur naturally. By identifying and defining specific criteria to measure values, the advocate is less likely to find her arguments dismissed out of hand because they were misunderstood.

However, the advocate must exercise good judgment. Remember that argumentation is an instrumental process, and consider the other party to the dispute as well as the audience. If the advocate and her audience share an understanding of the criteria that define a particular value at the outset, it is a waste of time and an insult to the audience's intelligence to use anything but a criteria discovery approach.

The advocate then establishes the necessary and sufficient characteristics of these criteria. For example, in the case arguing that drug XYZ is an effective treatment for cancer, the necessary characteristics were (1) that it could cure cancer, (2) that it could contain cancer, and (3) that it did not have seriously harmful side effects. Notice that these conditions individually are insufficient to warrant acceptance of the proposition. A drug that merely has no seriously harmful side effects is not acceptable as criteria for that drug's use. It must also possess some other properties. The criteria advanced by the advocate must include all necessary and sufficient properties of the value object being argued. How believable will argumentation concerning television's strong positive influence on the electoral process be if the only evaluative criteria concerns the number of people who are exposed to information about upcoming elections by television. While the extent of such exposure is probably a necessary condition for influence, it alone is insufficient to demonstrate such influence to be strongly positive.

In some instances, case construction must involve consideration of two other issues relevant to the criteria. If the connection between the criteria and the value object is not readily apparent, the advocate must establish the relevance. For example, if she wants to evaluate the quality of children's television using economic criteria, she has to explain their relevance. If she combines criteria from more than one field, but the proposition seems to lie in only one, she must explain their pertinence to the field of the proposition. Although questions of abortion, euthanasia, and genetic engineering lie in a scientific-medical field, the criteria you use to evaluate them could come from legal, ethical, or moral hierarchies. The advocate would have to explain how criteria from these fields are pertinent to the medical-scientific aspects of the quality of human life.

Measure the Object

Measuring the value object with the criteria for value judgment is the fourth step in the advocate's case construction. This is the heart of value advocacy and where argument development takes place. Three subissues must be addressed as the advocate confronts the third stock issue of value argumentation, the appropriateness of measuring the value object with the criteria. The amount of proof and the number of arguments used in establishing effect, extent, and inherency are matters of choice, but all three subissues must be discussed for a prima facie case to exist.

By **effect** we mean what the value object is purported to do. Arguments of effect result from analysis of the immediate causes of a controversy. For example, as a value object, children's television might be said to have some effect if it influences children's view of what the world, their nation, various groups of people, or appropriate behaviors are like. This effect can be judged as positive or negative, depending on what the evidence suggests. If the advocate is urging a change in attitude about the way children's television should be judged, she would develop effect arguments consistent with the judgment made by the value proposition she is arguing.

Extent relates to the severity or frequency with which the effect occurs. Does the object of the proposition do what it is purported to do with serious consequences or regularity? Arguments of extent also result from investigation of the immediate controversy; they show how significant or consequential the value object's effect is. For example, if only a very small portion of children watch television programs, the severity or potency of the effect may be insignificant or inconsequential. Although an effect may exist, if it doesn't have some significance, it may not be worth the audience's concern. Effect and extent arguments are both necessary elements of case construction. If a value object is shown to exist extensively, but it does not have much effect on society, concern may not be justified. Equally, if the effect of the value object is very serious but does not extend to a significant number of individuals, concern may not be justified.

Inherency pertains to causation. Are the effect and its extent the result of something intrinsic to the value object? In value argumentation, inherency often results from societal attitudes toward the value object. For example, if broadcasters do not feel children are influenced by what they see and hear on television, this attitude would cause a lack of concern about the content of children's television. Inherency arguments examine attitudes to determine what might produce these attitudes and the identified effects. Keep in mind that causality is often the consequence of complex, interrelated factors, so inherency arguments have to consider the possibility of multiple causes.

Effect, extent, and inherency arguments must be present for a case to be prima facie. This is only logical. If the extent of the effect is not inherent to the fundamental nature of this value object, then measurement of the value object by the criteria is invalid. Inherency arguments prove that the effect and extent attributed to a value object are central to the value system of society or some elements of it. The most carefully constructed arguments about the effect of children's television and the extent to which it gives children a particular perspective will not warrant a change in the audience's evaluation of children's television if the most probable reason for the existence of the effect and its extent can't be given.

Once again, the advocate is ready to develop a brief for the proposition, and choices have to be made. In this instance, she decides to apply existing criteria that appear to approach the status of being premises. Whenever the advocate is able to do this, it has the potential of reducing the opponent's options insofar as refutation is concerned.

Argument in Action

PROPOSITION: Television can be a beneficial educational force.
HIERARCHY: Education is essential to a free and democratic society, and literacy is its cornerstone.

(Ernest Boyer, Carnegie Foundation President, and principle author of *High School: A Report on Secondary Education in America*) wants to make sure that all students acquire the ability to think and communicate effectively in the English language. Literacy, he writes is "the essential tool," made all the more important by the advent of the information age; computer programs may be written in binary code, but they are displayed on the screen in English. (Dennis Williams, Barbara Burgower, Joe Contreras, Darby Junkin, Patricia King, and Dianne H. McDonald, "Rx for High Schools," *Newsweek*, September 26, 1983, p. 97)*

CRITERIA: That which improves the literacy of children is a beneficial educational force.

*References are fully cited only in the *Argument in Action* sections to show students the importance of fully documenting their evidence.

I. School-age children watch television.

Viewing time increases and peaks at about two and one-half hours per day just before elementary school. At first, the onset of school seems to diminish available TV time slightly. However, from about age eight viewing increases steadily to an average of almost four hours per day during early adolescence. Viewing then levels off in the later teens at two to three hours a day. (Robert M. Liebert, Professor of Psychology, State University of New York (SUNY) Stony Brook, Joyce N. Sprafkin, Director of the Laboratory of Communication SUNY Stony Brook, and Emily S. Davidson, Associate Professor of Psychology, Texas A&M University, *The Early Window: Effects of Television on Children and Youth* (2nd Ed.). New York: Pergamon Press, 1982, pp. 2–4)

II. The industry has furnished television-based instructional materials which are used in the schools.
    A. CBS's program is extensive.

The medium is a fact of life in the world of the child and can be harnessed as a mighty force for the use of educators. I cite one example for the teachers of secondary and older elementary school students. In the last five years almost 20 million students have participated in the CBS Television reading program, using specially prepared scripts to follow the drama of a telecast and, by using an accepted medium in their daily life, to enhance their reading abilities. A staggering achievement in television history was aired November 14 through 16 on CBS Television, an eight hour presentation of Bruce Catton's *The Blue and the Gray*. It could be enjoyed by itself but CBS furnished more than 1 million scripts and teacher's guides for American young people and their teachers participating in the reading program. (Bob Keeshan, also known as Captain Kangaroo, "Families and Television," *Young Children*, March 1983, 38, p. 53)

    B. NBC has a similar program.

NBC publishes and distributes a series of viewers guides which are designed to aid the entire audience and in particular young viewers to understand and take advantage of the many excellent programs on television. The guides contain descriptive materials about selected programs and among other things suggest questions implicit in them which would serve as the basis for class and home discussion. Last year, thousands of copies of over a dozen guides were distributed by NBC nationwide. (Phyllis Tucker-Vinson, Vice President, Children's Programming, NBC Television Network, "Children and Television," Hearings before the Subcommittee on Telecommunications, Consumer Protection, and Finance of the Committee on Energy and Commerce, House of Representatives, 98th Congress, First Session, March 16, 1983, p. 187)

    C. The schools use these materials.

The Television Information Office, an arm of the National Association of Broadcasters (NAB), provides a variety of services, including a teacher's guide for television which has been distributed since 1967. Today, tens of thousands of teachers and educators are using this publication to encourage the children to watch such specifically selected programs of educational value as "Fame," "The Changing Family," "The Wrong Way Kid," "The Edison Adventure," "The Secret World of Og," and the "National Student/ Parent Mock Election for 1984." (Edward O. Fritts, NAB President, "Children and Television," Hearings before the Subcommittee on Telecommunications, Consumer Protection, and Finance of the Committee on Energy and Commerce, House of Representatives, 98th Congress, First Session, March 16, 1983, p. 114)

III.   Television-based instruction has a beneficial effect on student literacy.
    A.   It has a beneficial effect on motivation

Currently I am hearing direct reports about children who lack school zeal now applying tremendous persistence on skill tasks based on popular TV shows. Teachers report increased interest in formerly reluctant learners when academic lessons were linked with television. These remarks come from teachers with students at many levels and from varied backgrounds. (Rosemary L. Potter, Ph.D., Reading Specialist, Pinellas County Schools, Clearwater, Florida, *The Positive Use of Commercial Television with Children.* Washington, D. C.: National Education Association, 1981, p. 111)

    B.   It has a beneficial effect on vocabulary.

The children paid unusually close attention to detail, listened more closely to other readers, read complex sentences, and attacked unknown and difficult words with great confidence. So interested did the children appear to be in the television-related reading materials developed, that those experiencing difficulty were happy to receive coaching from peers and teacher. In all, the children were willing to read stories whose vocabulary was drawn from oral dictation far more difficult than class texts. (Rosemary L. Potter, *The Positive Use of Commercial Television with Children.* Washington, D. C.: National Education Association, 1981, p. 1)

    C.   It has a beneficial effect on the climate of learning.

From reading and, especially, from classroom observation, my colleagues and I notice certain results when using TV scripts—low absentee rates, high attention spans, sincere interest in discussing motivation and details, and, best of all, high scores in applied specific reading skills and vocabulary taken from scripts. (Rosemary L. Potter, *The Positive Use of Commercial Television with Children.* Washington, D. C.: National Education Association, 1981, p. vi)

IV.   Therefore, television can be a beneficial educational force.

To be prima facie, this argument should contain all the following elements. Before going on to the next section of the chapter, decide for yourself whether or not the advocate's case is prima facie.

Summary of Value Advocacy

1. Define the terms of the proposition's value object.
2. Place the value object in the appropriate field and state the value hierarchy of that field in which the value object is now placed.
3. State the criteria for evaluation.
   A. Have the characteristics of the criteria been defined or described?
   B. Are the criteria identified as necessary and/or sufficient to warrant acceptance?
   C. Has the relevance of the criteria to the value object been established?
   D. Are the criteria consistent with placement of the value object in a given field?
4. Measure the value object against the value judgment criteria, demonstrating that the value object fits the criteria on the basis of the following:
   A. What element of the society is influenced by the value object? (arguments on effect)
   B. To what degree or in what amount does the effect occur? (arguments on extent)
   C. What is the cause that produces the effect and extent of the value object? (arguments on inherency)

OPPOSING VALUE PROPOSITIONS

The analysis of the proposition and search for issues and evidence is just as important for the opponent as it is for the advocate. To gain any advantage from presumption, the opponent must be aware of how the value object is presently viewed in its field in particular and by society in general. The opponent should investigate every possible aspect of the value object—how it is regarded in its field, what opinions respected sources have formed about it, what value standards are used to judge it, and what controversies exist concerning it. On the basis of this analysis, the opponent chooses his strategies for refuting the advocate's case.

Recall the discussion at the beginning of this chapter regarding how value change occurs. Since the advocate's task is to change existing values, the opponent may have a natural advantage in that change is often resisted. Examine value change theory in general to identify possible arguments that reflect the tendency of both individuals and society to resist value change. The advocate supports change on the basis of drawing new associations between presently held values and value objects. The opponent's task is to hold these new associations up to scrutiny and show either that they are invalid or that the existing associations are more valid and should not be rejected.

Establish Strategy

The opponent begins case construction with an overview of the value proposition reflecting the position he will take in presenting arguments refuting the advocate's case. This is sometimes referred to as a philosophy, and it expresses the essence of the opponent's perspective on the controversy and includes a preview of his strategy. It tells the listener or reader that he will defend present values, present alternative values, or demonstrate the weakness of proof and reasoning in specific areas of the advocate's case; in short, it elucidates whatever strategy he chooses to employ. The purpose is to clarify where he intends to stand on the proposition's value object.

Examine Definitions and Hierarchy

Since the first step in the advocate's case construction was to define the value object, that may be the opponent's next area of concern. Has the value object been properly defined? Does the opponent agree with the method of definition used by the advocate? If he feels that the value object should include elements the advocate has failed to consider, or exclude elements she has included, his first point of clash with the advocate will be over how to define the value object.

The opponent's next step in case construction will make use of the stock issues of value argumentation. Recall that the first stock issue asks by what value hierarchy the value object is best understood. There are two questions the opponent should ask himself in preparing arguments about this issue. First, is the hierarchy the advocate has chosen really valued by society as the advocate suggests? He may attempt to demonstrate that society or those in the field of the proposition do not accept the validity of the value hierarchy the advocate has identified. His arguments, using expert opinion, may attempt to prove that these experts do not recognize the validity of this value standard. Second, has the advocate identified a value hierarchy appropriate to better understanding the value object? Does he see other more appropriate value hierarchies that the advocate has failed to recognize? Does the advocate provide an adequate justification for her choice of a value hierarchy? Should the hierarchy be determined by some other standard or authoritative source?

Challenge Criteria

The opponent's next concern is with the appropriateness of the criteria used in measuring the value object in terms of its effect, extent, and inherency. Has the advocate established unique criteria for a value object for which other more commonly understood or accepted criteria exist? He may choose to argue that the value criteria are inappropriate to the value object because these criteria are too unusual or more appropriate to measuring some other object. He would then provide arguments establishing that better criteria exist, criteria that are more appropriate to the value object, or more widely recognized by experts in the field or society, or that the advocate has misinterpreted the value in question.

Refute Measurement

Finally, the opponent will turn to the third stock issue to determine if the value object is appropriately measured by the value criteria. With the concepts of effect, extent, and inherency clearly in mind, the opponent considers his strategies for opposition. First, remembering that the advocate must establish a prima facie case, he asks himself, "Have effect, extent, and inherency been argued by the advocate?" If one or more have not, a prima facie case has not been established. He should begin refutation by pointing this out. Second, since arguments of effect, extent, and inherency are advanced as claims, they require supporting proof and reasoning. He should examine the advocate's support for claims, asking, "Does the proof and reasoning offered by the advocate meet the tests established to determine its validity?" If it does not, the existence of a prima facie case would be in serious doubt.

If after analyzing the advocate's case construction strategy the opponent decides that the value criteria are fairly drawn, he must concentrate refutation on the goodness of fit between the criteria and the value object in the proposition. Since we have already discussed the use of the strategies of denial and extenuation against claims used to support propositions of fact, we shall not repeat that discussion here. Suffice it to say that factual and definitional claims are also advanced by the advocates of value propositions; so, opponents of value propositions should review the discussion of denial and extenuation in Chapter 8.

In employing denial and extenuation to oppose the value advocate, the opponent searches for proof and reasoning to ground (1) arguments stating that the effect suggested by the advocate occurs only in an exceptional case or that extenuating circumstances produce the effect, (2) arguments denying that the value object's influence is as extensive as the advocate suggests, (3) arguments showing that only a small segment of those who place value on this object are influenced, (4) arguments showing that prominent sources in the field do not consider the effect or the extent to be of great importance, (5) arguments showing that either the effect or the extent is a temporary phenomenon brought about by the unusual circumstances, and (6) arguments challenging inherency by demonstrating that the value in question is either not central to the society or is subject to change over time.

The opponent is now ready to respond to the advocate. In terms of the example of advocacy provided earlier in this chapter, we indicated that the advocate's choice of hierarchy and criteria, which bordered on being premises, restricted the opponent's options. That does not mean that he has no choices. He still could choose to dispute the value that she has placed at the pinnacle of the hierarchy of beneficial social forces, education, or more specifically literacy. This illustrates one of the fundamental differences between fact and value argumentation. While it would have been inappropriate for the opponent to respond to the advocate of fact by saying "Yes, but it doesn't cause violence," the opponent in value argumentation could propose an alternative candidate for the pinnacle of the hierarchy. He might suggest that promotion of cooperative endeavor is a more appropriate ultimate social force than literacy. He could also accept literacy as the criteria, and examine television's influence on it.

Argument in Action

PROPOSITION: Television is not a beneficial educational force.

I.   Television makes the attainment of literacy more difficult because of its effect on preschool-age children.
   A.   The advocate notes that preschoolers watch two and one-half hours of television per day.
   B.   At best, this stimulates the less capable at the expense of the more capable.

Heavy television viewers from low-IQ groups may actually be somewhat stimulated and may improve in world knowledge and readiness for school achievement. Brighter children, however, who watch a great deal of television, may indeed be reading less, generating less differentiated vocabularies, and may move to lower levels of school achievement than might be expected from their initial capacities. Television may be producing a homogenization effect around a lower central tendency, a result certainly in keeping with reductions in Scholastic Aptitude Test (SAT) scores over the last decades. (Jerome L. Singer, Department of Psychology, Yale University, and Dorothy G. Singer, Department of Psychology, Yale University, "Implications of Childhood Television Viewing for Cognition, Imagination, and Emotion." In Jennings Bryant and Daniel R. Anderson, editors, *Children's Understanding of Television: Research on Attention and Comprehension.* New York: Academic Press, 1983, p. 287)

   C.   At worst, this leaves young children ill prepared to begin school.
      1.   Television is a visual medium.

The basic mode of discourse of the TV curriculum is the analogic, nondiscursive visual image. People *watch* television. They don't read it, and what they hear is almost always subordinate to what they see. (Neil Postman, Professor of Education, New York University, "Engaging Students in the Great Conversation," *Phi Delta Kappan,* January 1983, 64, p. 311)

      2.   A visual medium emphasizes form, not content.

The printed page leads one away from the form of its symbols and *toward* their meaning. The TV image, because it is interesting in itself and continuously changing, leads one *toward* the form of its symbols and *away* from their meaning. There is no more important observation to be made about the difference between the two media than this: Print is content-oriented; TV is form-oriented. (Neil Postman, "Engaging Students in the Great Conversation," *Phi Delta Kappan,* January 1983, 64, p. 312)

3. A visual medium leaves the child ill prepared to begin school.

The lively visual quality of television may make it more difficult for children to shift from such a medium to making sense of purely verbal presentations such as teachers' lectures. The visual factor in television may also contrast with the more complicated decoding and encoding processes involved in reading. It is clear that children who watch television 3-4 hours a night are simply less likely to be practicing the necessary skills required to master reading in their early school years. (Jerome L. Singer and Dorothy G. Singer, "Implications of Childhood Television Viewing for Cognition, Imagination, and Emotion." In Jennings Bryant and Daniel R. Anderson, editors, *Children's Understanding of Television: Research on Attention and Comprehension.* New York: Academic Press, 1983, p. 271)

D. Therefore, exposure of preschool-age children to television makes the achievement of literacy more difficult.

II. The use of television-based instructional materials does not produce literacy as the advocate suggests.

A. Television's vocabulary is limited.

It is very likely that the lexicon of television programming is under 5,000 words. Children enter school with a lexicon about that large, probably furnished to a great extent by television. Students I encounter as college freshmen do not give evidence of a significantly larger vocabulary. (Michael Liberman, Professor of English, East Stroudsburg State College, Pennsylvania, "The Verbal Language of Television," *The Education Digest,* November 1983, XLIX, pp. 50-51)

B. Television's vocabulary is simple.

Opponents point out that the minimal degree of reading skill and concentration required by TV teaching is not adequate training for serious study of literature or history, or for the effort necessary to master subjects that cannot be easily popularized like math and chemistry. They also fear that television teaching may stimulate excessive viewing among a generation that watchs too much TV as it is. ("Learning to Live With TV," *Time,* May 28, 1979, p. 50)

C. Exposure to television is normally associated with decreases in literacy rather than increases.

1. This is the case in terms of verbal fluency.

Harrison and Williams analyzed data on 137 subjects in three Canadian towns: Notel (no television), Unitel (one channel), and Multitel (four channels). The study incorporated fairly careful controls to insure comparability of culture. . . . Children were tested in grades four and seven in all three towns; following the introduction of television, tests were given to children in grades six and nine who had been tested earlier in grades four and seven. When Notel children were divided at the median according to verbal associative fluency scores obtained before Notel was introduced to television, the authors found no difference in mean hours of *viewing* reported after two years exposure to television. This would argue against a differential viewing *preference* for high and low creatives. The Notel childrens' verbal fluency scores *decreased* significantly from the first to second phase of the study. Evidence was strong that television exposure is negatively related to children's performance on verbal fluency tasks. (Dorothy G. Singer and Jerome L. Singer, "Television and the Developing Imagination of the Child," *Journal of Broadcasting*, Fall 1981, 25, p. 376)

2. This is the case in terms of writing.

Heavy viewing is negatively related to writing to such an extent that, to predict writing ability, one should first examine viewing habits. Reading habits and the home environment also affect writing ability, though their contributions, while still significant, are not as great as that of television viewing. (Kate Peirce, Assistant Professor of Communication, University of Alabama, Birmingham, "Relation Between Time Spent Viewing Television and Children's Writing Skills," *Journalism Quarterly*, Autumn 1983, 60, p. 448)

D. Therefore, by the advocate's own criteria, television is not a beneficial educational force.

In this example, the strategy is one of denial. Notice the use of parallel cases in the last two arguments. While what the opponent argues does not pertain directly to television-based instruction, it touches on the relationship between television and literacy. In essence these arguments suggest that exposure to television reduces literacy, and the opponent would argue that all television-based instruction does is compensate for the medium's negative impact on literacy rather than raising it. This relationship would be made explicit through the opponent's oral or written argumentation in which he transforms the brief into a speech or essay. What you see in the brief is just the outline of his claims and the evidence he would use to ground them. This reemphasizes the difference between the brief and arguments presented orally or in writing in which points of clash between advocate and opponent are emphasized and arguments are fully explained.

Summary of Opposition Case Strategies

1. Give a statement of the opponent's philosophy that overviews the stand to be taken against the advocate's case.
2. Challenge or accept the advocate's definition of the value object.
3. Consider what criteria should be used to measure the value object.
   A. Is the asserted value as good as the advocate claims?
      1) Does society recognize it as good?
      2) Do experts in the field recognize it as good?
   B. Have the value criteria been correctly identified?
      1) Are there other values involved in the standard used?
      2) Does the advocate provide adequate justification for the value criteria selected?
      3) Is there a better standard by which to evaluate the value object?

4. Evaluate how appropriately the value object has been measured by the value criteria.
   A. Does the value object fit the stated criteria?
   B. Is the effect of the value object created by an exceptional case or extenuating circumstances?
   C. Is the extent temporary, insignificant, or improperly measured?
   D. Is the value inherent in the value hierarchy of society or the field of the value proposition? Is there some alternate causality?

Propositions of value attempt to establish how something or someone ought to be judged. They are argued by determining the criteria or standards by which the evaluation ought to be made and then determining the goodness of fit between the object being evaluated and these criteria. Advocates of value propositions must be sure their argumentation considers effect, extent, and inherency, regardless of whether they proceed by means of the criteria discovery or the criteria development approach. The opponent, besides employing techniques also applicable to propositions of fact may also use the strategies of proposing different criteria and charging improper classification. Understanding how propositions of both fact and value are argued provides important insight into the final chapter's subject—how policy propositions are argued.

LEARNING ACTIVITIES

1. John Naisbett's *Megatrends* (1982) hypothesizes ten directions in which the United States seems to be moving. Choose one of these trends, or the trend assigned by your instructor, and make a presentation to the class in which you explain the trend in terms of a value hierarchy it suggests. What values are implied by the trend? What degree of importance does society presently attach to these values? How will the future affect the present hierarchy of these values?
2. Discuss each of the following value propositions in terms of the value(s) to be supported by the advocate, the field(s) from which value criteria could be taken, and the specific judgmental criteria that might be used in measuring the value object.
   A. Students will benefit from classical literature studies in grades 6 through 12.
   B. The addition of a second professional football league has made the season longer, not better.
   C. For most people, buying a home computer is a waste of money.
   D. The rights of endangered species ought to take precedence over the rights of indigenous human populations.
   E. Humanitarian rather than geopolitical objectives ought to govern foreign policy decisions.
3. Review the two samples of value argumentation—advocacy and opposition— in this chapter. Identify the kinds of reasoning and proof used in constructing the arguments, and test their validity. Would other forms of proof or reasoning have been more effective?
4. Written/oral assignment: Frame your own proposition of value. Develop a prima facie case for the advocate's position. Respond in opposition to the

arguments advocating the value proposition, either your own or those of a classmate as assigned by your instructor.
5. Read the essay "Excuses, Excuses" by Helen C. Vo-Dinh in *Newsweek*, August 15, 1983, p. 13. Analyze the case using the stock issues of value argument. Which advocacy responsibilities does Ms. Vo-Dinh fulfill? Are there any that she omits? What is the value object, hierarchy, and criteria?

SUGGESTED SUPPLEMENTARY READINGS

CHURCH, R. T., AND BUCKLEY, D. C. Argumentation and Debating Propositions of Value: A Bibliography. *Journal of the American Forensic Association*, 1983, 19, 239-50.

> A comprehensive bibliography on value argumentation covering the work published in the field of speech and related disciplines.

NAISBITT, J. *Megatrends*. New York: Warner Books, 1982.

> Naisbitt predicts change based on social, economic, technical, and political shifts, and he identifies ten ways in which society will change between now and the end of this century. Among the areas of interest is how technology will influence what is valued. This is a very readable book and an excellent example of argumentation of future fact.

RIEKE, R. D., AND SILLARS, M. O. *Argumentation and the Decision Making Process*. Glenview, Ill.: Scott, Foresman and Co., 1984.

> Chapter 6 discusses the American value system and argues that understanding such systems are necessary if we are to understand how decisions are made. The book represents an audience centered approach to the study of argumentation, and the authors suggest means of discovering your audience's values.

WARNICK, B. Arguing Value Propositions. *Journal of the American Forensic Association*, 1981, 18, 109-19.

> The author examines the basic issues found in value propositions. She suggests that to be prima facie, the advocate's case must establish a set of values that, when applied to the value object, are shown to be more fundamental than those presently associated with the value object. As a result, analysis of value propositions must be centered on how the audience/society views that which is evaluated. An outline of the steps to follow in analyzing a value proposition is provided.

YOUNG, M. J. The Use of Evidence in Value Argument. In J. Rhodes & S. Newell (Eds.), *Proceedings of the Summer Conference on Argumentation*. ERIC Document ED 181 503.

> A very good discussion of what is necessary to ground value arguments. In particular, the concepts of *harm* and *significance* are discussed as value judgments intrinsic to policy argumentation.

10

HOW DO I ARGUE POLICY PROPOSITIONS?

Policy propositions concern a change in behavior, which may amount to the passage of new legislation, the creation of new institutions, or the course of action an individual should follow. Policy propositions imply that a critical decision to do or change something be considered. Making this decision is the result of considering the validity of a number of intermediate claims of fact and value. Your success in arguing a policy proposition rests on the skills you have developed in arguing both fact and value propositions. The procedure followed by advocates and opponents in constructing such cases will be used to construct policy cases as well.

Value argumentation often considers ideas that lead to policy formation. The relationship between fact, value, and policy is such that policy argumentation rests on consideration of issues of fact pointing to a particular value being attained or violated by adoption of a policy, or that, given certain facts, which among competing values favors adoption of an expressed policy (Young, 1980). When you consider your beliefs, they often make a series of statements about what you see as desirable or undesirable about a certain course of action. Your previous experience with value propositions may have involved using value criteria to judge the merits of a policy.

Policy argumentation contemplates a potential course of action. Where do we find examples of policy argumentation? In the field of law, we see examples of policy making as criminal codes are devised and revised, judges set penalties for those who are found to be guilty, and both professionals and ordinary citizens debate the merits of capital punishment or other issues involving the law and its implementation.

One of the more obvious places to see policy making and policy argumentation in action is in legislative bodies—national, state, and local. The establishment of new programs and the evaluation of existing ones takes place in city counsels and commissions, in state legislative houses, and in the U.S. House of Representatives and the Senate. Your school may have a decision-making body that sets university policy. Since many policy proposals have strong support and strong opposition, deliberation over a specific action can be quite lengthy, and even frought with emotion.

In business, management concerns itself with the creation and implementation of policy and the subsequent review of its effectiveness. Issues related to production, labor relations, purchasing, sales, and public relations are examples of the development of policy as it is considered, adopted, evaluated, and revised. The policy deliberations in business include definition and limitation of the problem, analysis of the problem, establishing criteria to evaluate possible solutions to the problem, and review of a particular solution once it has been implemented (Koehler, Anatol, & Applbaum 1981).

In academic argumentation, policy propositions have long been used as a tool for teaching skills and as competitive speaking activities. Much of academic argumentation considers proposed actions that "should" be undertaken by some agency, usually the federal government. These propositions usually involve looking at some broad change in domestic policy, such as a proposition urging greater freedom in the investigation and prosecution of crime; or in foreign policy, such as a proposition seeking to reduce foreign military commitments. You will recall that academic propositions are usually stated in such a way that they have more than one possible interpretation and can be argued by many students over the course of a semester, or even an entire year. Because of this, academic propositions offer you the chance to examine different ways of solving problems concerning the economy, welfare and human services, foreign trade deficits, and so forth.

Any group of people joined together for a purpose probably engage in some form of policy argumentation. In analyzing the propositions of policy from various fields of human endeavor, it is important to remember the particular characteristics of these propositions. Policy argumentation focuses on an action to be taken, and the analysis of policy propositions works backward to discover reasons, in the form of facts and values, justifying that course of action (Dudczak, 1983). As you analyze the policy proposition, you must remember that aspects of both fact and value are present in it.

ANALYZING THE POLICY PROPOSITION

As was the case with fact and value propositions, your analysis of the policy proposition will seek ideas, issues, and information in the four categories of the investigation: locating the immediate cause, investigating historical background, defining key terms, and determining the issues. Thorough analysis of the proposition prior to case construction is just as important for policy propositions as it is for fact and value. Give careful consideration to past, present, and contemplated policies that relate to your proposition's topic area. In policy argumentation, the change in policy suggested by the proposition is the contested ground. You will want to discover what reasons exist for making this change and what specific details might be included in such a policy. You will also want to know as much as possible about why such a change would be potentially beneficial or harmful.

Locating the Immediate Controversy

Immediate controversies are those events that bring attention to the topic area at present; they provide the answer to the question, why is this topic important at this time? Suppose that the problem you are addressing relates to the lack of cost-effectiveness in military spending. The immediate controversy which might have generated argumentation on the question of how to deal with the problem of the high cost of replacment parts might have resulted from the release of a report by Air Force auditors revealing that the cost of some 4,000 replacement parts for aircraft engines had increased by more than 500 percent (Cost Bombshells, 1983).

Policy argumentation often originates when some person or group of persons believes a problem exists. Immediate controversies stem from events that suggest the nature of the problem. Your research should look for significant, harmful events and explanations of why these events occurred. The analysis of immediate controversies is important to your development of inherency arguments for the policy proposition. Inherency arguments show the causal relationship between the absence of the policy suggested by the proposition and the continuation of the problem you have identified (Patterson & Zarefsky, 1983).

Investigating Historical Background

Learning the history of your topic can be useful in developing arguments. The notion of the "history" of a proposed change should be given a very liberal definition. History may be the last two years, or the last two hundred, depending upon the specific proposition. Your research may be restricted solely to the field of your proposition, or it may require you to look at other fields as well. Return to the example of military spending for a moment. Examining past efforts to solve the problems of the high cost of equipment maintenance might include examining the system by which military contracts for replacement parts are let to vendors and the history of those companies that win these contracts. The investigation might also include researching how the private sector deals with the same problem. How do civilian airlines cope with the high cost of replacement parts? Your answer might produce arguments from parallel case. Your investigation of the topic's historical background could even stretch beyond the field of aviation to include an evaluation of how other government agencies that use technologically sophisticated equipment obtain replacement parts.

In particular, you should research other attempts to institute a policy of this sort—attempts that seem identical or that embody the same principles as your policy proposition. Examine the field of your proposition to discover whether they succeeded or failed, whether authoritative sources support or oppose such a course of action, and whether or not legislation is pending in regard to the policy. For example, if your policy proposition concerns a balanced federal budget, investigate U.S. history for instances when the budget was in balance. How was balance achieved, and what caused the budget to go out of balance? What attempts were subsequently made to balance the budget? Why did they fail? What was said about them?

You must learn the history of the controversy. You want to know if the presence or absence of a policy has created dissatisfaction in the past. Because policy making is usually consistent with the traditions of a society, you must examine society's value hierarchies and predispositions toward the topic of argumentation. Policies are typically consistent with the past, so if an action has not been deemed appropriate in the past, it may not be regarded as such now. If you know a policy has not been regarded as appropriate, but it is the course of action you wish to advocate, you will need to discover a way to change attitudes.

Defining Key Terms

The advocate in policy argumentation must decide what portions of the proposition require definition. Since the most identifiable characteristic of a policy proposition is that it points toward a change in behavior, some new course of action, defining that course of action is one of the advocate's responsibilities in case construction. If at some point the advocate fails to define what is meant by this specified course of action, for listeners or readers a change in that direction will not only be unwarranted but also probably impossible because they will not know what they are being asked to do. We usually do not change our behaviors when we are unsure what the change involves. Equally, decision-implementing bodies are unlikely to change if the details of the decision are unclear.

In academic argumentation, defining the proposed action so that it conforms to the wording of the proposition is known as *being topical*. For those of you learning the techniques of policy argumentation this is a matter of some concern, as well as a question of ethics and good faith between you and your audience. By agreeing to argue a certain proposition, it becomes a matter of trust that you will indeed argue it. If you have consented to argue the advocate's side of the question, "should the federal government be required to operate on a balanced budget," you break faith with your audience when you twist the proposition by arguing in support of a nuclear freeze that would reduce international tension and the probability of a nuclear confrontation, and "Oh, by the way," balance the budget by reducing defense spending.

There are many legitimate methods for defining the terms of a policy proposition, and the advocate has choices to make regarding which other terms require definition. Whether or not to define more than the proposed action is one of those choices. In some propositions the subject—the agency that will undertake change or that will undergo change—may be clearly stated: "The International Olympic Committee should hold all future Summer Olympics in Greece." In other examples the subject is not as clearly identified: "The federal government should issue identity cards to all persons residing in the United States." Since there are many branches and agencies of the federal government that could be used to implement such a program—the Federal Bureau of Investigation, the Internal Revenue Service, the Bureau of Immigration and Naturalization, for example—the advocate would probably have to define in this case what is meant by the subject of the proposition.

The terms of the proposition may be defined individually, taking the subject of the proposition and the course of action as separate terms, or the entire proposition may be defined operationally—the meaning of the proposition is to be taken as engaging in this specific course of action. If you perceive an operational definition to be your best strategy, it is particularly important that your topic investigation include researching similar courses of action tried in the past. If you are defining key terms individually, recall the methods for defining terms offered in Chapter 3. In either case, the definition of terms of the operational plan of action would be one of the first elements to be presented in the advocate's case.

Determining the Issues

The stock issues for policy propositions are useful in making your preliminary analysis. As you research the topic area, whether from the perspective of advocate or opponent, you will be looking for claims and evidence in reference to the following questions:

1. Is there a reason for change in the manner generally specified by the policy proposition?
2. What policy is proposed to satisfy the reason for change?
3. What are the consequences of the proposed change?

Any topic will suggest some specific reasons why a change in policy or the creation of a new policy is desirable, some indications of what kinds of policies are feasible, and the merits of those potential policies. Using these stock issues can help you discover the specific arguments that will become part of the advocate's or the opponent's case structure. The range of potential arguments may vary greatly with propositions from different fields. The number of potential reasons for change might not be as extensive in some topics as in others. The range of potential new policies may be vast or narrow depending upon the topic area. Some proposed policies may cause more problems than they solve, or they may accrue benefits in a number of different areas. However, regardless of the field of the topic, the stock issues common to all policy propositions can be used to identify general areas of concern that you should research. Your research will yield specific arguments.

ADVOCATING POLICY PROPOSITONS

Creation of a prima facie case for a policy proposition begins with the advocate's identification of a disparity between things as they exist now, or are likely to exist in the future, and how they would be under a more ideal system (Sproule, 1980). The analysis of stock issues in a policy proposition leads to discovering the existence of this disparity. The first stock issue asks what unresolved problems exist or will exist in the future: *Is there a reason for change in the manner generally specified by the policy proposition?*

Advocacy of the First Stock Issue

Answering this question is important, because if no reason for change exists, change is unwarranted. If someone walks up to you and asks to borrow ten dollars, they are advocating the policy proposition, "You should give me ten dollars." Your probable response will either be "no," because they've given you no reason to warrant action on your part, or "why?" because you would like to know their reason. Inquiry into the reason for change involves us in a consideration of what the advocate perceives the disparity between actual and ideal to be.

The advocate's response normally takes the form of a value claim, and four subissues must be substantiated to win assent. These subissues provide the answers to questions customarily asked to determine the existence of a reason for change:

1. What is the nature of the alleged disparity?
2. How extensive is the alleged disparity?
3. Does the disparity cause harm to something or someone?
4. Is the disparity inherent in the present nature of things?

Advocacy of the first stock issue, reason for change, makes the listener or reader aware of an unresolved problem now, or in the future, which is a consequence of the way things are at present.

Identify the Disparity. The first subissue, the nature of the alleged disparity, requires the advocate to substantiate at least one definitional claim, that something which presently exists can be defined or classified as representing a disparity of a certain type. Because there is a natural resistance to change, people will usually be unresponsive unless the disparity is a serious one. The seriousness of the disparity is suggested in the definitional claim and further supported by arguments on the next two subissues, extent and effect. This should sound familiar, since it is basic value argumentation. The advocate may discover that more than one disparity must be identified to produce a compelling case. Although this may make the advocate's case complex, it is no more difficult than when a series of effects, or a number of different ways of measuring the extent of a single effect, is argued.

Quantify the Disparity. The second subissue explains or quantifies the extensiveness of the disparity, alleging the magnitude of this present or future problem. If the extent of the problem is demonstrable in quantitative terms, the advocate will advance and substantiate a factual claim. If the question is addressable only qualitatively, the claim will be definitional— that the disparity in question is to be classified as being of a certain qualitative type such as widespread or all-encompassing.

Characterize the Consequences. The third subissue concerns the effects, or consequences, of the disparity. An evaluative claim is presented, suggesting that the consequences are in some way harmful to those experiencing the disparity. Why is this important? We could probably prove that every person reading this book is not presently a student at the University of Tokyo, a disparity that is both serious and extensive; but unless we could demonstrate that as a result you are being hurt, our advocacy of the policy proposition "you should transfer to the University of Tokyo" would be unwarranted. Thus, the advocate uses the third subissue to examine the consequences of the present or future disparity. She evaluates them in negative terms by first establishing the criteria for harm and then demonstrating the goodness of fit between those criteria and the present disparity.

Establish Inherency. The final subissue used in developing argumentation on the first stock, reason for change, concerns itself with inherency. You might review the discussion of inherency in Chapters 2, 8, and 9. In policy propositions, inherency is argued to determine the cause of the serious, extensive, and harmful disparity. Blame for the existence of the disparity is placed at the doorstep of things as they are now—existing laws, institutions, or beliefs. A factual claim is used to establish the causal relationship between that which exists and the disparity. The demonstration of inherency is critical. Subscribing to the philosophy of "if it ain't broke don't fix it," the advocate's readers or listeners will be unwilling to assent to a change in something that is apparently innocent of having caused the problem for which a remedy is sought.

If the reason for change rests on the hypothesis that some more desirable future state will not be achieved because of things as they are now, the advocate must demonstrate that this state will probably not be reached because of the way things are now. People tend to give existing laws, institutions, or beliefs the benefit of the doubt, assuming they are likely to change naturally in ways that result in a future that is better than our past or present. The advocate must preclude this kind of thinking by demonstrating that existing barriers render the more desirable future state she supports, unavailable by any means other than those she will propose.

Having successfully upheld the burden of proof with regard to the first stock issue, reason for change, the advocate must now propose a way to remedy the disparity. The remedy is a new policy by which a preferred state, one in which the disparity would cease to exist, may be reached. *What policy is proposed to satisfy the reason for change?*

Advocacy of the Second Stock Issue

Assuming change is warranted because the advocate has proven the existence of a problem, she must provide the solution if she hopes to win assent. This solution, or proposed policy, should explain exactly what is to be done, and it should include the following elements:

1. **Change**—What behaviors are to be enacted that are not presently being enacted? What will be done differently?
2. **Mechanism**—On whose authority will these behaviors be undertaken? Will a new law be passed, a new agency or institution created, or will individuals do this on their own?
3. **Financing**—If the change or mechanism incurs any costs, how much will they be, and how will they be paid?
4. **Enforcement**—Unless everyone is willing to go along with the change, how will violations be detected? Who will be responsible for this detection, and how will violators be dealt with? What means are used to assure compliance?

Unless a separate definition of key terms in the proposition is provided, the advocate's proposal serves as an operational definition of the meaning of the proposition.

Suppose the advocate has suggested that present laws regarding drunk drivers should be changed because of the number of deaths and injuries attributable to them. The proposal for change might include the following:

The federal government will remove the requirement of probable cause and mandate that law enforcement officers randomly stop one vehicle per shift and administer a test of sobriety to the driver. Drivers with blood alcohol levels above the legal limit shall be subject to license revocation for one year. Persons caught driving during the period of revocation will receive a one-year jail sentence. Since this proposal involves the addition of no new manpower or facilities, it is essentially a free solution to the problem.

All four elements a policy proposal should have are contained in this example. After its details are spelled out, the advocate will be obliged to demonstrate how the reason for change has been satisfied. This involves considering the third stock issue: *What are the consequences of the proposed policy?*

Advocacy of the Third Stock Issue

At the very least, we expect solutions to work, to solve the problems that called them into being. If, in addition to this workability, other good things happen coincidentally, we are very pleased. The advocate guides the listener or reader through the consequences of the proposed policy by considering four questions:

1. How does the proposed policy address the disparity?
2. How does the proposed policy overcome its inherency?
3. How workable is the proposed policy?
4. What are the subsidiary effects of the proposed policy?

These four questions represent the subissues the advocate must develop in support of the third stock issue of policy argumentation, the consequence of change.

Demonstrate Solvency.   The first question pertains to the concept sometimes referred to as solvency. Does the proposed policy address the disparity in such a way that it eliminates or substantially minimizes it? Does the proposed policy get us to, or at least nearer to, the more ideal state the advocate seeks? The proposed solution to the problem created by drunk drivers rests on the laws of probability. If 10 percent of the people who are driving could not pass a sobriety test, then 10 percent of the random stops should result in arrests and convictions. The penalties are hoped to be severe enough to deter people from driving while intoxicated or to incapacitate them if they were not deterred but were caught. The advocate of this policy would have to offer proof and reasoning in support of these claims alleging the solvency of the proposal.

Overcome Inherency.   The second subissue is important. If existing institutions cannot address the reason for change because of inherent barriers, the advocate must demonstrate how her proposal is not hamstrung by these same barriers. Normally, the mechanism section of the policy proposal will fiat the necessary change. If the barrier was structural, for example the present requirement of having probable cause to stop a driver and administer a sobriety test, the advocate would argue that her proposal removed or revised it in such a way that it no longer constitutes an impediment. If inherency was a consequence of something's absence at present, for example the lack of a federal mandate and determinant sentencing for drunk drivers, the advocate must show how her proposal fills these gaps. If inherency resulted from attitudes, the advocate must be able to prove these same attitudes will not undermine the solvency of the proposal, or she must provide some means to change them. For example, if inherency was due to police attitudes, that catching murderers, rapists, and thieves is more important than stopping someone who may have had too much to drink, the advocate would be in serious trouble because those charged with enforcing her proposal still would not attach much importance to the task.

Establish Workability.   The third subissue turns the reader or listener's attention to the fundamental nature of the proposal itself and analyzes its workability. A proposal may solve problems and overcome inherent barriers but be totally unrealistic and unworkable. To suggest that the most effective solution to the problem of drunk driving would be to prohibit the manufacture and sale of alcoholic beverages may be true but absolutely unworkable. The nation tried that particular policy for moral reasons in the past and discovered that most Americans not only did not favor it, but willfully violated it. The advocate must develop and use criteria of effectiveness to argue the proposed policy is more workable than that which it replaces.

Identify Subsidiary Effects.   The fourth subissue, identifying the subsidiary effects of the proposed policy, allows the advocate to conclude discussion of the consequences of change by pointing to whatever desirable side effects occur as a result of assent to her proposal. Do the members of her audience get something for nothing? The advocate of tougher action against drunk drivers could claim they might. While her reason for change devolves from deaths and injuries attributable to those who drive while intoxicated, a problem the proposed policy is alleged to remedy; a subsidiary effect of the policy might be lower insurance premiums for everyone.

To be considered a subsidiary effect, something must be an inherent consequence of the success of the proposed policy, over and above remedying the disparity motivating it. Subsidiary effects are like fringe benefits, they are nice to have but they are not always available. Therefore, the absence of subsidiary effects does *not* render an advocate's case non–prima facie. Nor do subsidiary effects constitute a warrant for change in and of themselves. If a reason for change does not exist, or if the proposal for change fails to remedy the problem it is intended to resolve, the advocate's cause is lost even if her proposal produces some pleasant side effects.

Patterns of Organization

Before we turn to an example of policy advocacy, some comments about patterns of organization are in order. While we have labeled the stock issues first, second, and third, the logic of the advocate's approach should dictate the order in which they are presented. The pattern of case construction presented here reflects traditional organization, known as need-plan-advantage. It is used when the reason for change involves righting past wrongs and showing the subsidiary benefits of the proposed policy. For this type of case, the order in which the stock issues have been discussed in this chapter is most appropriate.

However, if the reason for change relates to the attainment of a more desirable future state, then the means to attain that state, the second stock issue, should be discussed first. This is called comparative advantage case structure, for it compares the advocate's proposed policy to existing policy and argues that the advocate's proposal should be considered more advantageous. It is used when serious present problems under the stock issue of reason for change cannot be discovered or are not widely accepted. It is also used when there is almost universal agreement that a reason for change exists, but controversy surrounds the question of what is the best means of change. This is often the case in legislative debate. Argumentation compares the proposed solution to existing policy. The stock issues on the proposed change and the consequences of change provide the structure for argument.

Although there is no rule regarding how many advantages are necessary for a policy change to be viable, the advantages must be demonstrated to result from the new policy and their value must by qualitatively or quantitatively measurable. The same is true of advantages claimed in the traditional need-plan-advantage case. The organizational structure of a comparative advantage case begins with the presentation of the policy proposal that specifies change, mechanism, financing, and enforcement. The advocate then indicates one or more advantages to be achieved by adopting this proposal. Each advantage should be unique, so that only the proposed policy, when compared to existing policy, is capable of achieving it. In addition to demonstrating uniqueness, the advocate establishes the quantitative and/or qualitative measure of each advantage's value to society.

A third type of case organization exists for policy advocacy that uses many of the features of value argumentation. A goals-criteria case begins by examining what society values and the goals it has set to achieve these values. If full employment is a goal of the society stemming from valuation of the work ethic, a proposal to achieve full employment might be advocated on the basis of how it better achieves the goal and, therefore, more fully realizes the relevant value. Criteria are used in the same manner as in value argumentation. The proposed policy is then examined in terms of value criteria that measure its ability to obtain the desired goal.

The advocate's case may be organized in accordance with different philosophies—traditional, comparative advantage, or goals-criteria—but her arguments will still address the same stock issues. As you read through the following example of policy advocacy, decide which pattern of organization the advocate is using. Also try to find the fatal flaw in the advocate's case. We will explain the pattern of organization right away, but you will have to wait to evaluate the opponent's arguments to find out if you spotted her error.

Argument in Action

PROPOSITION: The federal government should significantly increase the regulation of children's television.

PROPOSAL: The Federal Communications Commission will establish guidelines requiring that a minimum percentage of roles be created for characters representing racial minorities.

1. These guidelines will apply to those television programs produced by network, independent, cable, and public broadcasters for the children's market, age two to eleven.
2. Conformance with these guidelines can be demonstrated on a show-by-show basis or by the broadcaster's programming taken en toto.
3. Affiliates who preempt programming, or otherwise fail to carry the feed supplied to them, in such a way that their programming fails to conform to the guidelines will face license revocation.
4. Fifty percent of all lost profits, documented over three consecutive years, will be rebated to broadcasters out of general federal revenues.

I.   Increased federal regulation of children's television better serves the interests of all Americans.
    A.   Children's television is not representative of America's multiracial character.
        1.   It is not racially integrated.

The world of children's TV is not well integrated racially. White chracters most often appear without the company of blacks or other minorities, and animals are plentiful. (F. Earle Barcus, Director of the Communication Research Center, Boston University, *Images of Life on Children's Television.* New York: Praeger, 1983, p. 16)*

        2.   Minorities are underrepresented.
           a.   Blacks are underrepresented.

For a short while during the early 1970s, there was an increase in the number of minority characters on the television screen. Since then their numbers have

*References are fully cited only in the *Argument in Action* sections to show students the importance of fully documenting their evidence.

seemed to stabilize and, for some groups, have diminished. On children's television, minorities have appeared, but their number are still scarce. . . . The patterns in other areas of television correspond with the data observed in children's TV: that blacks may have made the most headway in terms of recognition, but this is still not reflective of their numbers in our society. Other minorities seem not to have fared even as well as blacks, since their numbers are barely noticeable. (F. Earle Barcus, *Images of Life on Children's Television.* New York: Praeger, 1983 p. 80–82)

    b. Asians are underrepresented.

In children's programming (weekend daytime and weekday afternoons) the same trends are reflected but cannot be analyzed reliably because of the even smaller number of minority characters. In a survey of racial and cultural groups portrayed on Saturday children's programs on three network-affiliated television stations in San Francisco, California, Asians appeared on only 1 of the 27 programs monitored; in contrast, whites appeared on 25 of the 27 programs. (Patti Iiyama, UCLA Center for Afro-American Studies, and Harry H. L. Kitano, UCLA Departments of Social Welfare and Sociology, "Asian Americans and the Media." In Gordon L. Berry and Claudia Mitchell-Kernan, editors, *Television and the Socialization of the Minority Child.* New York: Academic Press, 1982, pp. 156–57)

    3. Minority characters are stereotypical.
        a. Blacks are stereotyped.

During Saturday morning's programs no women or black males represented powerful institutions; in the afternoon programs there were 19 males and only 4 females; and in the evening there were eight males and only one female. Afternoon programs included 19 white representatives and four blacks, while evening viewers saw only two blacks representing powerful institutions. (Karin L. Sandell, Assistant Professor of Speech Communication, Bowling Green State University, and David H. Ostroff, Assistant Professor of Speech Communication, Bowling Green State University, "Political Information Content and Children's Political Socialization," *Journal of Broadcasting,* Winter 1981, 25, p. 57)

    b. Asians are stereotyped.

Thus, the Asian image presented on the television screen has been consistently stereotyped. The basic message is that Asians are inferior to white Americans and that the only way to become accepted by white society is for Asians to become passive, dependent, and respectful—that is, to know their place. (Patti Iiyama and Harry H. L. Kitano, "Asian Americans and the Media." In Gordon L. Berry and Claudia Mitchell-Kernan, editors, *Television and the Socialization of the Minority Child.* New York: Academic Press, 1982, p. 162)

    c. Indians are stereotyped.

The most common Indian characters viewed on the television screen are depicted as simple, lazy, wasteful, and humorless; they are shown as lacking intelligence and English-speaking skills and as believing in heathenistic nonsense for a religion. This portrayal was begun in the cheaply made western films and later carried over into television westerns. (Joann Sebastian Morris, American Indian Educational Commission, "Television Portrayal and the Socialization of the American Indian Child." In Gordon L. Berry and Claudia Mitchell-Kernan, editors, *Television and the Socialization of the Minority Child.* New York: Academic Press, 1982, p. 189)

B.   This nonrepresentativeness is harmful.
  1.   It harms minority self-concept.

The consequence for television programming may then be more crucial in regard to the self-concept development of minority group children than it is to that of white children. (Gloria Johnson Powell, University of California, Center for Health Sciences, Los Angeles, "The Impact of Television on the Self-concept Development of Minority Group Children." In Gordon L. Berry and Claudia Mitchell-Kernan, editors, *Television and the Socialization of the Minority Child.* New York: Academic Press, 1982, p. 123)

  a.   It harms black self-concept.

The predominance of minority characters in heavily or totally minority casts suggests that minorities should remain within, or are only important within, the context of their own minority group. Their occupational roles, actions within these roles, and lack of power in integrated settings suggests that in the larger American society "white is still right." (Aimee Dorr, UCLA Graduate School of Education, "Television and the Socialization of the Minority Child." In Gordon L. Berry and Claudia Mitchell-Kernan, editors, *Television and the Socialization of the Minority Child.* New York: Academic Press, 1982, p. 27)

  b.   It harms Asian self-concept.

If Asian American children identify strongly with Asian models on television, they have only stereotyped characters to imitate (Fu Manchu, Charlie Chan, or silent, passive types if male; prostitutes or shy housewives if female). If, on the other hand, they identify with the white characters, then they will be repudiating their racial identity because of the perception of the racism of this society. (Patti Iiyama and Harry H. L. Kitano, "Asian Americans and the Media." In Gordon L. Berry and Claudia Mitchell-Kernan, editors, *Television and the Socialization of the Minority Child.* New York: Academic Press, 1982, p. 172)

  c.   It harms Indian self-concept.

In most American Indian homes, parents attempt to instill a sense of pride in their young ones. And many American Indian communities across the country are revitalizing their ceremonies, language, and customs. Yet all the work of community and parents can be undermined from within the home by television. The view of themselves and their race that American Indian children receive from their parents is generally one that incorporates many positive characteristics. Yet that viewpoint is not compatible with the way the children see their tribesmen depicted by television networks. (Joann Sebastian Morris, "Television

Portrayal and the Socialization of the American Indian Child." In Gordon L. Berry and Claudia Mitchell-Kernan, editors, *Television and the Socialization of the Minority Child.* New York: Academic Press, 1982, p. 197)

   2.　It harms interracial understanding.
     a.　Many receive their information about minorities from television.

Since the real lives of most of us do not include much contact with ethnic groups other than our own, television could be especially potent in filling our experiential gaps with these groups—to the extent that television includes them in its world. Our essentially segregated society leaves this opening for television. (Aimee Dorr, "Television and the Socialization of the Minority Child." In Gordon L. Berry and Claudia Mitchell-Kernan, editors, *Television and the Socialization of the Minority Child.* New York: Academic Press, 1982, p. 29)

     b.　Many accept this information as true.

Regarding perceived reality, respondents were asked if blacks on TV "talk" like blacks in real life: eliminating "not sure" responses, 66% said yes and 34% no. . . . Black "teenagers" on TV were seen as realistic by 56%, and televised black "men" by 45%, and black "women" by 44%. (Charles K. Atkin, Professor of Communication, Michigan State University, Bradley S. Greenberg, Professor of Communication, Michigan State University, and Steven McDermott, Assistant Professor of Speech, University of Georgia, "Television and Race Role Socialization," *Journalism Quarterly,* Autumn 1983, 60, p. 412)

C.　Only the proposed federal regulation can remedy the problems of nonrepresentativeness.
   1.　Children's television is currently controlled by market forces rather than federal regulations.

Bluntly stated, American kidvid is a national disgrace. And according to most citizen watchdog groups, the blame can be traced to the laissez-faire policies of the Reagan administration. During the 1970s, they note, the Federal Communications Commission strongly pushed for an improvment in kidvid's air quality—even going so far as to consider mandatory programming requirments for local stations. But under Mark Fowler, the FCC's Reagan-appointed chairman and a fervent apostle of deregulation, the agency abruptly switched to a hands-off policy. From almost his first day on the job, Fowler sent out a clear message: the quantity and quality of children's TV should be decided by marketplace forces rather than by government pressure. (Harry F. Waters, "Kidvid: A National Disgrace," *Newsweek,* October 17, 1983, p. 82)

   2.　Market forces are inherently discriminatory against minorities.

American television is unabashedly profit-dominated and, because of this, discriminates in its programming against minorities, whether defined by age, ethnicity, or otherwise, in favor of audiences whose hugeness rests on heterogeneity. It specializes only to the degree imposed by audience availability—children on Saturday mornings; housewives in the daytime, Monday through Friday. (George Comstock, Syracuse University School of Public

Communication, and Robin E. Cobbey, Source Telecomputing Corporation, "Television and the Children of Ethnic Minorities: Perspectives from Research." In Gordon L. Berry and Claudia Mitchell-Kernan, editors, *Television and the Socialization of the Minority Child*. New York: Academic Press, 1982, p. 245)

3. Children's television is very profitable.

Advertising on children's programs accounts for between 6 and 9% of all advertising revenue or about $500 million yearly. The biggest spenders are toy manufacturers ($40 million yearly), followed by cereal companies ($35 million), and candy companies ($20 million). The average price per minute to advertise on a children's program is $20,000. Because programming costs and risks are far lower than with prime time shows, children's programming, on a percentage basis, is one of the more profitable segments of commercial television. (Robert M. Liebert, Professor of Psychology, State University of New York (SUNY) Stony Brook, Joyce N. Sprafkin, Director of the Laboratory of Communication SUNY Stony Brook, and Emily S. Davidson, Associate Professor of Psychology, Texas A&M University, *The Early Window: Effects of Television on Children and Youth* (2nd Ed.). New York: Pergamon Press, 1982, p. 18-19)

4. While it may become less profitable, the benefit to the public interest more than offsets the loss.

It is simply unacceptable to say that broadcasting is a business and must be guided by what is most profitable. As entities with an exclusive license to use the spectrum, broadcasters have benefitted substantially from the use of a public resource. In return, the public is entitled to a dividend. At a minimum, that dividend should include regular, diverse and enriching programming for children. (Henry M. Rivera, Commissioner, Federal Communications Commission, "Children and Television," Hearings before the Subcommittee on Telecommunications, Consumer Protection, and Finance of the Committee on Energy and Commerce, House of Representatives, 98th Congress, First Session, March 16, 1983, p. 6)

If you concluded that the advocate followed a comparative advantage pattern of organization you were right. If you were unable to find the flaw in this example, you may want to review it using the following summary of the stock issues of policy advocacy. In order to be prima facie, the advocate's case must include arguments that address the following questions:

Summary of Policy Advocacy

1. Is there a reason to change in the manner generally specified by the policy proposition?
   A. What is the nature of the alleged disparity?
   B. How extensive is the alleged disparity?
   C. Does the disparity cause harm to something or someone?
   D. Is the disparity inherent in the present nature of things?
2. What policy is proposed to satisfy the reason for change?
   A. What will be done differently?

    B.   Who will be responsible for doing it?
    C.   What will it cost, and how will costs be paid?
    D.   What means are used to assure compliance?
 3. What are the consequences of the proposed change?
    A.   How does the proposed policy address the disparity?
    B.   How does the proposed policy overcome its inherency?
    C.   How workable is the proposed policy?
    D.   What are the subsidiary effects of the proposed policy?

OPPOSING POLICY PROPOSITIONS

The opponent of the policy advocate attempts to demonstrate that good and sufficient reasons exist to consider the proposed policy unacceptable. Remember that the advocate must develop arguments in support of three stock issues. Although the second one becomes essentially noncontestable as soon as a proposal for change is advanced, she must win the two remaining stock issues. There must be a reason for change and the consequences of the proposed policy must be such that the reason for change is remedied. Must the opponent also win both these issues in order to defeat the advocate? No! In fact, he doesn't even have to contest both! Thus, the first strategic choice the opponent must make concerns whether to argue one or both of the remaining stock issues. If he feels one is clearly winnable and the other is not, he may choose to attack only where he has the advantage, focusing audience attention on that portion of the contested ground where his arguments are strongest.

    Why is this strategic choice possible? A prima facie case is one that can be taken at face value, meaning that the reason for change, the proposed change, and the proposed change's ability to resolve the reason for change must be present in the advocate's case before it can be termed prima facie. If the opponent can successfully attack the advocate's position on the first or last of these stock issues, the case is no longer considered to be prima facie. It no longer offers its listeners or readers good and sufficient reasons to assent to its viability. As a rule, the advocate's position will not be so clearly deficient in its development of the three stock issues to make this decision an easy one. Therefore, it is usually wisest for the opponent to attack on both fronts, and to determine the strengths and weaknesses of the advocate's case based on the arguments used to defend it.

Establish Strategy

    Construction of the opponent's case begins with an overview of his rationale for rejection. What will he defend? What does he oppose? How does he wish the listener or reader to view the proposed policy? The opponent should examine the advocate's case, identify the central idea behind the proposed change, and ask himself the following questions. Does the reason for change contain assumptions that are unwarranted because they have not been fully proven? Are there implied values the reader or listener is asked to accept without explanation? What is the advocate's burden of proof and has it been met? In addition to determining whether or not the advocate has met her responsibility of the burden of proof, the opponent should assess the evidence and reasoning contained in individual arguments, applying tests of evidence to the proof grounding and backing claims, and examining the reasoning for fallacies.

Examine Definitions

The opponent must also determine whether or not he wishes to contest the advocate's definition of terms. If the proposition has been defined operationally, his refutation of the ability of the proposal to do what the advocate claims it will do is equivalent to contesting the definition of terms. But if the advocate chooses to define the subject of the proposition independently, the opponent should apply the same tests of definitions as he employed in opposing fact and value propositions—has the advocate excluded something important or included too much?

Refute the Reason for Change

Opposing argumentation on the first stock issue may use the strategies discussed in Chapters 8 and 9, since the stock issue of reason for change is advanced by fact and value arguments. The opponent may choose to use arguments that deny that the alleged disparity exists or that it is not as great as the advocate suggests. The opponent may use arguments that deny the harmfulness of the disparity or he may attempt to prove the harm is insignificant. He may also offer arguments that demonstrate extenuating circumstances, which are only temporary, explain the existence of the disparity.

Challenge Inherency.   In regard to reason for change, the opponent may offer arguments showing that the disparity is not inherent to society, its institutions, or their policies. In arguing inherency, the advocate attempts to lead the reader or listener to believe that what presently exists causes the problem and, by implication, that the only remedy to this problem lies beyond the reach of existing laws, institutions, or patterns of belief. If this were absolutely true, society would be locked in place, totally incapable of change. In reality, that which exists at present is, to a certain degree, in a state of flux and in the process of becoming something else. The opponent may attempt to capitalize on this, denying the inherency of the reason for change on the basis of society's self-correcting abilities. This is normally referred to as a **minor repairs** argument.

The philosophy of minor repairs does not give the opponent license to claim whatever he wishes. Whatever minor repairs are suggested to that which exists must meet certain tests. First, *minor repairs must be attainable within the foreseeable future.* To assert that someday the state of the art in automotive safety technology will be such that people will no longer be killed or injured in an accident, thus rendering unnecessary the advocate's proposal to crack down on drunk drivers, stretches both the audience's credulity and the limits of the foreseeable future beyond their breaking points.

Second, *a minor repair must be attainable without benefit of a structural or attitudinal change*—it must be a natural consequence of that which presently exists. To argue that the states could decide to suspend probable cause without the federal mandate provided by the advocate would violate this second standard. However, arguing that there is a current trend toward tougher sentences for those convicted of drunk driving, which causes many to think twice before driving while intoxicated, and that this trend will continue into the future, conforms to the second standard.

Third, *minor repairs are subject to the same standards of proof,* insofar as their solvency, inherency, and workability are concerned, as the policy proposal presented by the advocate. Fourth, and finally, *minor repairs should not themselves be interpretable as a legitimate part of the policy proposition.* If the proposition calls for the prevention of drunk driving, the opponent could not suggest the installation of ignition interlock devices, which prevent intoxicated drivers from starting their cars, as a minor repair. While the suggestion differs from the specific interpretation of the proposition presented by the advocate, it still constitutes "advocacy" of the proposition's intent. Because it also constitutes a structural change in the way society attempts to control drunk driving, it is neither a defense of present policy nor a reasonable interpretation of what present policy is in the process of becoming.

Refute the Consequences of Change

Question Solvency. Opposing argumentation on the third stock issue requires creativity, along with a firm belief in the principle, "whatever can go wrong, will go wrong." What might preclude solvency? Almost anything or anyone, whose actions are necessary to remedy the problem, has the potential to interfere. In the drunk-driving example, the accuracy of some devices used to determine blood alcohol content is questionable. The advocate's proposal provides no funding to purchase the right kind of equipment. As a result, a police department with the wrong kind of equipment could find all the cases it brings to court being dismissed. In addition, if most police cars are not sent into the field with testing equipment because of the expense, how are the officers to make their daily determinations of sobriety?

Identify Barriers.   What might preclude inherency being overcome? While the proposal will normally fiat a means to overcome present barriers, two things must be remembered. First, attitudes cannot be legislated. Second, people resist change, especially when they are not sure that a change is in their best interests. This leads the opponent to an analysis of what are commonly called **circumvention arguments.** How might circumvention occur in the present example? Police are only human. Some of them may even have a drink from time to time. One of the current impediments in convicting drunk drivers is the "there but for the grace of God go I" syndrome. Enforcement relies on the police, and if they suffer from the aforementioned syndrome, they may choose to let marginal cases go or only stop those whose driving indicates they are obviously intoxicated, those for whom they would have had probable cause under the old system anyway.

Dispute Workability.   What renders a proposal unworkable? If the means by which it operates are so slow, so inconvenient, or so time-consuming that the cost of making a proposal work outweighs the benefits gained when it does, we deem it unworkable. Simple proposals are rarely all that simple. The efforts expended by those who make the system work should not be excessive. In the drunk-driving case, for example, requiring the police to spend time either waiting by the roadside for the car with the test equipment to arrive or driving around late at night on deserted streets looking for a car to stop suggests a relatively high proportion of wasted effort.

Present Disadvantages.   Up to this point we have said nothing about the fourth subissue, subsidiary effects. Proposals are like pebbles tossed into ponds, they make waves. Sometimes these waves are small, but usually one or more may be of epic proportions. The opponent should look for these, since they constitute the *disadvantages* to the advocate's proposal. Development of arguments of this kind rest on performing a "worst case" analysis of a situation in which the consequences of the proposal are portrayed to be as bad, or worse, than the problem the proposal was intended to remedy.

What would be a "worst case" situation in the proposal we have been discussing? A person who would not fail the sobriety test, but who has had a drink, is driving home. A police car pulls up behind him and turns on the red light. The person panics and flees, resulting in a high speed chase in a congested area. Or, more likely, a person who has lost his license but has continued to drive is the driver in our "worst case." Although he has not had a drink, he knows he will be arrested for driving without a license. The result is the same and the consequence is at least as potentially serious as the problem the policy was designed to remedy.

How are disadvantage arguments developed? The opponent begins by assuming the policy will do exactly what the advocate says it will. This means that solvency, inherency, and workability are, partially or wholly, granted to the advocate. The argument is then developed in the same manner that an argument advocating a value proposal would be. The opponent establishes criteria for evaluating the advocate's proposal as if it were in existence, and then he demonstrates the goodness of fit between these criteria and the proposal. This also means that he assumes a burden of proof similar to that of an advocate of a value proposition.

A final note of caution concerning disadvantage arguments. The opponent should resist using disadvantage indiscriminantly. To be effective, disadvantages must possess *uniqueness;* they must occur only in the presence of, and as a consequence of, the advocate's proposal. If the same disadvantage would occur as a result of a minor repair the opponent has suggested, or would occur even without the repair as a consequence of that which presently exists, its impact in dissuading the reader or listener from assenting to the advocate's proposal is diminished.

If the opponent has to concede so much, and be so careful, in arguing a disadvantage, why bother? Because disadvantages are the potential "service aces" of argumentation. The opponent can concede everything, the stock issues of reason for change and the ability of the proposed change to remedy the problem; but if he can convince the audience that a single disadvantage, or series of disadvantages, to the advocate's proposal represents a greater harm to society than the one the proposal remedies, he can win their assent.

Consider the relationship between the pharmaceutical industry and the Food and Drug Administration as a real-world example of the power of a disadvantage in the outcome of argumentation. A drug company makes a product intended to produce certain health-improving effects. Assume the drug produces these effects, along with some dangerous side effects. If it determines that these side effects are so harmful and extensive that they outweigh the benefits the drug produces, the Food and Drug Administration would force the company to take the product off the market.

The burdens placed on the advocate seem so great, and the opponent may defeat a policy proposal with one telling disadvantage so why bother to argue? Why risk advocacy? The advocate actually has a number of natural advantages, not the least of which is the ability to define the nature of the ground over which argumentation is joined. The policy advocate makes the best possible case for her proposal's adoption. However, if the good she could achieve would be outweighed by the greater evils that would occur, rational decision making suggests that the reader or listener ought to reject it.

Offering Counterproposals

One final strategy the opponent may elect to employ is to accept as valid the advocate's reason for change and offer a **counterproposal,** an equally acceptable alternative to it. This strategy is seldom used in academic argumentation but is quite common in real-world contexts. In law making, business, and family decision making situations, all parties may agree a problem exists which must be solved, but they may disagree over which policy would represent the best solution. However, unlike these groups, the opponent in academic argumentation may be constrained from making full use of this strategy. The requirement that the proposal must be nontopical applies to counterproposals and minor repairs alike. In addition, the counterproposal must be competitive, which means that its adoption must preclude the ability to adopt it in addition to the advocate's proposal. If the opponent chooses to use a counterproposal, he assumes the same burden of proof as an advocate and uses the subissues of the second and third stock issues in his argumentation to demonstrate the superiority of his proposal.

Patterns of Organization

A final suggestion to opponents—in organizing the case, follow the pattern of organization provided by the advocate. Argue first things first and proceed to subsequent arguments in an order that juxtaposes each with the advocate's argument it addresses. This helps listeners and readers clearly understand the points of clash and disagreement. The opponent has available a number of strategic options. However, all of these options can never be used simultaneously. The following example reflects one set of choices the opponent might make in constructing his case. Notice the manner of its organization.

Argument in Action

PROPOSITION: The federal government should not significantly increase the regulation of children's television.

    I.   There is no reason to increase the regulation of children's television.
        A.   The ethnic identity of minorities is not harmed.
           1.   Ethnic identity is influenced by other factors besides television.

The racial awareness and ethnic group identification of children are influenced by a wide variety of individuals, including parents, siblings, peers, teachers, and other adults as well as by children's direct encounters with the environment. (Ruby Takanishi, Columbia University Department of Psychology, "The Influence of Television on the Ethnic Identity of Minority Children: A Conceptual Framework." In Gordon L. Berry and Claudia Mitchell-Kernan, editors, *Television and the Socialization of the Minority Child.* New York: Academic Press, 1982, p. 81)

           2.   There are no studies to confirm television's harmful effect on ethnic identity.

There is a paucity of studies that have focused on the impact of television on children's ethnic identity. Studies of the social effects of television have been explored mainly at the surface level, for example, on sex- and race-role presentations. None of the existing studies on television and its influence on ethnic identity have actually measured ethnic identity. (Ruby Takanishi, "The Influence of Television on the Ethnic Identity of Minority Children: A Conceptual Framework." In Gordon L. Berry and Claudia Mitchell-Kernan, editors, *Television and the Socialization of the Minority Child*. New York: Academic Press, 1982, p. 82)

B.   Interracial understanding is not harmed.
   1.   The advocate's own source indicates that television only reenforces previously held stereotypes; it does not create them.

The more important factor is perceived attributes of TV performers; the viewer's interpretation of the content stereotypes is closely related to parallel beliefs about the real world. . . . Thus, it is the combination of exposure and interpretation that determines impact, which is consistent with the traditional conception that "what the child brings to TV" is just as crucial as "what TV does to the child." (Charles K. Atkin, Professor of Communication, Michigan State University, Bradley S. Greenberg, Professor of Communication, Michigan State University, and Steven McDermott, Assistant Professor of Speech, University of Georgia, "Television and Race Role Socialization," *Journalism Quarterly*, Autumn 1983, 60, p. 414)

   2.   The advocate's own source indicates that television is not a major source of information about minorities.

According to the self-reports of the young whites, TV is a major source of learning about the world. Almost half said most of what they learn about occupations and certain aspects of family relations and sex roles comes from television. Learning about blacks from TV is not so prevalent. When asked if they learn most of the things they know about "black people" from TV, 24% said yes and 76% said no (ignoring those who said "not sure"). (Charles K. Atkin, Bradley S. Greenberg, and Steven McDermott, "Television and Race Role Socialization," *Journalism Quarterly*, Autumn 1983, 60, p. 412)

II.   Even if a reason existed to increase the regulation of children's television, the advocate's proposal should not be adopted.
  A.   The advocate's proposal will not solve the problem of stereotyping.
    1.   The advocate only mandates the creation of a minimum percentage of minority roles.
    2.   The advocate indicates that at present minorities are stereotyped on children's television.
    3.   Since the advocate's proposal says nothing about the nature of these roles, only their number, it will result in children's television that just presents more stereotypical portrayals of minorities.
  B.   The advocate's proposal cannot overcome the inherent barrier to increased integration in children's television, the forces of the marketplace.
    1.   The advocate's proposal allows broadcasters to demonstrate compliance on either a show-by-show or an across-the-board basis.
    2.   The advocate indicates that at present children's television is very profitable.
    3.   Therefore, the advocate's proposal will not increase the integration of children's television. Circumventing it by dumping all minority characters into a single show is the easiest way to comply and the best way to protect current profits.

C.   The advocate's proposal is unworkable.
   1.   All television is children's television.

Only about 15% of children's viewing time is with so-called children's programs. Should the form and content of programs in prime time, watched by large numbers of children, be determined by the presumed needs of this younger audience? (Eli A. Rubinstein, Adjunct Research Professor in Mass Communication, University of North Carolina, Chapel Hill, "Research on Children and Television: A Critique," *Journal of Broadcasting*, Fall 1981, 25, p. 392)

   2.   Prime-time television has the same characteristics that the advocate identifies as problematical in daytime and weekend programming.

Results of their long-term analysis indicate that television drama presents a world in which men outnumber women three to one; blacks and Hispanics are underrepresented; most majority types get proportionally more leading roles than do minority types; weekend-daytime children's programs both conceal and exaggerate the inequalities reflected in prime time. (F. Earle Barcus, Director of the Communication Research Center, Boston University, *Images of Life on Children's Television*. New York: Praeger, 1983, p. 74)

   3.   Therefore, the advocate's proposal is unworkable. It either fails to deal with most of what children see or dooms society to endless litigation over whether broadcasters intended a particular program to attract the two- to eleven-year old audience.
D.   The advocate's proposal is disadvantageous because it undermines the First Amendment.
   1.   The First Amendment guarantees several freedoms, one of which is speech.
   2.   In terms of television, free speech suggests that it is better for several different broadcasters to establish program content than for a single central government to do so.

Each of us would like television to offer more of the kinds of programming which he or she thinks is important. But broadcaster time is finite. If one kind of program is put on, then another has to be excluded. Clearly the first amendment means that such value judgments will not be imposed by Government. (John Blessington, Vice President, Personnel, CBS/Broadcast Group, "Children and Television," Hearings before the Subcommittee on Telecommunications, Consumer Protection, and Finance of the Committee on Energy and Commerce, House of Representatives, 98th Congress, First Session, March 16, 1983, p. 149)

   3.   The advocate's proposal imposes governmental values on program content by mandating minority roles.
   4.   Even critics of children's television stop short of advocating such governmental intervention.

FCC guidelines should address the amount of programming and advertising designed for children, not its content. (Peggy Charren, Action for Children's Television, "Children and Television," Hearings before the Subcommittee on Telecommunications, Consumer Protection, and Finance of the Committee on Energy and Commerce, House of Representatives, 98th Congress, First Session, March 16, 1983, p. 50)

5.   Such intervention is inimical to the values of a free and democratic society.

The accumulated evidence (as well as our own experience) also suggests that it would be possible to design TV entertainment for children on a conscious basis that, given their level of viewing (15 to 20 hours a week, week in week out, from infancy to adulthood) would exert great influence. This, apparently, is the strategy for socializing the young employed in some dictatorships. Such systematic use of television entertainment to influence children is undoubtedly a subtle but effective type of brainwashing. (Robert M. Liebert, Professor of Psychology, State University of New York (SUNY) Stony Brook, Joyce N. Sprafkin, Director of the Laboratory of Communication SUNY Stony Brook, and Emily S. Davidson, Associate Professor of Psychology, Texas A&M University, *The Early Window: Effects of Television on Children and Youth* (2nd Ed.). New York: Pergamon Press, 1982, p. 211)

6.   On balance, no matter how bad children's television may be, any form of governmental content control is more harmful to the best interests of society.

Were you right, did you find the same flaw in the advocate's case that her opponent did? The example of policy advocacy was specifically structured to allow us to demonstrate argumentation on the third stock issue, and to reemphasize the importance of the stock issues to both advocates and opponents as they analyze propositions and construct cases. If the advocate's case was not so clearly flawed, the opponent might have had less to say about the third stock issue and more about the first. He might have argued that programs presently exist that teach children how to be critical viewers, that these programs work, and that they are capable of being expanded. In other words, he could have discussed a minor repair. He didn't in this case because it would have weakened his solvency argument on stereotyping. He decided it was better to leave the advocate in a dilemma, having to accept either that stereotyping was not very harmful or that her proposal would not solve it.

Summary of Policy Opposition

1.   Is the advocate's case prima facie, and does it fulfill the burden of proof?
  A.   Has the advocate failed to provide a rationale for change?
  B.   Has the advocate failed to provide a specific proposal for change?
  C.   Has the advocate failed to consider the consequences of change?
2.   Will the opponent choose to argue both the first and third stock issues or only one of them?
3.   What is the philosophy on which opposition rests?
  A.   What will the opponent defend?
  B.   How does the opponent wish the audience to view the proposed change?
4.   Will the opponent accept the advocate's definition of terms?
  A.   Has the advocate "broken faith" with the audience by distorting the meaning of the proposition?

   B. Has the advocate improperly included or excluded things in defining terms?
5. How will the reason for change be opposed?
   A. Is the disparity as great as the advocate has alleged? (challenges to extent arguments)
   B. Is the disparity as severe as the advocate has alleged? (challenges to effect arguments)
   C. Are there extenuating circumstances that produce the disparity? (challenges to inherency arguments)
   D. Are there other possible causes for the alleged disparity? (challenges to inherency arguments)
6. Will existing institutions ameliorate the disparity?
   A. Will the normal pattern of societal change resolve the disparity given time?
   B. Short of the change called for by the advocate, what minor repairs are available to remedy the disparity?
7. What are the deficiencies in the proposed solution?
   A. Is the solution capable of solving the problem?
   B. Are conditions necessary for the solution to work present or will something preclude the proposal's ability to solve the problem? Can the proposal be circumvented?
   C. Is the solution workable?
8. What are the consequences of the proposed solution?
   A. Will the proposal bring about the advantages claimed by the advocate?
   B. Will the proposal cause disadvantages, or greater evils?
   C. Are these disadvantages unique to the advocate's proposal?
9. Will a counterproposal be offered?
   A. Is it an equally acceptable alternative to the advocate's proposal?
   B. Is it nontopical and competitive with the advocate's proposal?

LEARNING ACTIVITIES

1. In class, present a brief description of a topic you believe suitable for policy argumentation. Lead your classmates in a discussion of which approach to case construction for policy advocacy (traditional, comparative advantage, or goals-criteria) would be most feasible for the topic you described.
2. From the *Congressional Record,* choose a recent example of a legislative debate that addressed some disparity. In a written or oral report, discuss the argumentation. How were the issues of reason for change, proposal for change, and consequences of change handled by both advocates and opponents?
3. Identify the disparity implied in each of the following policy propositions. In small groups, brainstorm possible fact and value arguments that could be used in developing the advocate's case, and proposals to achieve the change. Now discuss the arguments you would use in opposing the cases just brainstormed.
   A. Puerto Rico should be granted statehood.
   B. The federal government should institute a national sales tax.
   C. The ability to pass a nationally standardized proficiency test of basic skills should be a requirement for high school graduation.
   D. Private ownership of firearms should be more rigorously controlled.
   E. The United States should significantly decrease its military commitments in the Middle East.

4. Go back and examine the advocate's case for increased federal regulation of children's television. In small groups, brainstorm alternative proposals for change that would address the reason for change she established while avoiding the workability problems and disadvantages of her proposal.
5. Written/oral assignment: Frame your own proposition of policy. Develop a prima facie case for the advocate's position. Respond in opposition to the arguments advocating the policy proposition, either your own or those of a classmate, as assigned by your instructor.

SUGGESTED SUPPLEMENTARY READINGS

CHESEBRO, J. W. Beyond the Orthodox: The Criteria Case. *Journal of the American Forensic Association*, 1971, 7, 208–215.

Chesebro discusses the requirements and strategies of the goals-criteria case. He provides a rationale for using this approach to policy argumentation, suggesting it embodies value principles that are necessary conditions for policy formation. The article contains an excellent discussion of the standards of proof such a case must meet in order to be prima facie, along with a description of the pattern of case construction.

PATTERSON, J. W., AND ZAREFSKY, D. *Contemporary Debate*. Boston: Houghton-Mifflin, 1983.

This book's focus is policy argumentation, its emphasis is competitive debate, and it probably represents the state of that art. Chapters 7 through 13 are devoted to the theory and practice of affirmative and negative case building, refutation, cross-examination, and judging. This book is good resource for the nondebater who is interested in learning more about policy argumentation.

SMITH, C. R., & HUNSAKER, D. M., *The Bases of Argument*. Indianapolis: Bobbs-Merrill, 1972.

This book presents a broad view of the use of argument in everyday situations, although it is primarily concerned with policy propositions. We especially recommend Chapters 8 and 9 for their discussion of the strategy of refutation and attack, and the options available to arguers.

APPENDIX

One specialized format for argumentation is competitive debate. The setting in which argumentation takes place is formalized, and specific time limits and responsibilities are imposed on those who participate. Debates may take place in argumentation classes as a learning experience, or you may find yourself involved in debate in an intercollegiate contest between teams representing different schools. There are even national debate championship tournaments.

Since the orientation of this book has precluded a focus on the specialized form that is competitive debate, this appendix provides an introduction to debate. Entire books are devoted to the tactics and strategies of competitive debate, as well as numerous articles in the *Journal of the American Forensic Association.* Once you have learned the basic skills of arguing, you may choose to delve further into debate technique. This appendix will assist you in recognizing debate formats and introduce you to debate technique. Winning debates is a matter of your skill and preparation. Had we cast this appendix in the interrogative paradigm of our chapter titles, we would have called it *What Are the Rules of the Game?*

DEBATE FORMATS

While there are many different debate formats, and there are different kinds of propositions argued, academic debate in general has the following characteristics:

1. Teams of debaters, usually two to a side, will be prepared to argue both sides of a proposition. In debate parlance, they are called affirmative and negative rather than advocate and opponent.
2. All teams will argue the same proposition, often a policy proposition, for the entire year, although value topics that change at midyear are used by the Cross Examination Debate Association (CEDA). Propositions address broad issues of national concern.
3. The debate is judged by a single individual or a panel of three, five, or seven individuals who determine the "winner" of the debate based on which team demonstrated the greater skill or had the better arguments.

Like all communication, debate is rule-governed behavior. One set of rules pertains to the order in which members of both teams make their presentations and the length of time they have for each presentation. This is commonly referred to as the **format** for the debate. While slight variations may be found, most debates use one of two formats. The first is called the **traditional format,** in which each team member presents a constructive and a rebuttal speech. While the time limits for the speeches may vary, the format looks like this:

Traditional Format

First Affirmative Constructive Speech	10	minutes
First Negative Constructive Speech	10	minutes
Second Affirmative Constructive Speech	10	minutes
Second Negative Constructive Speech	10	minutes
First Negative Rebuttal Speech	5	minutes
First Affirmative Rebuttal Speech	5	minutes
Second Negative Rebuttal Speech	5	minutes
Second Affirmative Rebuttal Speech	5	minutes

Notice that the affirmative team has the first and last speeches, and that the negative team has two speeches in a row. (We will have more to say about this when we discuss the responsibilities of the speakers.) We should also point out that the debate may take longer than an hour to complete, since it has become customary to allow both teams a total of five or ten minutes preparation time during the course of the debate. This is time that may be used as the team members see fit.

The second commonly used format is the **cross-examination format.** The order and length of constructive and rebuttal speeches stays roughly the same, but both teams are given the opportunity to interrogate each other. The format looks like this;

Cross-Examination Format

First Affirmative Constructive Speech	10 minutes
Cross-Examination of the First Affirmative Speaker	3 minutes

First Negative Constructive Speech	10 minutes
Cross-Examination of the First Negative Speaker	3 minutes
Second Affirmative Constructive Speech	10 minutes
Cross-Examination of the Second Affirmative Speaker	3 minutes
Second Negative Constructive Speech	10 minutes
Cross-Examination of the Second Negative Speaker	3 minutes
First Negative Rebuttal Speech	5 minutes
First Affirmative Rebuttal Speech	5 minutes
Second Negative Rebuttal Speech	5 minutes
Second Affirmative Rebuttal Speech	5 minutes

The length of constructive and rebuttal speeches are sometimes shortened to eight and four minutes respectively to reduce the amount of time that it takes to complete the debate, since preparation time is generally provided. The Cross Examination Debate Association does this in its debates on value propositions. Regardless of the subtle variations, debate formats establish fixed amounts of speaking and preparation time and give equal time to both parties to the dispute.

Less common than either of these formats for debates between teams of individuals is the **Lincoln-Douglas Format,** named after the historical one-on-one debates between these two candidates for the Senate. This format is often favored for in-class debating. The variations in this format are numerous. The basic rules for Lincoln-Douglas debating are that "each speaker presents a constructive position, questions the opponent, replies to questions, refutes the opponent's position, and defends his or her own position" (Patterson & Zarefsky, 1983, p. 13).

SPEAKER RESPONSIBILITIES

In both the traditional and cross-examination styles of debating, each speaker has certain duties he or she must perform. The order of presentation, with affirmative speakers beginning and ending the debate, is based on presumption, which lies with the negative, and the requirements of the burden of proof, which fall on the affirmative. The debate begins with the **first affirmative constructive speech.** This presentation establishes the basis of the affirmative case and normally includes all the claims, evidence, and reasoning that would, if unanswered, allow the judge to vote in favor of adopting the proposition.

In value debate, this would involve presenting a case as discussed in Chapter 9. Identifying the value object, establishing the criteria by which it is to be evaluated, and providing arguments supporting the appropriateness of judging the value object in this manner. In policy debate, the first affirmative speaker may only discuss the first stock issue, reason for change, if the affirmative is employing the traditional need-plan pattern of organization. However, if one of the other patterns of organization is used, the first affirmative is responsible for presenting both a proposal and a reason for change. Regardless of whether the proposition is one of value or policy, and irrespective of the pattern of organization followed, the first affirmative speaker establishes her team's interpretation of the proposition. The second affirmative may add new arguments that further develop, or in the case of the traditional organization pattern complete, that interpretation, but if the first affirmative speech fails to establish a prima facie position the affirmative has lost before the debate has even begun.

Assuming a prima facie case has been presented, what are the duties of the **first negative constructive speech?** The first negative speaker establishes the philosophy of the negative team—their stand on the proposition. If the negative team plans to question the definitions of key terms offered by the affirmative, those questions are raised in this speech and alternative definitions are offered. If the affirmative definitions are so outrageous that their case appears to be nontopical, the first negative speaker normally argues this as well. If the negative team intends to defend the present system of values or policies, the first negative presents these arguments. This speech responds directly to the first affirmative presentation and establishes the points of clash between the two teams. In policy debating, this speech usually focuses on the first stock issue, leaving the second and third stock issues to the second negative speaker. This is called division of labor, and you will see the wisdom of it when we discuss the rebuttal speeches.

The **second affirmative constructive speech** attempts to repair the damage done to the affirmative case by the first negative speaker. Since the initial points of clash between the two teams were defined by the first negative, the second affirmative must respond point by point—for three reasons. First, if there are arguments relating to definitions or topicality, the affirmative will be unable to carry argumentation forward successfully unless an attempt is made to resolve these disputes in the affirmative's favor. Second, the negative team is about to get two turns at bat, back to back. If the second affirmative does not respond to the first negative arguments, the first affirmative rebuttalist will be swamped. Third, it is a rule in debate that while new evidence may be introduced in rebuttal speeches, new arguments may not be. The constructive speeches are the appropriate place for presenting original arguments.

In addition to repairing any damage, the second affirmative should point out arguments that still stand, arguments with which the first negative chose not to clash. This is best accomplished if the second affirmative responds to the negative arguments in terms of the basic case structure used in the first affirmative constructive speech. Finally, in policy debating, the second affirmative must present the proposal for change if it was not included in the first affirmative's speech. In general, the second affirmative has the responsibility of rebuilding and extending the affirmative case.

The **second negative constructive speech** is the final speech in the constructive phase of the debate. The second negative generally deals with the stock issues that his or her partner left unargued. In value debate this frequently takes the form of examining society's willingness to accept the new value hierarchy proposed by the affirmative. In policy debate this means examining the affirmative proposal in terms of solvency, circumvention, workability, and disadvantages.

The second negative speaker must be careful to listen to his or her partner so that their arguments are not contradictory. The easiest way for the affirmative team to get off the hook on a disadvantage or solvency argument is to point out that one of the first negative's inherency or minor repair arguments reduces the disadvantage's impact or solves the solvency problem. Affirmative speakers have to listen to each other as well, but they usually do not have as much of a problem with contradictions, since they know where they want to go, and don't want to go, with their case. They have argued it many times before. The negative may be hearing it for the first time, grasping for anything to defeat it.

The **first negative rebuttal speech** begins the final phase of the debate. These back-to-back speeches are sometimes called the negative block. If the negative speakers do not maintain a clear division of labor, the first negative will waste time repeating what the second negative has just said; thus, any advantage that might have been gained from consecutive speeches will have been squandered. The first negative rebuttalist's responsibilities are similar to the second affirmative constructive speaker's—rebuild and extend on the points of clash established in the constructive speeches. It is important for the first negative rebuttalist to respond to the second affirmative's arguments, not merely repeat his own. This rebuttal should identify arguments the negative has "won" outright because they were not contested by the second affirmative. It should crystalize the important arguments to which the affirmative, during their rebuttals, must respond with new evidence and further reasoning, but no new arguments. If it suddenly dawns on the first negative that all the affirmative's evidence is over twenty years old, too bad. These are rebuttal speeches and no new arguments can be advanced.

The **first affirmative rebuttal speech** is, strategically speaking, the most important and most difficult speech in the entire debate. Attacks that took the second negative ten minutes to present must be answered in half the time, and the first affirmative rebuttalist cannot totally ignore what the first negative has had to say, especially if definitions and/or topicality are still in dispute. In policy debate, the fire drill goes like this: First, answer challenges on definitions and/or topicality. Second, respond to second negative constructive arguments. Third, respond to key issues extended in the first negative rebuttal. In value debate, the order of priority is the same, although the nature of the issues discussed is different.

The **second negative rebuttal speech** is the negative team's last speech. While he or she should respond to what the first affirmative rebuttalist had to say about arguments presented in the second negative constructive speech, the second negative rebuttalist must remember that his or her primary mission is to give the judge a reason to vote for the negative team. This speech should cover the main arguments favoring rejection of the affirmative team's arguments, regardless of whether they were initiated by the first or second negative speaker. This is the only point in the debate where observing the division of labor between the negative speakers hurts the team.

The **second affirmative rebuttal speech** is the final speech in the debate. Like the second negative rebuttal, it summarizes the debate but from the affirmative team's perspective. The second negative rebuttalist probably established reasons why the decision should favor the negative. The second affirmative rebuttalist should respond to these, as well as pointing out things the negative team has not contested that suggest an affirmative decision. In essence, both final rebuttal speakers attempt to provide the judge with a set of rules or criteria on which to decide the debate, which favors their side's interpretation of the proposition.

BURDEN OF CLASH

As already indicated, the order of speeches reflects the exigencies of presumption and burden of proof. The order of speaking also puts certain obligations on both teams in terms of going forward with the debate. Recall that the first affirmative speech must be prima facie, otherwise the debate is over before it really begins, although the rest of the speeches will be given. The negative team must move the debate forward by **establishing clash.** The negative is obligated to respond to what the affirmative has presented in some way, even if their only argument is that the affirmative case is so far off the topic that topicality is the only thing they have to argue.

Successive speakers have the responsiblity of **maintaining clash.** Each speech moves the judge closer to making a decision by responding to what the other side has just said. The only exception might be the second negative constructive speech, which, because of division of labor, usually leaves second affirmative constructive arguments to the first negative rebuttalist. It is not sufficient merely to repeat your arguments. You must respond to your opponent's arguments to move the controversy toward resolution. Not only must arguments be presented but the points of clash between the two teams must be identified. In so doing, both sides have the obligation to make an honest effort to develop arguments that do not distort, deceive, or misrepresent what they know to be true.

CROSS-EXAMINATION

The responsibilities of the speakers and the obligations to establish and maintain clash are relevant to both traditional and cross-examination debating. You may have known much about speaker responsibilities from having read this book. However, cross-examination places some unique opportunities at the disposal of debaters. You should approach the opportunity to ask and answer questions as a chance to advance the debate in a way that favors your side.

Cross-examination usually covers the speech immediately preceding it, although it might cover lines of argument extending from several preceding speeches. You use cross-examination for various purposes.

Cross-examination allows you to gain information about your opponent's reasoning. What kinds of inferences link evidence to claims, and what kinds of inferences link one argument to another? If they are illogical, you can point this out in a later speech.

Cross-examination allows you to prevent possible misunderstandings. If you are not sure whether the speaker said "million" or "billion," ask. In this way you ensure that the argument you advance in a later speech cannot be dismissed because it is based on a misinterpretation.

Cross-examination allows you to probe for and point out inconsistencies either within a single speech or between two speakers. If you are a first affirmative rebuttalist, remember that negative teams are especially vulnerable to contradictions if they do not listen to each other. Finding the contradictions makes your task much easier.

Cross-examination allows you to advance your own position. You can ask questions whose answers point toward the conclusion you wish the judge to draw.

Notice that all these purposes represent means to an end, rather than an end in and of themselves. Cross-examination is used to set up arguments in subsequent speeches. No one ever won a debate with an imitation of Perry Mason during cross-examination. Debates are won in the constructive and rebuttal speeches. Whatever gains you think you may have made will be realized only if you capitalize on them in your speeches.

Preparation is as important to success in cross-examination debate as it is in traditional debate. Preparation begins with a thorough understanding of your topic. Cross-examination quickly exposes limited knowledge. Be prepared to take the role of both questioner and respondent. In terms of the first three purposes discussed here, you obviously have to listen to what your opponent is saying and decide on the spot what you need to ask. However, in regard to the fourth, you can plan a series of questions in advance. A series of questions is needed because even the dullest respondent will not readily admit to something favoring your position. If your positon is that the poor are denied access to cable television because of its cost, asking "Don't you agree that the poor are denied access to cable because of cost?" will probably elicit a no. Assuming you had the supporting evidence, you would be better served by asking the following series of questions:

> The poor own just as many television sets, proportionally speaking, as the rest of the population, don't they?
> They watch television just about as much as everyone else, don't they?
> The majority of them live in urban areas served by cable systems, don't they?
> Yet few poor people are cable subscribers. Doesn't this suggest that the cost of cable service is a barrier access for the poor?

Even though this last question might still elicit the same answer, your position would be advanced for two reasons. First, you would have planted a seed in the judge's mind that the signs point to your conclusion. Second, you could always ask one more question: "OK, you tell me why the poor don't subscribe to cable?"

You may want to think twice before you ask that question. When attempting to advance your position through cross-examination, always ask questions to which you already know the answer. Your motive is to educate the judge, not yourself. Thus, if you do not know the answer to a question, it is sometimes safer not to ask it, else you will find you have presented your opponents with an opportunity to advance their position. While you will be fairly sure of the answers your questions will elicit, you still need to listen to the answers and adapt subsequent questions or even abandon a line of questioning if it is going nowhere.

Like the role of questioner, which allows for some prior planning, the role of respondent allows you to prepare your position. While you cannot anticipate every question that might be asked, you can anticipate the kinds of questions that will probably be asked about your affirmative case and the negative arguments you typically use. Prepare for answering by having your partner interrogate you.

Just as the various speaker positions in the debate have different responsibilities, so the roles of questioner and respondent carry with them specific requirements. Neither questioner nor respondent may confer with colleagues during the cross-examination period. The questioner is in charge during cross-examination. He or she asks the questions, being careful that the respondent does not try to turn the tables. Questions should be as brief and clear as possible, to encourage brief and clear responses. While the questioner cannot require yes or no responses, he or she need not tolerate filibustering by the respondent. The respondent should attempt to be as direct as possible but may qualify answers if necessary and refuse to answer questions that are patently unfair. If it becomes necessary to qualify an answer or refuse to provide one, it is important that the respondent explain why.

Both the questioner and respondent should remember that the debate is a public-speaking situation. Both parties should refrain from making speeches, and questions and answers should be addressed clearly and distinctly so that the judge may understand both. The most important thing to remember is to remain composed. Do not become hostile or defensive, and do not do things that would produce these behaviors in the other person.

To know what to ask in cross-examination, or what to argue in your next speech, requires not only argumentative skills but a sense of what is going on in the debate as a whole. What is your team's position? What has the other team disputed? What has the other team conceded? What has your partner said? What are you going to say? No matter how good your memory is, learning how to keep a flow sheet of the debate as it unfolds is your best memory aid. A flow sheet tracks the progress of arguments during a debate and is nothing more than a specialized outline.

FLOW SHEETING

In class, you fill page after page with notes on what your professor has to say. Now suppose that you have two professors who constantly disagree with each other. The only way you can keep things straight when you study is to have two sets of notes side by side. Suddenly you realize things would be much easier if you drew a line down the middle of each page in your notebook, and put what one professor has to say on one side and what the other says on the other. If you wrote notes for one class in black ink, and the other in red, you could tell at a glance who said what. You have just discovered the flow sheet.

Instead of two columns, most people divide their paper into as many as eight columns, one for each speech. Unless you are able to write very small and have very good eyesight, something bigger than the standard eight and one-half by eleven notebook paper is helpful; contest debaters often use large artist's sketch pads. Outline each successive speech in the next column to the right, placing opposite each other arguments that clash and connecting them with an arrow. If nothing is to the right of an argument, it probably means it has gone uncontested. To cram lots of information into a narrow column, use special symbols and abbreviations. You will have to develop your own because there is no standard set. For instance, one of your authors uses the acronym NAIR for "new argument in rebuttals." With a little practice you will quickly develop your own shorthand.

DEBATE JUDGES

Debates are judged and winners and losers are determined, but unlike the audiences for argumentation, which may vary considerably, the audience that counts in debate is somewhat more predictable. For the most part, debate judges are normally trained professionals, who engaged in the activity themselves as undergraduates, presently coach, or have coached debate teams, and teach courses in argumentation and debate. For debaters this means that concepts like presumption and burden of proof will not be alien to the judge of a debate as they might be to a lay audience for oral or written argumentation. Debaters are well advised to avoid "teaching" the debate judge in the same way they would the lay audience. If you intend to make a topicality argument, make it and go on. Debate judges dislike being lectured on theory, so they need not be informed of the gravity of a successful challenge to topicality. Unlike the lay audience, debate judges make a sincere effort to leave their biases at the door and judge the debate round on the basis of which team debated better, rather than which team they agreed with most. For debaters this means that an idea that could have passed unproven or undeveloped before a lay audience, because it approached the status of a premise, must be proven to the debate judge. If, for example, the topic relates to unemployment, a trained debate judge will expect proof for the notion that full employment is a national goal and listen to counter arguments that it is not a goal.

That is not to say that debate judges are bias-free. In regard to style, some judges dislike what is sometimes referred to as NDT (National Debate Tournament) style, which is characterized by rapid rates of delivery, the reading of large quantities of evidence at the expense of explanation, and the excessive use of debate jargon ("On PMA 1 . . ."); other judges may not object to this style. The formation of CEDA was, in part, a reaction to some of the perceived excesses of NDT debate. While it is unlikely that many teams have ever lost rounds for talking too fast, rate can undermine your understandability and credibility with a particular judge. In regard to the judging philosophy that shapes their decisions, some judges of policy debate see their role as that of a hypothesis tester while others see themselves as policy makers. Some judges will not consider successfully advanced topicality arguments as sufficient, in and of themselves, to warrant voting for the negative team. Other judges have a very narrow view of the range of possible meanings for the debate topic and seem to go out of their way to accept topicality arguments as a means of registering their displeasure with narrow interpretations of the topic. For debaters, the only saving grace is that they have to adapt only to one person, the judge, instead of to a group of people with undisclosed biases. The key is to learn the tendencies of those who judge and be flexible enough to adapt.

REFERENCES

BARCUS, E. F. *Images of Life on Children's Television.* New York: Prager, 1983.

BAROL, B., BAILEY, E., AND ZABARSKY, M. Tuning in on Kiddie Videos. *Newsweek,* June 25, 1984, p. 48.

BOLLER, P. F., Jr. *Presidential Anecdotes.* New York: Penguine, 1981.

BOORSTIN, D. Americans are "Haunted by a Fear of Technology." *U.S. News & World Reports,* March 17, 1980, p. 70.

BROCKRIEDE, W. E., AND EHNINGER, D. E. Toulmin on Argument: An Interpretation and Application. *Quarterly Journal of Speech,* 1960, 46, pp. 44-53.

BRYDON, S. R. Presumption in Value Topic Debates: The Three Faces of Eve. Western Speech Communication Association, Albuquerque, N.Mex., February 19-22, 1983. Unpublished Paper.

CHERUBIN, J. Toys are Programs Too. *Channels,* May-June 1984, p. 31-33.

COMMUNICATION RESEARCH ASSOCIATES. *A Workbook for Interpersonal Communication* (3rd ed.). Dubuque, Iowa: Kendall/Hunt, 1983.

COMSTOCK, G. Juvenile Crime. In Meg Schwartz (Ed.) *TV & Teens.* Reading, Mass.: Addison-Wesley, 1982.

COST BOMBSHELLS, *Time,* July 25, 1983, p. 16.

COWAN, J. L. The Uses of Argument—An Apology for Logic. In D. Ehninger (Ed.), *Contemporary Rhetoric.* Glenview, Ill.: Scott, Foresman, 1972.

CRABLE, R. E. *Argumentation as Communication: Reasoning with Receivers.* Columbus, Ohio: Chas. E. Merrill, 1976.

DUDCZAK, C. A. Value Argument in a Competitive Setting: An Inhibition to Ordinary Language Use. In D. Zarefsky, M. O. Sillars, & J. Rhodes (Eds.), *Argument in Transition: Proceedings of the Third Summer Conference.* Annandale, Va.: Speech Communication Association, 1983.

EHNINGER, D. E. *Influence, Belief, and Argument.* Glenview, Ill.: Scott, Foresman, 1974.

EHNINGER, D. E., AND BROCKRIEDE, W. *Decision by Debate.* New York: Dodd, Mead, & Co., 1963.

EISENBERG, A. M., AND ILARDO, J. A. *Argument: A Guide to Formal and Informal Debate* (2nd ed.). Englewood Cliffs, N.J.: Prentice-Hall, 1980.

FISHER, W. R., AND SAYLES, E. M. The Nature and Functions of Argument. In G. R. Miller & R. Nilsen (Eds.), *Perspectives on Argumentation*. Chicago: Scott, Foresman, 1966.

GODFREY, L. R. (Ed.). *Scientists Confront Creationism*. New York: Norton, 1983.

GOLDEN, J. L., BERQUIST, G. F., AND COLEMAN, W. P. *The Rhetoric of Western Thought* (3rd ed.). Dubuque, Iowa: Kendall/Hunt, 1983.

HART, R. P., AND BURKS, D. M. Rhetorical Sensitivity and Social Interaction. *Speech Monographs*, 1972, 39, pp. 75-91.

HECHINGER, C. Happy Mother's Day. *Newsweek*, May 11, 1981, p. 19.

HOLT, F. L. An Olympic-Size Delusion. *Newsweek*, July 16, 1984, p.16.

JENSEN, J. V. *Argumentation: Reasoning in Communication*. New York: D. Van Nostrand, 1981.

JOHNSTONE, H. W., JR. Introduction. In M. Natson & H. W. Johnstone, Jr. (Eds.), *Philosophy, Rhetoric, and Argumentation*. University Park, Pa.: Pennsylvania State University Press, 1965.

KARP, W. Where the Do-Gooders Went Wrong. *Channels*, March-April 1984, pp. 41-47.

KELLERMAN, J. Big Brother and Big Mother. *Newsweek*, January 12, 1981, p. 15.

KOEHLER, J. W., ANATOL, K. W. E., & APPLEBAUM, R. L. *Organizational Communication*. New York: Holt, Rinehart & Winston, 1981.

KOHAN, J. The Vocabulary of Confrontation. *Time*, January 2, 1984, pp. 42-43.

KORDA, M. How to Be a Leader. *Newsweek*, January 5, 1981, p. 7.

LAGRAVE, C. W. Inherency: A Historical View. In David A. Thomas (Ed.), *Advanced Debate*. Skokie, Ill.: National Textbook Company, 1975.

LIEBERT, R. M., SPRAFKIN, J. W., AND DAVIDSON, E. S. *The Early Window: Effects of Television on Children and Youth* (2nd Ed.). New York: Pergamon Press, 1982.

LIPKIN, M. On Lying to Patients. *Newsweek*, June 4, 1979, p. 13.

MATLON, R. J. Debating Propositions of Value. *Journal of the American Forensic Association*, 1978, 14, pp. 194-204.

MILLS, G. E. *Reason in Controversy*. Boston: Allyn & Bacon, 1968.

MINNICK, W. C. *The Art of Persuasion*. Boston: Houghton-Mifflin, 1968.

MORRIS, L. Let the Eskimos Hunt. *Newsweek*, May 21, 1979, p. 13.

MORRIS, J. S. Television Portrayal and the Socialization of the American Indian Child. In G. L. Berry & C. Mitchell-Kernan (Eds.), *Television and the Socialization of the Minority Child*. New York: Academic Press, 1982.

NAISBITT, J. *Megatrends*. New York: Warner Books, 1982.

NILSEN, T. R. *Ethics of Speech Communication* (2nd ed.). Indianapolis: Bobbs-Merrill, 1974.

PATTERSON, J. W., AND ZAREFSKY, D. *Contemporary Debate*. Boston: Houghton-Mifflin, 1983.

PHILLIPS, G. M., BUTT, D. E., AND METZGER, N. J. *Communication in Education: A Rhetoric of Schooling and Learning*. New York: Holt, Rinehart & Winston, 1974.

RESCHER, N. *Introduction to Value Theory*. Englewood Cliffs, N.J.: Prentice-Hall, 1969.

RIEKE, R. D., AND SILLARS, M. O. *Argumentation and the Decision Making Process*. Glenview, Ill.: Scott, Foresman, 1984.

RIVES, S. G. Ethical Argumentation. *Journal of the American Forensic Association*, 1964, 1, pp. 79-85.

ROBERTS, R. (Trans.). *Aristotle, the Rhetoric*. New York: Modern Library, 1954.

ROKEACH, M. *The Nature of Human Values*. New York: MacMillan, Free Press, 1973.

SANDELL, K. L., AND OSTROFF, D. E. Political Information Content and Children's Political Socialization. *Journal of Broadcasting*, 1981, 25, pp. 49-59.

SINGER, J. L., AND SINGER, D. E. Come Back, Mister Rogers, Come Back. *Psychology Today*, March 1979, pp. 56-60.

SPROULE, J. M. The Psychological Burden of Proof: On the Evolutionary Development of Richard Whately's Theory of Presumption. *Communication Monographs*, 1976, 43, pp. 115-29.

SPROULE, J. M. *Argument: Language and Its Influence*. New York: McGraw-Hill, 1980.

TALBOTT, S. The Case Against Star Wars Weapons. *Time*, May 7, 1984, pp. 81-82.

TOULMIN, S. *The Uses of Argument*. London: Cambridge University Press, 1958.

TOULMIN, S., RIEKE, R., AND JANIK, A. *An Introduction to Reasoning* (2nd ed.). New York: MacMillan, 1984.

VASILIUS, J. Presumption, Presumption, Wherefore Art Thou Presumption. Desert Argumentation Symposium, Tucson, Ariz.: March 2, 1980. Unpublished Paper.

WALTER, O. M., AND SCOTT, R. L. *Thinking and Speaking* (5th Ed.). New York: MacMillan, 1984.

WARNICK, B. Arguing Value Propositions. *Journal of the American Forensic Association,* 1981, 18, pp. 109-19.

WENZEL, L. Reach Out and Write Someone. *Newsweek,* January 9, 1984, p. 14.

WHATELY, R. *Elements of Rhetoric,* Douglas Ehninger (Ed.). Carbondale, Ill.: Southern Illinois University Press, 1963. (Originally Published, 1828)

WILCOX, J. R. The Argument from Analogy: A New Look. Central States Speech Association, Minneapolis, April 1973. Unpublished Paper.

WILL, G. F. "Peacekeeping" in War. *Newsweek,* January 5, 1981, p. 7.

WILSON, B. A. *The Anatomy of Argument.* Lanham, Maryland: University Press of America, 1980.

WINDES, R. R., AND HASTINGS, A. *Argumentation and Advocacy.* New York: Random House, 1965.

YOUNG, M. J. The Use of Evidence in Value Argument. In J. Rhodes & S. Newell (Eds.), *Conference on Argumentation.* Falls Church, Va.: Speech Communication Association, 1980.

ZAREFSKY, D. A Reformulation of the Concept of Presumption. Central States Speech Association Convention, Chicago, April 7, 1972. Unpublished Paper.

ZAREFSKY, D. Criteria for Evaluating Non-Policy Argument. Western Speech Communication Association, San Francisco, November 24, 1976. Unpublished Paper.

ZIEGELMUELLER, G. W., AND DAUSE, C. A. *Argumentation: Inquiry and Advocacy.* Englewood Cliffs, N.J.: Prentice-Hall, 1975.

Index

Absurdity, reducing a claim to, 125-26
Academic argument:
  claims in, 54
  presumption in, 137
  prima facie cases in, 24
  propositions for, 44-46, 152, 176
Accuracy of evidence, 75-76, 81
Action, belief and, 175, 178
Actual issues, 139
Adaptation rule, 39
Ad hominem argument, 119
Ad ignorantum argument, 121
Ad populum argument, 122
Advocate:
  burden of proof and the, 21
  defined, 17
  definition of terms and the, 134
  presumption and the, 20
  proposition of fact and the, 131, 136-42
  proposition of policy and the, 180-90
  proposition of value and the, 155, 159-66
Affective response, 4
Agent of change, 179
Ambiguity, 127
Analogy, 103-5
Analysis:
  phrasing the proposition and, 48

  proposition of fact and, 133-36
  proposition of policy and, 177-80
  proposition of value and, 156-59
  stock issues and, 131, 158-59, 179-80
  topicality and, 178-79
Appeal:
  to authority, 124
  to emotion, 121-23
  to humor, 125-26
  to ignorance, 121-22
  to the people, 122
  to tradition, 125
Argument:
  as agency of change, 2
  from analogy, 103-5
  from authority, 105-8
  from cause, 92-97
  from definition, 108-9
  from dilemma, 109
  field of, 52 (see also Context of argument)
    and analysis of policy propositions, 178-80
    values and the, 157, 160
  from generalization, 99-101
  generic, 146
  inference in, 91
  as instrumental communication, 2

Argument (*cont.*)
  in interpersonal communication, 2, 34, 59-60
  in intrapersonal communication, 3, 5
  from parallel case, 101-3
  preemptive, 139-40, 146
  as probability, 11
  from sign, 97-99
  structure, 53-64
Argumentation:
  abuse, 7-8
  criteria for evaluating effectiveness, 4
  defined, 2
  persuasion and, 4-5
  probability and, 15
  reasons to study, 5-6
  rhetoric and, 11
  risks of engaging in, 6-7
  rule governed behavior, 5
Artifacts, 71, 78, 156-7
Artificial presumption, 18-19, 122
Assumptions, 119
Attitude:
  inherency and, 25
  natural presumption and, 18-19
  value claims and, 55
Attitudinal inherency, 184
Audience analysis:
  and backing warrants, 61-62
  and burden of proof, 22
  and evidence, 67, 83
  and inherency, 137
  and issue selection, 135
  and presumption, 19
Audience for argument, 2-3, 9
Authority:
  argument from, 105-6, 124
  definition by, 42
  fallacy of appealing to, 124
  tests of, 106-8
Averages, 70
Avoiding the issue, 119-20

Backing, 53, 60-62, 64
  fallacy of composition and, 117
  hasty generalization and, 116
  warrant and, 61
Begging the question, 119
Belief, 43-45, 175
Bias, 80, 107
Bible, abuse of authority and the, 124
Books, 84 (*see* Research)
Briefs, 140
  sample of fact advocacy, 140-42
  sample of fact opposition, 146-47
  sample of policy advocacy, 186-90
  sample of policy opposition, 196-99

sample of value advocacy, 164-66
sample of value opposition, 170-72
Burden of proof:
  audience analysis and the, 22
  counterproposals and the, 196
  in legal argument, 21
  minor repairs and the, 193
  opponent and the, 27, 192
  order of presentation and the, 23, 28
  presumption and the, 22
  prima facie case and the, 22
  proposition and the, 30, 32-33, 48

Card catalog, 84 (*see* Research)
Case construction:
  criteria development and, 161-62
  criteria discovery and, 161-62
  measurement of the value object in, 163-64
  organization in policy advocacy, 185-86
  value criteria in, 163
  value hierarchy in, 160-61
Causal reasoning, 92-97
Cause:
  analyzing propositions and, 133, 156, 177
  false, 96
  inherency and, 24, 164, 177, 181-82
  necessary, 96, 117
  sufficient, 96, 117
Change:
  agent of, 179
  consequences of, 183-84
  coping with, 6
  policy proposals and, 182
  propositions and, 32-34, 175-76, 178
  reasons for, 180-82
  resistance to, 6, 167, 178
  tradition and, 125
  value conflict and, 154
Choice making, 109
Circular reasoning, 119
Circumvention argument, 194
Claim:
  appeal to ignorance and, 121
  circular reasoning and, 119
  fallacy of refutation and, 118
  as a hypothesis, 57
  issues and, 54
  phrasing the, 55-56, 126
  proof of, 54
  qualifying the strength of, 62-63, 117
  rebuttals and, 63
  reduced to absurdity, 125-26
  relevance of evidence to, 82
  types, 54-55
Clarity, 36, 40, 82
Clash, 207

Cognitive response, 4
Coined terms, 41
Common good, 13-14
Common ground:
    argument from definition and, 109
    criteria discovery and, 161-62
    supporting a claim with, 57
Communication rules, 5, 14-15
Comparability, 76
Comparative advantage organization, 185
Comparison, analogy as, 103
Competitiveness of counterproposals, 196
Composition, fallacy of, 117
Consequences of change, 183-84, 193-95
Consistency, 78
Constitution, abuse of authority and the, 124
Constructive speeches in debate, 204-6
Context, 107
Context of argument, 8, 20
    business, 176
    government, 176
    law, 9, 11, 21, 33, 176
    political campaigns, 9-10
    science, 10
Counterproposal, 195-96
Credibility:
    accuracy of evidence, 13, 81
    argument from authority and, 105-6
    ethical behavior and, 12
    evidence as a means of enhancing, 68
    expert opinions and, 72-73
    minority views and, 107
    scientific evidence and, 71
    tests of evidence and, 74
Criteria:
    defining value judgment to provide, 158
    disadvantages as, 195
    fields of argument and, 157
    propositions of policy and, 186
    propositions of value and, 44-45, 155,
        159-163, 168
    relevance to the value object, 163
Criteria development case, 161-62
Criteria discovery case, 161-62
Cross-examination debate, 203-4, 208-10
Custom, appeal to, 125

Data significance, 76-77
Debate:
    constructive speeches in, 204-6
    cross-examination, 208-10
    flow sheets in, 210
    formats for, 202-4
    judges, 210-211
    in political campaigns, 9-10
    propositions, 203
    rebuttal speeches in, 206-7

rules, 203-7
    time limits in, 203-4
Decision rules:
    definition of terms and, 32
    presumption as a, 18-20, 137, 144
    value hierarchies and, 160-161
Definition:
    argument from, 108
    claims, 55
    fallacies of language and, 126-27
    methods of, 41-43 (*see also* Methods of
        definition)
    questions of, 11
    terms needing, 40-41
    tests of, 109
    of value object and judgment, 158
Definitional claims, 55, 181
Definition of terms:
    action and the, 178
    adaptation rule, 39
    advocate and the, 134
    agent of change and the, 179
    analysis and the, 134, 158, 178-79
    burden of proof and the, 31
    clarity and the, 36
    clarity rule, 40
    decision rules for, 32
    exclusionary rule, 39
    inclusionary rule, 38-39
    issues and the, 35
    neutrality rule, 39
    opponent and the, 31-32, 35, 143, 168, 192
    presumption and the, 31, 33-34
    primary inference and the, 137
    proposition and the, 31, 38
    specificity rule, 39-40
    topicality and the, 178-79
Denial, refutation by, 144-45, 169, 192
Dependent variable, 71, 77
Descriptive statistics, 69-70
Dialectic, 7
Dichotomy, forcing a, 120
Dilemma, 109, 120
Disadvantage argument, 194-95
Division, fallacy of, 117-18
Division of labor, 205-7
Duties of the speakers, 204-7 (*see also*
        Debate)

Effect, argument of, 163-64, 181
Emotional appeal, 7-8, 121-23, 127-28
Enforcement, 182
Equivocal terms, 40
Equivocation, 127
Erosion and value change, 154
Establishing clash, 207

Ethical behavior, 12–14
  deception and, 115
  topicality and, 178–79
  value argument concerning, 152
Evasiveness, 119–20
Evidence:
  appeal to ignorance and, 121
  credibility of, 67–68
  ethics and the use of, 115
  grounds and, 57
  organizing, 88–89
  paraphrasing, 81
  probability and the absence of, 122
  quality of, 81
  recording, 87–89
  tests of, 74–83 (*see also* Tests of evidence)
  types of, 68–74 (*see also* Evidence from
      opinion, evidence of fact)
Evidence from opinion:
  credibility of, 72–73
  interpretation of fact in, 74
  secondary sources and, 73–74
Evidence of fact:
  artifacts as, 71
  example as, 68–69
  illustration as, 68–69
  premises as, 71–72
  scientific evidence as, 70–71
  statistics as, 69–70
Example:
  atypical, 116
  definition by, 42
  evidence of fact from, 68–69
  tests of, 75
Exclusionary rule, 39
Expertise:
  argument from authority and, 106
  fallacy of appeal and, 124
  nature of, 107
  test of opinion evidence, 80
Expressive communication, 2–3
Extent, argument of, 163–64, 181
Extenuation, refutation by, 144–45, 169, 192
External consistency, 78, 82, 107

Fact:
  arguing propositions of, 131–148 (*see also*
      Proposition of fact)
  argument from authority and, 107
  claims, 54–55, 99, 155, 159, 181–82
  evidence of, 68–72 (*see also* Evidence of
      fact)
  interpretation of, 74
  opinion evidence and, 80
  propositions of, 43–44, 47
  questions of, 11

Fallacy:
  of appeal, 121–26
  of composition, 117
  of division, 117–18
  in language, 126–29
  in reasoning, 116–21
  of refutation, 118
Fear, appeal to, 123
Field experiment, 71
Field of argument, 52
  analysis and the, 178, 180
  values and the, 157, 160
Financing, 182
Flow sheets, 210
Forced dichotomy, 120
Formats for debate, 202–4
Function, definition by, 42

Generalizability, 77
Generalization:
  argument from, 99–101
  in causal reasoning, 95
  fallacy of, 116, 117
  restricted, 100
  tests of, 100–1, 116
  universal, 100
Generic argument, 146
Genuineness, 78
Goals-criteria organization, 185–86
Government documents, 86 (*see* Research)
Grounds, 60
  argument from parallel case and, 101
  claim and, 56–57
  strength of, 99
  sufficiency of, 95
  types of, 57
Ground shifting, 120
Guides, 84 (*see* Research)

Habits of language, 126
Harm, 133, 163, 181, 192
Hasty generalization, 116–17
Hierarchy of values, 151, 154, 159–61, 168–69
Historical research, 133–34, 156–57, 177–78
Humor, 125–26
Hypothesis testing, 19, 57, 137

Ignorance, appeal to, 121–22
Illustration, 68–69, 74–75
Immediate cause, 156, 177
Inclusionary rule, 38–39
Independent variable, 71, 77
Inductive reasoning, 99

Inference:
  in argument, 91
  circular reasoning and, 119
  primary, 137, 139, 143
  propositions and, 132, 135
  reasoning and, 135
  warrant as, 58
Inferential statistics, 70
Information and value change, 153
Inherency:
  attitudinal, 25, 184
  cause and, 24-25, 137-39, 177, 181-82
  consequences of change and, 183-84
  disadvantage arguments and, 195
  minor repairs and, 193
  permanence and, 25
  prima facie case and, 24, 26, 138-39, 164
  reform and, 25
  refutation of, 144, 192, 194
  structural, 25, 184
Instrumental communication, 2-4
Internal consistency, 82
Irrelevant arguments, 118-19
Issues:
  actual, 139
  analysis of, 135, 158-59, 179-80 (*see also*
    Stock issues)
  claims and, 54
  definition of terms and, 35
  fallacy of avoiding the, 119-20
  locus of disagreement and, 36
  potential, 134-35
  primary inference and, 173
  proposition and, 35, 48

Jargon, 128
Judges, 203, 210-11
Judgment, criteria of, 150-51, 155
Justification, questions of, 11

Kitchen sink preempts, 140

Laboratory experiment, 71, 77
Language fallacies, 126-28
Lincoln-Douglas debate, 204
Locus of disagreement, 36, 59

Maintaining clash, 207
Meaning fallacies, 126-27
Mechanism in policy proposals, 182
Methodology in scientific research, 77-78
Methods of definition:
  by authority, 42
  by behavior, 43

by example, 42
by function, 42
by negation, 43
by operation, 42-43
by synonym, 41, 42
Microfilm, documents on, 85
Minor repairs, 192-93, 195
Modal qualifier, 62

Natural presumption, 18-19
Necessary:
  cause, 96, 117
  criteria, 159, 162
Need-plan organization, 185
Negation, definition by, 43
Negative instances, 101
Neutrality rule, 39
New arguments in debate, 205
New evidence in debate, 205
Newspapers, 85 (*see* Research)
New terms, 41
Non sequitur, 118
Nuisance variable, 71, 77

Operation, definition by, 42-43
Opponent:
  burden of proof and the, 27, 192
  defined, 17
  definition of terms and the, 31-32, 35, 192
  inherency and the, 144, 192
  presumption and the, 20, 27, 143-44
  prima facie case and the, 27, 169, 191
  proposition of fact and the, 142-48
  proposition of policy and the, 191-200
  proposition of value and the, 155, 167-72
  refutation and the, 144-45, 192-95
  stock issues and the, 168-69, 191
Order of speeches in debate, 203-7
Organization:
  of evidence, 88-89
  flow sheets and, 210
  patterns of, 185-86, 196
Overgeneralization, 116-17

Parallel cases, 101-3
Paraphrasing evidence, 81
Patterns of organization, 185-86, 196
People, appeal to the, 122
Periodicals, 84 (*see* Research)
Personal attacks, 119
Persuasion, 4, 9
Pity, appeal to, 123
Policy:
  arguing propositions of, 177-200 (*see also*
    Proposition of policy)

Policy (*cont.*)
  causal reasoning and, 95
  claims, 55
  fact and, 181-82
  proposals, 182-83
  propositions of, 43-47, 176, 203
  value and, 175
Political change and value change, 154
Potential issues, 134-35
Preemptive arguments, 139-40, 146
Prejudice, 99, 122
Premises, 71-72, 74, 79
Presumption:
  artificial, 18, 122
  burden of proof and, 20, 22
  as a decision rule, 144
  definition of terms and, 31, 33-34
  inherency and, 144
  in legal argument, 9, 33
  natural, 18
  opponent and, 20, 27, 143-44
  prima facie case and, 23
  proposition and, 30, 32, 48, 137, 167
  tradition and, 125
Prima facie argument, 9
Prima facie case, 22, 131
  briefs and the, 140
  burden of proof and the, 139
  defined, 23
  inherency and the, 24, 26, 137-39
  in legal argument, 23
  opponent and the, 27, 169, 191
  presumption and the, 23, 137
  stock issues and the, 23, 164, 180-84
  topicality and the, 24, 136
Primary cause, 25-26
Primary inference, 137, 139, 143
Primary issues, 67
Probability:
  absence of evidence and, 122
  analogy and, 104
  estimate of in scientific evidence, 71
  future fact and, 44, 138
  policy and, 46
  reasoning and, 110
  statistical significance and, 78
  value and, 45
Problem, 177
Procedure, questions of, 11
Proof:
  grounds as, 56-57
  propositions of fact and, 44
  stock issues and, 135
  supporting claims with, 54
Proposition:
  for academic argument, 33-37, 44-46
  burden of proof and the, 32-33
  change and the, 32

  claims and the, 53-54
  defined, 30
  definition of terms and the, 31, 36, 38
  issues and the, 35
  for legal argument, 33
  locus of disagreement and the, 31
  phrasing the, 47-49
  presumption and the, 32
Proposition of fact, 43-44, 47
  advocate and the, 136-42
  analysis of, 133-36
  examples of, 131-32
  hypothesis testing and the, 137
  inference in, 132
  inherency and the, 137-39
  opponent and the, 142-48
  presumption and the, 137
  prima facie case and the, 137
  stock issues and, 135
Proposition of policy, 43, 45-47
  action and the, 178
  advocate and the, 180-90
  analysis of, 177-80
  definitional claims and, 181
  factual claims and, 181-82
  inherency and the, 181-82
  opponent and the, 191-200
Proposition of value, 43-45, 47
  advocate and the, 159-66
  analysis of, 156-59
  arts and, 151-52
  characteristics of, 155
  concerning ethical behavior, 152
  opponent and the, 167-72
  religion and, 151
  value object and judgment in, 155

Qualifier, 53, 60, 62-64
  hasty generalization and, 116-17
  modifying claim with, 94
  restricted generalization and, 100
Questions, 118

Random sampling, 101
Reason for change, 180-82
Reasoning:
  circular, 119
  fallacies in, 116-21
  as inference, 91-92, 110, 135
  rebuttals and, 63
  tests of, 95-104 (*see also* Tests of
    reasoning)
  warrant as, 58-60
Rebuttal, 53, 60, 63-64
Rebuttal speeches in debate, 206-7
Recency, 81

Reducto ad absurdum, 125
Reference guides, 83-84 (*see* Research)
Refutation:
  by denial, 144-45, 169, 192
  by extenuation, 144-45, 169, 192
  fallacy of, 118
  of inherency, 192, 194
  of solvency, 193
  of workability, 194
Relevance, 82
Reliability, 98
Representativeness, 78, 81-82
Representative sampling, 100
Research:
  biographical information, 86
  books, 84
  card catalog, 84
  ethical responsibility and, 12
  government documents, 86
  guides to reference materials, 83-85
  historical, 133-34, 156-57, 177-78
  periodicals, 84-85
  statistical information, 86
  techniques of, 87-89
Resistance to change, 22, 178, 181
Restricted generalization, 100
Rhetoric, 11
Rule-governed behavior:
  communication as, 5, 14-15
  debate as, 203, 209-10

Sampling, 76
Scientific evidence, 70-71, 74, 77-78, 138
Secondary sources, 73-74
Shifting ground, 120
Significance arguments, 163, 181, 192
Sign reasoning, 97-99
Similarity, 104
Solvency:
  consequences of change and, 183
  disadvantage arguments and, 195
  refutation of, 193
Source qualifications, 75
Source reliability, 76
Speaker duties in debate, 204-7
Specificity rule, 39-40
Statistics, 69-70, 74, 76-77
Stock issues:
  analysis and the, 135, 158-59, 179-80
  consequences of change and the, 183-84
  defined, 23
  inherency and the, 139
  opponent and the, 168-69, 191
  organization and the, 185-86
  policy proposal and the, 182-83
  prima facie case and the, 23

proof and, 135
reason for change and the, 179-82
value criteria and, 162
value hierarchy and the, 161
value object measurement and the, 163
Straw man argument, 118
Structural inherency, 184
Structure of argument, 53-64
Style:
  analogy and, 104
  briefs and, 140
  humor and, 126
  warrant and, 62
Subsidiary effects, 184
Sufficiency, 81
Sufficient:
  cases, 100
  cause, 96, 117
  criteria, 159, 162
Synonym, definition by, 41-42

Technical terms, 41, 128
Terms, definition of, 31-32, 38-43 (*see also*
    Definition of terms)
Testimonials, 124
Tests of evidence:
  for artifacts, 78
  for examples, 74-75
  general, 81-83
  for illustrations, 74-75
  for opinion, 80
  for premises, 79
  for scientific evidence, 77-78
  for statistics, 76-77
Tests for reasoning:
  for analogy, 104
  for cause, 95-97
  for generalization, 100-1
  for parallel case, 102
  for sign, 98-99
Time limits in debate, 203-4
Topicality:
  counterproposals and, 196
  ethical behavior and, 178-79
  minor repairs and, 193
  opponent and, 143
  prima facie case and, 24, 136
Toulmin model of argument, 53-64
Traditional debate format, 203
Traditional organization, 185
Tradition, appeal to, 125
Transfer fallacies, 117-18
Trivial point, seizing on a, 120

Unethical behavior, 7, 13-14

Uniqueness, 185, 195
Universal generalization, 100

Vague terms, 40-41
Value:
arguing propositions of, 156-72 (*see also*
    Proposition of value)
change, 152-54
claims, 55, 155, 180, 195
conflict, 13, 34, 151, 154
criteria, 157, 161-63, 168
examples of, 150-51
hierarchy, 151, 154, 159-61, 169
judgment, 155, 158
object, 155, 158-60, 163-64
policy and, 175, 185
propositions of, 43-45, 47
systems, 175
tradition and, 125

Value emphasis and change, 152-53
Value implementation and change, 153
Value redistribution and change, 152-53
Variable control, 77
Variable manipulation, 77

Warrant:
in argument from authority, 105-6, 108
backing for the, 61
in causal reasoning, 93
fallacy in the use of, 116-17
fallacy of composition and, 117
fallacy of division and, 117-18
hasty generalization and the, 116-17
importance of, 59-60, 110
as inference, 58, 91-92
reliability of the, 61
Workability, 184, 194-95